N. Naveen

EXAM CRAM™

P9-CBS-083

RHCE Linux

Kara J. Pritchard

CORIOLIS

The Coriolis Group, LLC
14455 N. Hayden Road
Suite 220
Scottsdale, Arizona 85260

480/483-0192
FAX 480/483-0193
http://www.coriolis.com

Library of Congress Cataloging-in-Publication Data
Pritchard, Kara J.
    RHCE Linux Exam Cram / Kara J. Pritchard
        p. cm.
    Includes index.
    ISBN 1-57610-487-7
    1. Electronic data processing personnel--Certification. 2. Operating systems (Computers)--Examinations--Study guides. 3. Linux. I. Title.
QA76.3.P75   1999
005.4'469 21--dc21   99-045281
                                                                 CIP

President, CEO
Keith Weiskamp

Publisher
Steve Sayre

Acquisitions Editor
Shari Jo Hehr

Marketing Specialist
Cynthia Caldwell

Project Editor
Michelle Stroup

Technical Reviewer
Michael Maher

Production Coordinator
Kim Eoff

Cover Design
Jesse Dunn

Layout Design
April Nielsen

Printed in the United States of America
10 9 8 7 6 5 4 3 2 1

14455 North Hayden Road, Suite 220 • Scottsdale, Arizona 85260

Coriolis: The Training And Certification Destination™

Thank you for purchasing one of our innovative certification study guides, just one of the many members of the Coriolis family of certification products.

Certification Insider Press™ has long believed that achieving your IT certification is more of a road trip than anything else. This is why most of our readers consider us their *Training And Certification Destination*. By providing a one-stop shop for the most innovative and unique training materials, our readers know we are the first place to look when it comes to achieving their certification. As one reader put it, "I plan on using your books for all of the exams I take."

To help you reach your goals, we've listened to others like you, and we've designed our entire product line around you and the way you like to study, learn, and master challenging subjects. Our approach is *The Smartest Way To Get Certified ™*.

In addition to our highly popular *Exam Cram* and *Exam Prep* guides, we have a number of new products. We recently launched Exam Cram Live!, two-day seminars based on *Exam Cram* material. We've also developed a new series of books and study aides—*Practice Tests Exam Crams* and *Exam Cram Flash Cards*—designed to make your studying fun as well as productive.

Our commitment to being the *Training And Certification Destination* does not stop there. We just introduced *Exam Cram Insider*, a biweekly newsletter containing the latest in certification news, study tips, and announcements from Certification Insider Press. (To subscribe, send an email to **eci@coriolis.com** and type "subscribe insider" in the body of the email.) We also recently announced the launch of the Certified Crammer Society and the Coriolis Help Center—two new additions to the Certification Insider Press family.

We'd like to hear from you. Help us continue to provide the very best certification study materials possible. Write us or email us at **cipq@coriolis.com** and let us know how our books have helped you study, or tell us about new features that you'd like us to add. If you send us a story about how we've helped you, and we use it in one of our books, we'll send you an official Coriolis shirt for your efforts.

Good luck with your certification exam and your career. Thank you for allowing us to help you achieve your goals.

Keith Weiskamp
President and CEO

Look For This Other Book From The Coriolis Group:

General Linux I Exam Prep
Dee-Ann LeBlanc

In memoriam of my grandfather, Hershell Enlow (1926–1999)
Your strength has guided me where I am today,
and will carry me forever…
—Kara J. Pritchard

❧

About The Author

Kara J. Pritchard is currently a systems administrator for an Internet Service Provider in Springfield, Illinois and is a project manager for VA Linux Systems, developing the Linux User Group resource on Linux.com. In an ongoing consulting endeavor, Kara has been promoting the use of Linux in both corporate and educational facilities since late 1995.

Kara began participating in the Linux community in fall of 1995, when introduced to the Southern Illinois Linux Users Group (SILUG), founded by her husband in 1994. Together with her husband, Kara founded the Linux Users of Central Illinois (LUCI) in 1997 and has since been involved with several projects including a Linux mentoring program for youth. She was elected president of a technology show held annually at the Illinois State Fairgrounds in late 1998. She may be contacted via email at kara@linux.com.

Acknowledgments

First, accreditation goes to the Linux community of developers, supporters, and activists who have made Linux what it is today. May the source be with you!

I would like to thank the Project Editor, Michelle Stroup, for being brave enough to battle this new topic to the Exam Cram series with me, and for helping me deal with the trials of being a new author. I would also like to thank the Coriolis team for giving me the opportunity to be one of the leaders in their new series of books dedicated to Linux and Linux certification. Thank you for providing this service to the Linux community.

An extra-special thanks goes to my husband, Steven, who has spent many a sleepless night helping on the project (or listening to me talk about it). Without him, I'd never have been introduced to Linux, or been given the opportunity to work on this book.

Thanks and dedication belong most to my family. To my mother, father, and sister who have supported me in everything I have ever done—and to Grandma Enlow who showed me I could accomplish anything I put my mind to; *thank you*.

Contents At A Glance

Table Of Contents

Introduction

Welcome to the *RHCE Linux Exam Cram*! This book aims to help you get ready to take—and pass—the Red Hat certification exam RHCE 300. This Introduction explains Red Hat's certification programs in general and talks about how the Exam Cram series can help you prepare for Red Hat's certification exams.

Exam Cram books help you understand and appreciate the subjects and materials you need to pass Red Hat certification exams. Exam Cram books are aimed strictly at test preparation and review. They do not teach you everything you need to know about a topic (such as the ins and outs of building your own RPMs). Instead, I present and dissect the questions and problems I've found that you're likely to encounter on a test. I've worked from Red Hat's own training materials, preparation guides, and tests. My aim is to bring together as much information as possible about Red Hat certification exams.

Nevertheless, to completely prepare yourself for any Red Hat test, I recommend that you begin by taking the Self-Assessment included in this book immediately following this Introduction. This tool will help you evaluate your knowledge base against the requirements for an RHCE under both ideal and real circumstances.

Based on what you learn from that exercise, you might decide to begin your studies with some classroom training, or that you pick up and read one of the many Linux guides available from Red Hat or third-party vendors. We also strongly recommend that you install and configure the software and tools that you'll be tested on, because nothing beats hands-on experience and familiarity when it comes to understanding the questions you're likely to encounter on a certification test. Book learning is essential, but hands-on experience is the best teacher of all! Especially because two-thirds of the exam is hands-on!

The Red Hat Certified Engineer (RHCE) Program

The RHCE exam is comprised of three separate parts. The three parts include:

➤ Installation and Configuration Lab Exam

➤ Debugging Lab Exam

➤ Written Exam

The three exams are taken on the same day and are each graded individually. The RHCE exam taker must receive a composite score of 80 percent on all three exams, with no single score dropping below 50 percent.

The best place to keep tabs on the RHCE program and its various certifications is on the Red Hat Web site. The current URL for the RHCE program is located at **http://www.redhat.com/products/training_exam.html**. Red Hat's Web site changes frequently, so if this URL doesn't work, try using the Search tool on Red Hat's site with either "RHCE" or the quoted phrase "Red Hat Certified Engineer Program" as the search string. This will help you find the latest and most accurate information about the company's certification programs.

Taking A Certification Exam

Alas, testing is not free. Your exam day could cost from $349 to $749 (depending if you participate in the training program, or take the exam-only approach). Currently, exams are administered by Red Hat itself (though training is now offered from Global Knowledge as well). To reach the RHCE team, contact (919) 547-0012, or email training@redhat.com.

To schedule an exam, call at least 10 days in advance. Exam seats are limited, and are often booked solid two months in advance. To cancel or reschedule an exam, you must call at least 2 days before the scheduled test time, to receive any sort of refund. (For 2 days advanced, you are billed 80 percent; for 3 to 10 days advanced, you are billed 50 percent; and for more than 10 business days, you are given a full refund.)When calling Red Hat, please have the following information ready for the RHCE staffer who handles your call:

➤ Your name, organization, and mailing address.

➤ A method of payment. (The most convenient approach is to supply a valid credit card number with sufficient available credit. Otherwise, payments by check, money order, or purchase order must be received before a test can be scheduled. If the latter methods are required, ask your order taker for more details.)

When you show up to take a test, try to arrive at least 15 minutes before the scheduled time slot. You must bring and supply two forms of identification, one of which must be a photo ID.

All exams are completely closed-book. In fact, you will be required to stow anything you brought with you under your desk. You will be furnished with a blank sheet of paper, pencil, and any other tools you may need for your exam. We suggest that you immediately write down on that sheet of paper all the information you've memorized for the test.

When you complete a Red Hat certification exam component, you will report to your instructor, and either have him sign off on your lab exam, instructing you on the next step, or turn in your written exam and be excused for a break. All exam components are scored on a percentage basis.

How To Prepare For An Exam

Preparing for any Linux exam requires that you obtain and study materials designed to provide comprehensive information about Red Hat Linux and the specific exam for which you are preparing. The following list of materials will help you study and prepare:

➤ The Red Hat Linux 6.0 manuals (or online documentation found on Red Hat's Web site)

➤ The Linux Documentation Project (online resource found at **http:// metalab.unc.edu/LDP**)

In addition, you'll probably find the following training courses useful in your quest for Windows Red Hat Linux expertise:

➤ **RHCE 300 Certification Training**   Red Hat Inc. (Durham, NC) offers an RHCE 300 Certification course. The course is a week-long adventure and includes a full day of examinations. Current perks of the course include daily-catered lunches and all the soda and juice you can handle. You pay for it in the long run, however; the week-long course (includes exam fee) is currently priced at $2,498.

➤ **Other Red Hat Inc. Training**   Red Hat Inc. offers three additional courses to help you with learning Red Hat Linux. They include the RH033 (Introduction to Red Hat Linux I and II), RH133 (Red Hat Linux System Administration I and II), and RH253 (Red Hat Linux Networking and Security Admin). Each class is a four day program, and prices range from $1,098 (RH033) to $2,198 (RH253).

➤ **Global Knowledge, Inc**   Red Hat has recently partnered with Global Knowledge to provide Red Hat Linux training services all over the world. For a list of classes (for the US) and prices, visit **http:// am.globalknowledge.com/authorized/redhatmail.html**.

I anticipate that you'll find that this book will easily complement your studying and preparation for the exam, either on your own, or with the aid of the previously mentioned study programs. In the section that follows, I explain how this book works, and give you some good reasons why this book counts as a member of the required and recommended materials list.

About This Book

Each topical Exam Cram chapter follows a regular structure, along with graphical cues about important or useful information. Here's the structure of a typical chapter:

➤ **Opening Hotlists**   Each chapter begins with a list of the terms, tools, and techniques that you must learn and understand before you can be fully conversant with that chapter's subject matter. We follow the hotlists with one or two introductory paragraphs to set the stage for the rest of the chapter.

➤ **Topical Coverage**   After the opening hotlists, each chapter covers a series of at least four topics related to the chapter's subject title. Throughout this section, we highlight topics or concepts likely to appear on a test using a special Exam Alert layout, like this:

This is what an Exam Alert looks like. Normally, an Exam Alert stresses concepts, terms, software, or activities that are likely to relate to one or more certification test questions. For that reason, any information found offset in Exam Alert format is worthy of unusual attentiveness on your part. Indeed, most of the information that appears on the Cram Sheet appears as Exam Alerts within the text.

Pay close attention to material flagged as an Exam Alert; although all the information in this book pertains to what you need to know to pass the exam, I flag certain items that are really important. You'll find what appears in the meat of each chapter to be worth knowing, too, when preparing for the test. Because this book's material is very condensed, I recommend that you use this book along with other resources to achieve the maximum benefit.

In addition to the Exam Alerts, I have provided tips that will help build a better foundation for Red Hat Linux knowledge. Although the information may not be on the exam, it is certainly related and will help you become a better test taker.

This is how tips are formatted. Keep your eyes open for these, and you'll become a Linux guru in no time!

➤ **Practice Questions**   Although we talk about test questions and topics throughout each chapter, this section presents a series of mock test questions and explanations of both correct and incorrect answers. We also try to point out especially tricky questions by using a special icon, like this:

Ordinarily, this icon flags the presence of a particularly devious inquiry, if not an outright trick question. Trick questions are calculated to be answered incorrectly if not read more than once, and carefully, at that. Although they're not ubiquitous, such questions make regular appearances on the Red Hat exams. That's why we say exam questions are as much about reading comprehension as they are about knowing your material inside out and backwards.

➤ **Details And Resources**   Every chapter ends with a section titled "Need To Know More?", which provides direct pointers to Red Hat and third-party resources offering more details on the chapter's subject. In addition, this section tries to rank or at least rate the quality and thoroughness of the topic's coverage by each resource. If you find a resource you like in this collection, use it, but don't feel compelled to use all the resources. On the other hand, I only recommend resources I use on a regular basis, so none of my recommendations will be a waste of your time or money (but purchasing them all at once probably represents an expense that many network administrators and would-be RHCEs might find hard to justify).

The bulk of the book follows this chapter structure slavishly, but there are a few other elements that we'd like to point out. Chapters 12, 13, and 14 represent what you should expect for the three elements of the RHCE 300 exam. Chapter 12 discusses objectives and elements involved during the Installation and Configuration Lab exam. Chapter 13 discusses methods for handling the Debugging Lab exam. Chapter 13 includes a sample written test that provides a good review of the material presented throughout the book to ensure you're ready for the exam. Chapter 14 is an answer key to the sample test that appears in Chapter 13. You'll notice that no answer key is provided for the exams that appear in Chapters 12 and 13. This is because performance-based exams test your ability to accomplish a specific task, not necessarily how you accomplish it. Therefore there is no specific right or wrong, yes or no answer. Additionally, you'll find a glossary that explains terms and an index that you can use to track down terms as they appear in the text.

Finally, the tear-out Cram Sheet attached next to the inside front cover of this Exam Cram book represents a condensed and compiled collection of facts, figures, and tips that we think you should memorize before taking the test. Because you can dump this information out of your head onto a piece of paper before answering any exam questions, you can master this information by brute force—you only need to remember it long enough to write it down when you walk into the test room. You might even want to look at it in the car or in the lobby of the testing center just before you walk in to take the test.

How To Use This Book

If you're prepping for a first-time test, I've structured the topics in this book to build on one another. Therefore, some topics in later chapters make more sense after you've read earlier chapters. That's why I suggest you read this book from front to back for your initial test preparation. If you need to brush up on a topic or you have to bone up for a second try, use the index or table of contents to go straight to the topics and questions that you need to study. Beyond the tests, I think you'll find this book useful as a tightly focused reference to some of the most important aspects of Red Hat Linux and Linux networking services.

Given all the book's elements and its specialized focus, I've tried to create a tool that will help you prepare for—and pass—Red Hat's "Red Hat Certified Engineer" exam. Please share your feedback on the book with me, especially if you have ideas about how I can improve it for future test-takers. I'll consider everything you say carefully and will respond to all suggestions.

Please send your questions or comments to us at **cipq@coriolis.com** or to the author at kara@linux.com. Please remember to include the title of the book in your message; otherwise, we'll be forced to guess which book you're writing about. Also, be sure to check out the Web page at **http://www.certificationinsider.com**, where you'll find information updates, commentary, and clarifications on documents for each book that you can either read online or download for use later on.

Thanks, and enjoy the book!

Self-Assessment

The reason we included a self-assessment in this *Exam Cram* book is to help you evaluate your readiness to tackle RHCE certification. It should also help you understand what you need to master the topic of this book—namely, RHCE 300. But before you tackle this self-assessment, let's talk about concerns you may face when pursuing an RHCE, and what an ideal RHCE candidate might look like.

RHCEs In The Real World

In the next section, we describe an ideal RHCE candidate, knowing full well that only a few real candidates will meet this ideal. In fact, our description of that ideal candidate might seem downright scary. But take heart: although the requirements to obtain an RHCE may seem pretty formidable, they are by no means impossible to meet. However, you should be keenly aware that it does take time, requires some expense, and consumes substantial effort to get through the process.

Just introduced in the Spring of 1999, the RHCE program is very young. Demand for this certification is growing, and the limited seating for the testing makes the RHCE even more valuable. However, if you're willing to tackle the process seriously and do what it takes to obtain the necessary experience and knowledge, you can take—and pass—all the certification tests involved in obtaining an RHCE. In fact, we've designed these *Exam Crams* to make it as easy on you as possible to prepare for these exams. But prepare you must!

The Ideal RHCE Candidate

Just to give you some idea of what an ideal RHCE candidate is like, here are some relevant statistics about the background and experience such an individual might have. Don't worry if you don't meet these qualifications—this is a far from ideal world, and where you fall short is simply where you'll have more work to do:

➤ Academic or professional training in network theory, concepts, and operations. This includes everything from networking hardware and software through the Linux operating system, services, and applications.

➤ Two-plus years of professional networking experience, including experience with Ethernet, modems, and other networking media. This must include installation, configuration, upgrade, and troubleshooting experience.

➤ Two-plus years in a networked environment that includes hands-on experience with Red Hat Linux, or other Linux distributions such as Caldera, Debian, or SuSE. A solid understanding of each system's architecture, installation, configuration, maintenance, and troubleshooting is also essential.

➤ Familiarity with key Linux-based TCP/IP-based services, including HTTP (Web servers), DHCP, DNS, plus familiarity with one or more of the following: FTP, Samba, Squid, NFS, or ipchains.

Put Yourself To The Test

The following series of questions and observations is designed to help you figure out how much work you must do to pursue Red Hat certification and what kinds of resources you may consult on your quest. Be absolutely honest in your answers, or you'll end up wasting money on exams you're not yet ready to take. There are no right or wrong answers, only steps along the path to certification. Only you can decide where you really belong in the broad spectrum of aspiring candidates.

Two things should be clear from the outset, however:

➤ Even a modest background in computer science will be helpful.

➤ Hands-on experience with Linux, Linux products and technologies is an essential ingredient to certification success.

Educational Background

1. Have you ever taken any computer-related classes? [Yes or No]

   If Yes, proceed to question 2; if No, proceed to question 4.

2. Have you taken any classes on Unix operating systems? [Yes or No]

   If Yes, you will probably be able to handle Red Hat's architecture and system component discussions. If you're rusty, brush up on basic Unix concepts, especially virtual memory, multitasking regimes, user mode versus superuser mode operation, filesystems, and general computer security topics.

   If No, consider some basic reading in this area. I strongly recommend a good general operating systems book, such as *Essential System*

Administration, by Æleen Frisch (O'Reilly & Associates, 1995, ISBN 1-56592-127-5). If this title doesn't appeal to you, check out reviews for other, similar titles at your favorite online bookstore.

3. Have you taken any TCP/IP based networking concepts or technologies classes? [Yes or No]

If Yes, you will probably be able to handle Red Hat Linux's networking terminology, concepts, and technologies (brace yourself for frequent departures from normal usage). If you're rusty, brush up on basic networking concepts and terminology, especially networking media, transmission types, the OSI Reference model, and networking technologies such as Ethernet, and WAN links.

If No, you might want to read one or two books in this topic area. The two best books that we know of are *Computer Networks*, *3rd Edition*, by Andrew S. Tanenbaum (Prentice-Hall, 1996, ISBN 0-13-349945-6) and *Computer Networks and Internets*, by Douglas E. Comer (Prentice-Hall, 1997, ISBN 0-13-239070-1).

Skip to the next section, "Hands-On Experience."

4. Have you done any reading on the Linux operating system or networks? [Yes or No]

If Yes, review the requirements stated in the first paragraphs after questions 2 and 3. If you meet those requirements, move on to the next section. If No, consult the recommended reading for both topics. A strong background will help you prepare for the Red Hat exams better than just about anything else.

Hands-On Experience

The most important key to success on all types of certification exams is hands-on experience. If I leave you with only one realization after taking this self-assessment, it should be that there's no substitute for time spent installing, configuring, and using Red Hat Linux and its components upon which you'll be tested repeatedly and in depth.

5. Have you installed, configured, and worked with:

   ➤ Linux? [Yes or No]

   ➤ Red Hat Linux? [Yes or No]

   If Yes, make sure you understand the methods used in Red Hat Linux 6.0, the differences between Red Hat Linux 6.0 and other

Red Hat Linux versions, as well as the differences between Red Hat Linux 6.0 and other vendor distributions (such as Caldera, SuSE, and Debian).

If No, you will want to obtain a copy of Red Hat Linux 6.0 and learn how to install, configure, and maintain it. You can use this book to guide your activities and studies.

6. For any specific Linux product that is not itself an operating system (for example, the X Window system or Apache), have you installed, configured, used, and upgraded this software? [Yes or No]

If the answer is Yes, skip to the next section. If it's No, you must get some experience. Read on for suggestions on how to do this.

Experience is a must with the RHCE 300 exam, be it something as simple as pine or as challenging as NFS or Apache.

 If you have the funds, or your employer will pay your way, consider taking a class from Red Hat Software, Inc. or at an Authorized Training Partner. In addition to classroom exposure to the topic of your choice, you get a copy of the Red Hat Linux version that is the focus of your course, along with the training materials for that class.

Before you even think about taking any exam, make sure you've spent enough time with the related software to understand how it may be installed and configured, how to maintain such an installation, and how to troubleshoot that software when things go wrong. This will help you in the exam, as well as in real life!

Testing Your Exam-Readiness

Whether you attend a formal class on a specific topic to get ready for an exam or use written materials to study on your own, some preparation for the Red Hat Certified Engineer exam is essential. At $749 a try, pass or fail, you want to do everything you can to pass the exam on your first try. That's where the importance of studying comes in.

We have included practice objectives, goals and exams in this book, so if you don't score that well on the first test, you can study more and then tackle the second test. If you still don't hit a score of at least 85 percent after the second test, you'll want to investigate the other practice test resources we mention in this section.

For any given subject, consider taking a class if you've tackled self-study materials, taken the test, and failed anyway. The opportunity to interact with an instructor and fellow students can make all the difference in the world, if you can afford that privilege. For information about Red Hat classes, visit the Training and Certification page at **http://www.redhat.com/products/training.html**.

Onward, Through The Fog!

Once you've assessed your readiness, undertaken the right background studies, obtained the hands-on experience that will help you understand the products and technologies at work, and reviewed the many sources of information to help you prepare for a test, you'll be ready to take a round of practice tests. When your scores come back positive enough to get you through the exam, you're ready to go after the real thing. If you follow our assessment regime, you'll not only know what you need to study, but when you're ready to make a test date. Good luck!

Red Hat
Certification Exams

. . . .

Terms you'll need to understand:

√ Exhibit

√ Multiple-choice question formats

√ Careful reading

√ Process of elimination

Techniques you'll need to master:

√ Assessing your exam-readiness

√ Preparing to take a certification exam

√ Practicing (to make perfect)

√ Making the best use of the testing software

√ Budgeting your time

√ Saving the hardest questions until last

√ Guessing (as a last resort)

Exam taking is not something that most people anticipate eagerly, no matter how well prepared they may be. In most cases, familiarity helps ameliorate test anxiety. In plain English, this means you probably won't be as nervous when you take your fourth or fifth Red Hat certification exam as you'll be when you take your first one. Granted, every certification exam—whether it is a Red Hat exam, a Caldera exam, or another certification program—will be different, the overall process for preparation will be very similar and you will become more comfortable with each experience.

Whether it's your first exam or your tenth, understanding the details of exam taking (how much time to spend on questions, the environment you'll be in, and so on) and the exam software will help you concentrate on the material rather than on the setting. Likewise, mastering a few basic exam-taking skills should help you recognize—and perhaps even outfox—some of the tricks and gotchas you're bound to find in some of the exam questions.

This chapter, besides explaining the exam environment and software, describes some proven exam-taking strategies that you should be able to use to your advantage.

Assessing Exam-Readiness

Before you take your Red Hat exam, we strongly recommend that you read through and take the Self-Assessment included with this book (it appears just before this chapter, in fact). This will help you compare your knowledge base to the requirements for obtaining an RHCE, and it will also help you identify parts of your background or experience that may be in need of improvement, enhancement, or further learning. If you get the right set of basics under your belt, obtaining Red Hat certification will be that much easier.

Once you've gone through the Self-Assessment, you can remedy those topical areas where your background or experience may not measure up to an ideal certification candidate. But you can also tackle subject matter for individual tests at the same time, so you can continue making progress while you're catching up in some areas.

Once you've worked through an *Exam Cram*, read the supplementary materials, completed the chapter tasks, and taken the practice test, you'll have a pretty clear idea of when you should be ready to take the real exam. We strongly recommend that you keep practicing until your scores top the 80 percent mark; 85 percent would be a good goal to give yourself some margin for error in a real exam situation (where stress will play more of a role than when you practice). Once you hit that point, you should be ready to go. But if you get through the practice exam in this book without attaining that score, you should keep taking practice tests and studying the materials until you get there. You'll find more information about other practice test vendors in the Self-Assessment, along with even more pointers on how to study and prepare. But now, on to the exam!

The Exam Situation

When you arrive at the testing center where you scheduled your exam, or Red Hat's training facility itself, you'll need to sign in with an exam coordinator. He or she may ask you to show two forms of identification, one of which must be a photo ID. After you've signed in you will be escorted to your testing station and you will be asked to deposit any books, bags, or other items you brought with you below your desk. Typically, the room will be furnished with anywhere from a half a dozen to a dozen computers.

You'll be furnished with a pen and pencil and a blank sheet of paper. You're allowed to write down any information you want on both sides of this sheet. Before the exam, you should memorize as much of the material that appears on The Cram Sheet (inside the front cover of this book) as you can so you can write that information on the blank sheet as soon as you are seated in front of the computer. You can refer to your rendition of The Cram Sheet anytime you like during the test. Keep in mind, however, that most of the RHCE exams are performance based, and not multiple choice. This means that you will be facing time constrictions that you have to balance between your physical system time, task coordination, and more. So use your time wisely.

The exam situation will be manned at all times by the instructor or exam coordinator to monitor the test takers, and give instructions when necessary. In addition, the instructor is available as a last resort for help. Please note, asking the instructor for help does impact your score by a very large percentage (even as much as 25 percent for one question!). If you are running out of time and can't get past a specific portion of the exam, you may opt to take the point reduction to complete the exam. Depending on which part of the exam you begin, the instructor will have preloaded or prepared the appropriate Red Hat certification exam set up. You'll be testing with a number of other students, and will be asked to start at the same time.

All Red Hat certification exams allow a certain maximum amount of time in which to complete your work. The RHCE 300 Exam consists of three sections. The sections are presented in random order, meaning that one time they may present the written exam first, another the Installation Lab, and another the Debugging Lab, so make sure you are very prepared before entering the exam area. You may not be able to take advantage of the breaks in between exams to prepare for the next one. The exam comprises two performance based sections and one written section. The performance based debugging section is allotted three hours. The performance based installation and configuration section is allotted two hours. The written element is given one hour.

Red Hat certification exams are performance based. Although this may sound quite simple, the exam comprises three elements, two of which are hands on. You are given a task assignment for each section, as well as a non-disclosure agreement stating you won't disclose the information and questions on the exam. With the debugging element, you will be asked to fix a system with a problem that the instructor has set up. There are two tasks to this element, with individual goals assigned to each task. You are graded for each goal in each task you reach.

The installation and configuration element of the exam is also hands on. It also provides you with a task list of multiple scenarios, goals, and system processes to set up on an uninstalled, unconfigured machine.

The least stressful part of the exam is the written element, comprised of 50 multiple choice questions. Do not let the simplicity of a multiple choice exam fool you, however. You might be asked to select the best or most effective solution to a problem from a range of choices, all of which technically are correct. In addition, you can almost guarantee that you will be presented with questions that were not made available in any preparation material, or even to those individual who participate in the RHCE 300 preparation course! Taking the exam is quite an adventure, and it involves real thinking, skill, and time management. This book shows you what to expect and how to deal with the potential problems, puzzles, and predicaments.

Exam Layout And Design

For the multiple choice exam, questions are typically structured with a question, and four or five options. The written exam is expected to change continuously (to provide the ultimate testing experience to fully test the exam taker), so you never know when you're going to get a curve ball. To get you comfortable with all types of questions, we've thrown in some differently-formatted question types in our end-of-chapter questions (the "Practice Questions" section in each chapter). For example, in this book, at least, you'll have to answer questions that have multiple correct answers, such as "What are three video configuration tools used on Red Hat 6.0?"

Exam-Taking Basics

The most important advice about taking any exam is this: Read each question carefully. Some questions are deliberately ambiguous, some use double negatives, and others use terminology in incredibly precise ways. The author has taken numerous exams—both practice and live—and in nearly every one has missed at least one question because she didn't read it closely or carefully enough.

Here are some suggestions on how to deal with the tendency to jump to an answer too quickly:

➤ Make sure you read every word in the question. If you find yourself jumping ahead impatiently, go back and start over.

➤ As you read, try to restate the question in your own terms. If you can do this, you should be able to pick the correct answer(s) much more easily.

➤ When returning to a question after your initial read-through, read every word again—otherwise, your mind can fall quickly into a rut. Sometimes, revisiting a question after turning your attention elsewhere lets you see something you missed, but the strong tendency is to see what you've seen before. Try to avoid that tendency at all costs.

➤ If you return to a question more than twice, try to articulate to yourself what you don't understand about the question, why the answers don't appear to make sense, or what appears to be missing. If you chew on the subject for awhile, your subconscious might provide the details that are lacking or you might notice a "trick" that will point to the right answer.

Above all, try to deal with each question by thinking through what you know about Red Hat Linux and Linux in general—the characteristics, behaviors, facts, and figures involved. By reviewing what you know (and what you've written down on your information sheet), you'll often recall or understand things sufficiently to determine the answer to the question.

Question-Handling Strategies

Based on exams the authors have taken, some interesting trends have become apparent. For the multiple choice element, questions taking only a single answer, usually two or three of the answers will be obviously incorrect, and two of the answers will be plausible—of course, only one can be correct. Unless the answer leaps out at you (if it does, reread the question to look for a trick; sometimes those are the ones you're most likely to get wrong), begin the process of answering by eliminating those answers that are most obviously wrong.

Things to look for in obviously wrong answers include spurious menu choices or utility names, nonexistent software options, and terminology you've never seen. If you've done your homework for an exam, no valid information should be completely new to you. In that case, unfamiliar or bizarre terminology probably indicates a totally bogus answer.

Numerous questions assume that the default behavior of a particular utility is in effect. If you know the defaults and understand what they mean, this knowledge will help you cut through many Gordian knots.

Budget your time by making sure that you've completed one-quarter of the questions one-quarter of the way through the exam period (or the first 12 or 13 questions in the first 14 or 15 minutes) and three-quarters of them three-quarters of the way through (36 or 37 questions in the first 45 to 47 minutes).

If you're not finished when 55 minutes have elapsed, use the last 5 minutes to guess your way through the remaining questions. Remember, guessing is potentially more valuable than not answering, because blank answers are always wrong, but a guess may turn out to be right. If you don't have a clue about any of the remaining questions, pick answers at random, or choose all a's, b's, and so on. The important thing is to submit an exam for scoring that has an answer for every question.

Mastering The Inner Game

In the final analysis, knowledge breeds confidence, and confidence breeds success. If you study the materials in this book carefully and review all the exam prep questions at the end of each chapter, you should become aware of those areas where additional learning and study are required.

Next, follow up by reading some or all of the materials recommended in the "Need To Know More?" section at the end of each chapter. In addition, check out some of the online resources listed in Chapter 4. The idea is to become familiar enough with the concepts and situations you find in the sample questions that you can reason your way through similar situations on a real exam. If you know the material, you have every right to be confident that you can pass the exam.

After you've worked your way through the book, take the practice written exam in Chapter 14. This will provide a reality check and help you identify areas you need to study further. Make sure you follow up and review materials related to the questions you miss on the practice exam before scheduling a real exam. Only when you've covered all the ground and feel comfortable with the whole scope of the practice exam should you take a real one.

If you take the practice written exam and don't score at least 85 percent correct, you'll want to practice further.

Armed with the information in this book and with the determination to augment your knowledge, you should be able to pass the certification exam. However, you need to work at it, or you'll spend the exam fee more than once before you finally pass. If you prepare seriously, you should do well. Good luck!

Additional Resources

A good source of information about Red Hat certification exams comes from Red Hat itself. Because its products and technologies—and the exams that go with them—change frequently, the best place to go for exam-related information is online.

If you haven't already visited the Red Hat Certified Engineer site, do so right now. The RHCE home page resides at **www.redhat.com/products/training.html** (see Figure 1.1).

> *Note: This page might not be there by the time you read this, or it might have been replaced by something new and different, because things change regularly on the Red Hat site.*

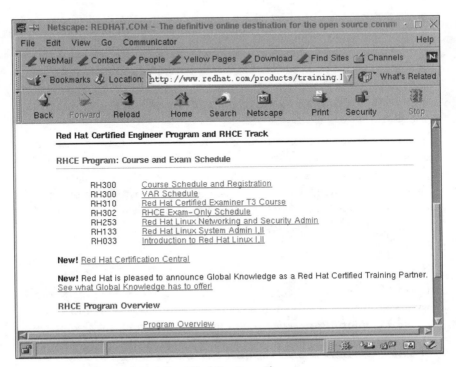

Figure 1.1   The Red Hat Certified Engineer home page.

The options on the home page's menu point to the most important sources of information in the RHCE pages. Check out the Certification Choices menu entry to read about the various certification and training programs that Red Hat offers.

These are just the high points of what's available in the Red Hat certification and training pages. As you browse through them—and we strongly recommend that you do—you'll probably find other informational tidbits mentioned that are every bit as interesting and compelling.

Coping With Change On The Web

Sooner or later, all the information we've shared with you about the Red Hat Certified Engineer and training pages and the other Web-based resources mentioned throughout the rest of this book will go stale or be replaced by newer information. In some cases, the URLs you find here might lead you to their replacements; in other cases, the URLs will go nowhere, leaving you with the dreaded "404 File not found" error message. When that happens, don't give up.

There's always a way to find what you want on the Web if you're willing to invest some time and energy. Most large or complex Web sites—and Red Hat's qualifies on both counts—offer a search engine. Looking back at Figure 1.1, you can see that a Search button appears along the top edge of the page. As long as you can get to Red Hat's site (it should stay at **www.redhat.com** for a long while yet), you can use this tool to help you find what you need.

The more focused you can make a search request, the more likely the results will include information you can use. For example, you can search for the string "training and certification" to produce a lot of data about the subject in general, but if you're looking for the installation guide for Red Hat 6.0" you'll be more likely to get there quickly if you use a search string similar to the following:

```
Installation Guide Red Hat 6.0
```

Finally, feel free to use general search tools—such as **www.google.com, www.search.com, www.altavista.com**, and **www.excite.com**—to search for related information. The bottom line is this: If you can't find something where the book says it lives, intensify your search.

General Linux Information

Terms you'll need to understand:

√ Open Source

√ Copyright

√ Free software

√ Usenet

√ Minix

Techniques you'll need to master:

√ Being familiar with the history and development of Open Source Software (OSS)

√ Being familiar with the history and development of Linux

√ Preparing to learn and install Linux

Open source software (OSS) and Linux in general have come a long way since Linus Torvalds began his hobbyist project called "Linux" back in 1990. In order to understand Linux at all, it's imperative that you learn both the history and the general concepts behind the development of OSS and Linux. So before you get engrossed with all the technical details of Linux, let's learn about where it started and how it developed. This chapter will help you understand where Linux came from and what it's all about, and where to look when you need more information.

Understanding OSS

OSS is software whose source code is available to the public. Having publicly available source code doesn't necessarily mean there are no copyright issues, however. In fact, OSS typically is copyrighted with restrictions meant to preserve its open source status, authorship, and control.

OSS is usually developed by the mass effort of programmers all over the world. Universities, government agencies, and not-for-profit organizations (as well as individual programmers) develop OSS.

Although companies and individuals had released their software source code for years, the actual label "Open Source" wasn't used until early 1998. On one early February day, a group of individuals met to discuss Netscape's January 1998 announcement that it was going to release the source code for its popular Web browser, Netscape Navigator. The members of this group included Todd Anderson, Chris Peterson (of the Foresight Institute), Jon "maddog" Hall and Larry Augustin (of Linux International), Sam Ockman (from the Silicon Valley Linux Users Group), and Eric S. Raymond.

These individuals recognized the impeccable timing that would be needed to respond to Netscape's actions. The Linux and "free software" community would need to react appropriately to seize the moment to gain corporate recognition for the open development process. After brainstorming about tactics, the corporate community, and Netscape's recent actions, they finally agreed on the "Open Source" label. Peterson had suggested this title instead of "free software."

Many things have happened to the open source community since it was adopted as "open source" instead of "free software." Shortly after the announcement regarding the new movement toward OSS, a feverish debate between hackers all over the world began about the use of the new term instead of "free software." In fact, even Richard Stallman, founder of the GNU project, considered using the new term, if only for a little while.

By the end of that February, however, the roar died down over the "Open Source" label issue. All attention was diverted back to the corporate world as both Netscape and O'Reilly and Associates had agreed to begin referring to OSS in their press releases and on their Web sites.

At the end of March, Netscape Navigator's source was made freely available, spawning a massive download over the Internet. Within a few hours of its release, hackers all over the world began returning code fixes and enhancements.

In April, the press began its stream of non-technical coverage of open source for the public's benefit. *Salon* magazine interviewed Eric S. Raymond (ESR) and published an article on the details of Open Source.

May was an exciting month for the open source community. Corel announced that it was going to port WordPerfect and its office products to Linux. In addition, Sun Microsystems and Adaptec were the first two large, established vendors to join Linux International.

OSS began to heat up in July when an article was published in *Forbes* magazine. The focus of the article? An interview with Linus Torvalds himself.

The number of open source projects continued to escalate into the end of the year. In October, Microsoft helped give an exciting end to Linux's first year. In response to its impending antitrust case, it released a formal statement claiming that Linux's existence proved that Microsoft didn't in fact have an OS monopoly. The year closed up with a bang after IDG announced that the Linux market share had increased by 212 percent in 1998!

The Free Software Foundation (FSF)

Before the OSS project began, the FSF, founded to help protect and pursue the rights of free software, was already established. The FSF, which supports the free software movement, is currently a tax-exempt charity that raises funds to work on the GNU Project.

According to the FSF, free software is a matter of liberty, not price. It says that to understand the concept, you should think of "free speech," not "free beer." The FSF believes that free software is the freedom for the user to run, copy, distribute, study, change, and improve software.

The GNU Project

The GNU Project was started in 1984 to develop a completely free Unix-like operating system. GNU's founder, Richard Stallman (also fondly

known by his email handle RMS), is the best one to explain its begin-
nings, so here (quoted verbatim) is his original post to Usenet on
September 1983 in which he explains his plans for the GNU Project:

```
From CSvax:pur-ee:inuxc!ixn5c!ihnp4!houxm!mhuxi!eagle!mit-
vax!mit-eddie!RMS@MIT-OZ
From: RMS%MIT-OZ@mit-eddie
Newsgroups: net.unix-wizards,net.usoft
Subject: new UNIX implementation
Date: Tue, 27-Sep-83 12:35:59 EST
Organization: MIT AI Lab, Cambridge, MA


Free Unix!


Starting this Thanksgiving I am going to write a complete
Unix-compatible software system called GNU (for Gnu's Not
Unix), and give it away free to everyone who can use it.
Contributions of time, money, programs and equipment are
greatly needed.

To begin with, GNU will be a kernel plus all the utilities
needed to write and run C programs: editor, shell, C compiler,
linker, assembler, and a few other things. After this we will
add a text formatter, a YACC, an Empire game, a spreadsheet,
and hundreds of other things. We hope to supply, eventually,
everything useful that normally comes with a Unix system, and
anything else useful, including on-line and hardcopy
documentation.

GNU will be able to run Unix programs, but will not be
identical to Unix. We will make all improvements that are
convenient, based on our experience with other operating
systems. In particular, we plan to have longer filenames, file
version numbers, a crashproof file system, filename completion
perhaps, terminal-independent display support, and eventually
a Lisp-based window system through which several Lisp programs
and ordinary Unix programs can share a screen. Both C and Lisp
will be available as system programming languages. We will
have network software based on MIT's chaosnet protocol, far
superior to UUCP. We may also have something compatible
with UUCP.

Who Am I?
I am Richard Stallman, inventor of the original much-imitated
EMACS editor, now at the Artificial Intelligence Lab at MIT. I
have worked extensively on compilers, editors, debuggers,
```

command interpreters, the Incompatible Timesharing System and
the Lisp Machine operating system. I pioneered terminal-
independent display support in ITS. In addition I have
implemented one crashproof file system and two window systems
for Lisp machines.

Why I Must Write GNU
I consider that the golden rule requires that if I like a
program I must share it with other people who like it. I
cannot in good conscience sign a nondisclosure agreement or a
software license agreement.

So that I can continue to use computers without violating my
principles, I have decided to put together a sufficient body
of free software so that I will be able to get along without
any software that is not free.

How You Can Contribute
I am asking computer manufacturers for donations of machines
and money. I'm asking individuals for donations of programs
and work.

One computer manufacturer has already offered to provide a
machine. But we could use more. One consequence you can expect
if you donate machines is that GNU will run on them at an
early date. The machine had better be able to operate in a
residential area, and not require sophisticated cooling or
power.

Individual programmers can contribute by writing a compatible
duplicate of some Unix utility and giving it to me. For most
projects, such part-time distributed work would be very hard
to coordinate; the independently-written parts would not work
together. But for the particular task of replacing Unix, this
problem is absent. Most interface specifications are fixed by
Unix compatibility. If each contribution works with the rest
of Unix, it will probably work with the rest of GNU.

If I get donations of money, I may be able to hire a few
people full or part time. The salary won't be high, but I'm
looking for people for whom knowing they are helping humanity
is as important as money. I view this as a way of enabling
dedicated people to devote their full energies to working on
GNU by sparing them the need to make a living in another way.
For more information, contact me.

```
Arpanet mail:
  RMS@MIT-MC.ARPA
Usenet:
  ...!mit-eddie!RMS@OZ
  ...!mit-vax!RMS@OZ
US Snail:
  Richard Stallman
  166 Prospect St
  Cambridge, MA 02139
```

Linux is composed of the Linux kernel and many GNU programs and utilities. Some popular GNU tools that are used frequently are Bash, CVS, ed, Emacs, finger, GCC, ghostview, the Gimp, gzip, ispell, mtools, screen, and tar. These are just a few of the existing GNU programs available, however. In fact, the GNU tools are often available for other commercial versions of Unix as well. Due to the large amount of GNU tools that are used within Linux, and those that help make the Linux distribution, some Linux advocates and evangelists differ on their opinions of what to actually call Linux itself. Many GNU evangelists insist on calling Linux "GNU/Linux" or "Lignux". Personally, I simply call it "Linux." However, I do credit the GNU tools for making Linux work. Therefore, as in the battle of how to pronounce Linux, I have no preference about what you call Linux either.

The GNU General Public License (GPL)

The GPL is the license that most open source projects use for their software. Developed in the late 1980s, it has not been revised since its publication in 1991. The GPL is quite extensive, and many of its users interpret the document in different ways. The GPL's text is shown in this book's Appendix. Read it for a better understanding of the foundation of the Open Source community.

Although you are not tested on this information in the RHCE Exam 300, you are required to have working knowledge of it.

History Of Linux

Linus Torvalds started Linux as a hobbyist project in 1990. Torvalds, a college student from Finland, began the project after purchasing a computer to run Minix, a Unix-like operating system that was included in Andrew Tanenbaum's textbook *Operating Systems: Design and Implementation*. Shortly after, Linus decided to learn more about some of the low-level features of the Intel 80386 processor, and he then began working on what would eventually develop into the Linux kernel.

Within two months of starting the project, Linus released kernel 0.01 shortly after he posted this to comp.os.minix:

```
From: torvalds@klaava.Helsinki.FI (Linus Benedict Torvalds)
Newsgroups: comp.os.minix
Subject: What would you like to see most in minix?
Message-ID: <1991Aug25.205708.9541@klaava.Helsinki.FI>
Date: 25 Aug 91 20:57:08 GMT

Hello everybody out there using minix -

I'm doing a (free) operating system (just a hobby, won't be big
and professional like gnu) for 386(486) AT clones.  This has
been brewing since april, and is starting to get ready. I'd like
any feedback on things people like/dislike in minix, as my OS
resembles it somewhat (same physical layout of the file-system
(due to practical reasons) among other things).

I've currently ported bash(1.08) and gcc(1.40), and things seem
to work. This implies that I'll get something practical within a
few months, and I'd like to know what features most people would
want.  Any suggestions are welcome, but I won't promise I'll
implement them :-)

        Linus (torvalds@kruuna.helsinki.fi)

PS. Yes - it's free of any minix code, and it has a multi-threaded
fs. It is NOT protable (uses 386 task switching etc) and it
probably neverwill support anything other than AT-harddisks as
that's all I have :-(
```

Nearly three years after Torvalds started this project, Linux 1 was released. By this time, several Linux distributions had begun packaging the Linux kernel with basic support programs, the GNU utilities and compilers, the X Windowing system, and other useful programs. The mass numbers of Linux kernel hackers had managed to develop all the things expected from a current Unix system, including preemptive multitasking, virtual memory, shared libraries, TCP/IP support, NFS, Ethernet, and so on.

In 1995, the Linux 1.2 kernel was released. The new kernel supported kernel modules, the PCI bus, kernel-level firewalling, non-TCP/IP networking protocols, and so on. By this time, Linux had become as stable as any commercial version of Unix on the x86 platform, and was even being ported to the DEC Alpha, Sun SPARC, and SGI mips.

In 1996, the Linux 2 kernel was released. Version 2 saw the preliminary support for SMP (symmetric multi-processor) machines. It also was fully functional on multiple platforms including the x86, Alpha, Sparc, Motorola 68k, PowerPC, and MIPS.

In 1999 the latest stable kernel, version 2.2, was released. The 2.2 kernel fully supports the SMP machines as well as more fully supports multiple platforms including the 64-bit platforms. In addition, version 2.2 also had a large improvement for speed.

Red Hat History

Red Hat was started in early 1995 when two entrepreneurs, Bob Young and Mark Ewing, decided to venture into beginning a commercial Linux distributor. In just one short year, Red Hat's distribution was taking the market by storm and was even voted desktop operating system of the year by *InfoWorld*. In 1997, Red Hat won another *InfoWorld* award when its distribution of Red Hat version 5 was named Network Operating System of the Year. It won it again in 1999 with Red Hat Linux 5.2, for three years running. This was a feat no other software product had achieved in the *InfoWorld* awards history.

In September 1998, the popular trend of large technology firms investing into Red Hat started. Some of the first included Intel and Netscape Communications. In addition to technical firms, venture capital firms decided to invest. The two first were Benchmark Capital and Greylock Management. Red Hat continues to grow in its investment base, and even entered the stock market in June 1999. In addition to financial growth, the company outgrew its living quarters in an office building in Research Triangle Park in North Carolina. In February 1999, it moved into its own building, gaining five times more space!

Red Hat has expanded, changed, and adapted many times in its short five years. Since beginning as simply a "packager" of Linux, Red Hat has gained many important developers for the project, including Alan Cox, on its payroll. In addition, Red Hat is quickly expanding its install base by being the most popular Linux distribution to be sold and supported by existing vendors such as IBM, Compaq, Dell, and Hewlett-Packard. Before these vendors began shipping Linux, however, many Linux vendors, including VA Linux Systems and Penguin Computing, were already shipping Red Hat Linux-configured machines.

Linux Resources

When you get stuck, your machine breaks, or you just want to learn about something, the best skill you can learn is RTFM (Read the Fine Manual). Many good online resources are available. In fact, some Web sites and Linux vendors (such as Red Hat) host very helpful mailing lists. Here are some of the many online resources for general Linux information, vendors, distributors, software, projects, news, download, and newsgroup information.

General Information And HOWTOs

➤ http://metalab.unc.edu/LDP/   The Linux Documentation Project

➤ http://www.ssc.com/glue/   Groups of Linux Users Everywhere (GLUE)

➤ http://www.linux.org/   Linux On-Line

➤ http://www.ssc.com/linux/   Linux resources Web site

➤ http://www.redhat.com/products/training.html   Red Hat Certified Engineer Program

➤ http://www.linux-howto.com/   Linux HOWTOs

➤ http://linuxkb.cheek.com/   Linux Knowledge Base

➤ http://www.tux.org/   General Info

➤ http://www.w3.org/   World Wide Web Consortium

➤ http://www.linux.com/   Linux Information

➤ http://www.tuxedo.org/   General Information

➤ http://www.penguinservices.com/   Linux Seek

➤ http://www.linuxstart.com/   Linux resource site

➤ http://www.isc.org   Internet Software Consortium

Linux Vendors

➤ http://www.linuxmall.com/   The Linux Mall

➤ http://www.lsl.com/   Linux System Labs

➤ http://www.varesearch.com/   VA Research

➤ http://www.infomagic.com   Info Magic

➤ http://www.cheapbytes.com/   On-line Store

➤ http://www.linuxcentral.com/   Linux Central

➤ http://www.linuxgeneralstore.com/   Linux General Store

➤ http://www.linux-hw.com/   Linux Hardware

➤ http://www.pht.com/   Pacific Hi-Tech

➤ http://www.aslab.com/   Linux Hardware Provider

➤ http://linux.corel.com/   Corel's Linux Projects

Linux Distributors

➤ http://www.redhat.com/   Red Hat Software

➤ http://www.caldera.com/   Caldera Software

➤ http://www.debian.org/   Debian

➤ http://www.suse.com/   SuSE

➤ http://www.turbolinux.com/   TurboLinux

Software Information

➤ http://www.apache.org/   Apache Web Server

➤ http://www.sendmail.org/   Sendmail

➤ http://www.mozilla.org/   Mozilla Internet Browser

➤ http://www.vim.org/   VIM Homepage

➤ http://www.xemacs.org/   XEMACS Homepage

➤ http://www.estinc.com/   Enhanced Software Technologies, Inc. (BRU)

➤ http://www.software.ibm.com/data/db2/linux/   DB2 for Linux

➤ http://www.informix.com/informix/solutions/linux/freelx.html   Informix

➤ http://www.interbase.com/   Interbase

➤ http://www.dosemu.org/   DOS Emulator

➤ http://www.myxa.com/elm.html   ELM Mail Reader

➤ http://www.tuxedo.org/~esr/fetchmail/   Fetchmail

➤ http://squid.nlanr.net/squid/   Squid Proxy

➤ http://www.applix.com/   ApplixWare

➤ http://www.abisource.com/   AbiWord

➤ http://www.gimp.org/   Gimp

➤ http://www.washington.edu/pine/   Pine Mail Reader

➤ http://www.netscape.com/   Netscape

➤ http://www.realaudio.com/   Real Audio

➤ http://www.stardivision.com/   Star Office

➤ http://www.adobe.com/   Adobe PDF Viewer

Project Information

➤ http://www.kernel.org/   Linux Kernel Web site

➤ http://www.opensource.org/   Open Source Software

➤ http://www.fsf.org/   Free Software Foundation

➤ http://www.xfree86.org/   XFree86 Development

➤ http://www.kde.org/   KDE Desktop System

➤ http://www.gnome.org/   Gnome Desktop

➤ http://www.rpm.org/ Red Hat Package Manager

➤ http://www.jargon.org/   Mirror of the Jargon File

➤ http://www.beowulf.org/   Beowulf Cluster Project

➤ http://www.kernelnotes.org/   Linux Kernel Information

➤ http://www.li.org/   Linux International

Linux News

➤ http://www.linuxjournal.com/   The *Linux Journal*

➤ http://www.slashdot.org/   Slashdot, News for Nerds

➤ http://www.freshmeat.org/   Freshmeat, more News for Nerds

➤ http://www.ssc.com/lg   Linux Gazette

➤ http://www.lwn.net/   Linux Weekly News

➤ http://www.linux-radio.com/   Linux Radio Show

➤ http://www.thelinuxshow.com/ The Linux Show

➤ http://www.linux-mag.com/ Linux Magazine

➤ http://www.linuxtoday.com/ Linux Today

➤ http://www.linuxworld.com/ Linux World

➤ http://www.linuxresources.com/ Linux Resources On-line

Download Sites

➤ ftp://ftp.redhat.com Red Hat

➤ ftp://ftp.luci.org Popular sites mirror

➤ ftp://metalab.unc.edu Popular site

➤ ftp://ftp.debian.org Debian

➤ ftp://ftp.xfree86.org X Windowing System

➤ ftp://ftp.kernel.org Linux Kernel

➤ ftp://ftp.caldera.com Caldera

➤ ftp://ftp.linux.org Popular sites

➤ ftp://prep.ai.mit.edu/pub/gnu/ Official GNU site

➤ http://www.linuxberg.com/ Popular download site

➤ http://www.binaries.org/ Download site for software binaries

Newsgroups

➤ comp.os.linux.announce

➤ comp.os.linux.answers

➤ comp.os.linux.hardware

➤ comp.os.linux.misc

➤ comp.os.linux.setup

➤ comp.os.linux.x

Practice Questions

Question 1

> Who developed Linux?
>
> ○ a. Linus Torvalds
>
> ○ b. Richard Stallman
>
> ○ c. Bob Young
>
> ○ d. None of the above

Answer a is correct. This is a tricky question because both answers a and d would be correct by today's definition. However, though a very large community helps to develop Linux today, the original developer was Linus.

Question 2

> What is the GPL and what is its purpose?

The GPL is the General Public License. Its purpose is to protect the copyright and open source or free software characteristics that the author of a software package wishes to keep. This license prevents other authors, companies, and so on from using the software source, making modifications, and redistributing it without redistributing the code as well.

Question 3

> Who founded the FSF and began the GNU Project?
>
> ○ a. Linus Torvalds
>
> ○ b. Richard Stallman
>
> ○ c. Bob Young
>
> ○ d. None of the above

Answer b is correct. Richard Stallman, founded the FSF and began the GNU Project.

Question 4

Who founded Red Hat?

Red Hat was a cooperative project between two entrepreneurs, Bob Young and Mark Ewing.

Question 5

What online resource could you use for text documentation and links for help with Linux-related programs, hardware, and more?

- ○ a. **www.microsoft.com**
- ○ b. **http://metalab.unc.edu/LDP/**
- ○ c. **www.compaq.com**
- ○ d. **www.slashdot.org**

Answer b is correct. All of these sites offer interesting Linux information of sorts; however, the best place to find help and documentation for your Linux issues is the Linux Documentation Project, found at **http://metalab.unc.edu/ LDP/**.

Question 6

Red Hat develops Linux.

- ○ a. True
- ○ b. False

Answer b is correct. Linux is developed by teams, companies, and programmers from all over the world. Although Red Hat does have staff members who develop parts of Linux, its main business is not to develop Linux. Rather, Red Hat helps the community by packaging, testing, bug fixing, developing, and supporting different parts of Linux.

Question 7

> What is the FSF?

The FSF is the Free Software Foundation. It was founded by Richard Stallman to promote and support free software development and developers of free software.

Question 8

> What does GNU stand for?
>
> ○ a. Greek Noble Unix
>
> ○ b. Genius Native Unix
>
> ○ c. Geek Needed Unix
>
> ○ d. GNU's Not Unix

Answer d is correct. Although some of the other answers could be accurate, they aren't what GNU stands for. GNU actually stands for GNU's Not Unix.

Need To Know More?

 Dibona, Chris, Sam Ockman, Mark Stone, eds. *Open Sources*. Sebastapol, CA, O'Reilly & Associates, 1999. ISBN: 1-56592-582-3. This entire book focuses on the roots of open source software, including where it came from and where it is going.

 http://www.fsf.org/

This Web site covers information regarding both the GNU Project and the Free Software Foundation. Visit the link **http://www.fsf.org/gnu/gnu-history.html** to learn more about the GNU Project. Visit the link **http://www.fsf.org/fsf/fsf.html** to learn more about the Free Software Foundation.

 http://www.opensource.org/

This Web site covers information and projects that are associated with open source software.

 http://www.redhat.com/

This Web site covers information related to Red Hat Software, Inc. To learn more about Red Hat Software, follow the "About" link (**http://www.redhat.com/about/**).

Red Hat
Prerequisites

Terms you'll need to understand:
√ Filesystem
√ Partition
√ Shell
√ Filter
√ Compile
√ Source

Techniques you'll need to master:
√ Partitioning hard disks
√ Manipulating text files
√ Compiling a kernel
√ Reading shell scripts
√ Reading a log file
√ Starting and stopping services

Before pursuing your dreams of becoming a Red Hat Certified Engineer (RHCE), or just becoming a Linux "power user", you should have extensive knowledge of Linux, Linux tools, and TCP/IP networking basics. These prerequisites are also required if you opt to take part in the Red Hat Certified Engineering training program, which is scheduled for the four days before you take your exam. This chapter will discuss many of the general Linux and Unix concepts that you need to be familiar with before tackling your RHCE preparation.

Unix Basics

Linux is a Unix-like operating system. Therefore, it's essential for you to know basic Unix commands in order to become an RHCE. You must have working knowledge of Unix concepts such as the filesystem hierarchy, mounting and administering filesystems, basic shell configuration, and basic file operations. In addition, filters, wildcards, vi, and other operations are file operations. They manipulate and edit files.

Unix Filesystem Hierarchy And Structure

Unix filesystems are structured in a directory tree. Although these structures differ slightly on each flavor of Unix system, the directories I describe here are standard on Linux.

The main directory, called the *root directory*, is denoted with a simple forward slash (/). All directories on a Unix system are subdirectories of the root. Directly under the root directory are the following subdirectories:

➤ **/bin** The typical location for executable and binary files for Unix commands and utilities. It also contains executables used by users.

 Several commands located in /bin are actually symlinks to /usr/bin. If you cannot find the command you are looking for in /bin, be sure to look in /usr/bin.

➤ **/dev** The device directory. The /dev directory is divided up into subdirectories that contain files for a specific device. These directories are named based on the type of device files they contain. Some examples of these directories are hda1 (for the first IDE hard drive), fd0 (for the floppy disk), and cdrom, which is a symlink created to whatever cdrom device that Red Hat was installed from, if installed via cdrom.

➤ **/etc**   The location for configuration files. More importantly, the /etc directory contains the system boot scripts. These boot scripts are located under the /etc/rc.d/ directory. The services that run at bootup are located under /etc/rc.d/init.d/.

It is rumoured that this method will be changing in upcoming versions of Red Hat Linux to reflect Debian's locations for the boot scripts. Therefore, these files may be represented under /etc/init.d rather than /etc/rc.d/init.d. This is still different than other distributions and other commercial versions of Unix who place these files under /sbin/init.d.

➤ **/sbin**   The location of some system configuration and system administrator executable files. Most of your general administration commands—such as **lilo, fdisk, fsck,** and **route**—are located here.

➤ **/home**   The location of the home directories for your general users. Under /home, each user can set up his own email, public_html, and personal files.

➤ **/lost+found**   The system's directory for placing lost files that are found or created by disk errors or improper system shutdowns. At boot, programs such as fsck find the inodes, which have no directory entries and reattaches them as files in this directory. In addition to the root filesystem, there should be one of these directories located on every filesystem created on the system.

➤ **/mnt**   The default mount directory. Under /mnt, you mount your devices such as cdrom and floppy disk.

➤ **/proc**   Your process directory. Under /proc, you will find information about running processes, as well as system configuration information such as interrupt usage, I/O port use, and CPU type.

➤ **/tmp**   A default directory created to house temporary files. This is a good directory to keep an eye on if you are trying to limit disk space.

➤ **/usr**   The location for subdirectories for local programs and executables for user and administrative commands. /usr contains the binaries for X, games, your shared libraries, and more.

➤ **/var**   The location for your spooling, logging, and other data (the "var" is short for various). Some common applications that use /var for spooling and logging are mail, printing, and cron.

➤ **/opt** The location for optional packages. Many programs, such as Applixware and even KDE, install packages in this directory.

➤ **/usr/local** The location where the administrator can install programs to the system. This is usually reserved for system related programs. Linux distributions do not heavily use this directory, as most Linux distributions come packaged with the most popular utilities, and such packages are not needed to be installed by the administrator.

Mounting Filesystems And Devices

You can mount devices, partitions, and separate disks to directories (called *mount points*) within the filesystem. To read from a device, such as a floppy disk or a CD-ROM, you use the **mount** command. The **mount** command's syntax is: **mount** *–t type /dev/device mountpoint*. For example, to mount a CD-ROM drive, type

```
mount -t iso9660 /dev/cdrom /mnt/cdrom
```

To access the CD-ROM drive, simply change into the /mnt/cdrom directory and then type "ls" for a list of files found on the CD-ROM.

Your default filesystem types and mount points are set in /etc/fstab. The fstab file sets the default device, mount point, filesystem type, type of mount, and filesystem dump and mount order options. Here is an example of a fstab file:

```
/dev/hda3        /            ext2      defaults          1  1
/dev/hda1        /boot        ext2      defaults          1  2
/dev/hda4        swap         swap      defaults          0  0
/dev/fd0         /mnt/floppy  ext2      noauto            0  0
/dev/cdrom       /mnt/cdrom   iso9660   noauto,ro,user    0  0
```

Settings in /etc/fstab also allow you to use the defaults when you are mounting filesystems manually. For instance, rather than typing

```
mount -t iso9660 /dev/cdrom /mnt/cdrom
```

you'd simply type

```
mount /dev/cdrom
```

or even

```
mount /mnt/cdrom
```

and mount automatically mounts the cdrom device, based on the defaults in your /etc/fstab file.

When mounting filesystems with settings other than the defaults, or to mount filesystems that aren't listed in the /etc/fstab file, you need to specify the type, device, and mount point. For instance, to mount separate partitions on a single drive, such as an msdos partition, you can type

```
mount -t msdos /dev/hda1 /dos
```

To access this partition, simply change into the /dos directory, treating it like any local filesystem. The **t** option after the **mount** command is used to specify the type.

Filesystem Administration Commands

The Unix filesystem is unique because in order for it to function properly, it must be structured, formatted, partitioned, checked, and mounted/unmounted cleanly. With this in mind, you must understand the basics of administration tools such as fdisk, mkfs, and fsck.

fdisk

The administration tool fdisk, which has a command-line interface, is used to partition your hard drive. After you become accustomed to using the interface, you'll see that it allows for quick and simple partitioning. Running fdisk opens a screen that looks similar to this:

```
Using /dev/hda as default device!
The number of cylinders for this disk is set to 1240.
This is larger than 1024, and may cause problems with:
1) software that runs at boot time (e.g., LILO)
2) booting and partitioning software from other OSs
             e.g., DOS FDISK, OS/2 FDISK)

Command (m for help):
```

Pressing "m" at the command prompt gives you a list of command options, as shown here:

```
Command (m for help): m
Command action
   a    toggle a bootable flag
   b    edit bsd disklabel
   c    toggle the dos compatibility flag
```

```
d    delete a partition
l    list known partition types
m    print this menu
n    add a new partition
o    create a new empty DOS partition table
p    print the partition table
q    quit without saving changes
t    change a partition's system id
u    change display/entry units
v    verify the partition table
w    write table to disk and exit
x    extra functionality (experts only)
```

As you can see from the list in this code block, pressing "p" prints the partition table. The output will look something similar to the following code block, if you have three partitions, including one FAT32, one Linux native, and one Linux swap. Also, this code is reporting for a 10GB IDE drive:

```
      Disk        /dev/hda: 255 heads, 63 sectors, 1240 cylinders
Units = cylinders of 16065 * 512 bytes

   Device Boot    Start      End   Blocks   Id  System
/dev/hda1    *        1      765  6144831    b  Win95 FAT32
/dev/hda2            766     1015  2008125   83  Linux native
/dev/hda3           1016     1024    72292+  82  Linux swap
```

You can edit these partitions by using the commands listed when you type "m". Pressing "d" deletes a partition, prompting you for the partition number. The "n" option adds a new partition, prompting you for primary or extended, and the number. Pressing "t" changes the type of partition from the current type to a new type (for instance, changing a Linux native to Linux swap). The "l" option gives you a list of supported types and their codes. The "q" command will quit fdisk without saving changes, and "w" writes to the table and exits.

mkfs

mkfs is used to build a Linux filesystem on a device, usually a hard disk partition. mkfs is simply a front end for the various filesystem builders available under Linux. Typical usage of mkfs looks like this:

```
mkfs  [ -V ] [ -t fstype ] [ fs-options ] filesys [ blocks ]
```

The following is an explanation of the typical options used with mkfs as well as some additional options available.

➤ **-V**   Produces verbose output, including all filesystem-specific commands that are executed. This is useful only for testing.

➤ **-t fstype**   Specifies the type of filesystem to be built. If the type is not specified, the default filesystem type (currently ext2) is used.

➤ **fs-options**   Specifies filesystem-specific options to be passed to the real filesystem builder.

➤ **-c**   Checks the device for bad blocks before building the filesystem.

➤ **-l filename**   Reads the bad blocks list from the file name.

➤ **-v**   Produces verbose output.

➤ **filesys**   Is either the device name (for example, /dev/hda1 or /dev/sdb2) or the mount point (for example, /, /usr, or /home) for the filesystem.

➤ **blocks**   Is the number of blocks that will be used for the filesystem.

fsck

fsck is used to check and repair Linux filesystems. It is typically used like this:

```
fsck [ -AVR ] [ -s ] [ -t fstype ] [ fs-options ] filesys
```

The following explains the options used in the previous snippet of code as well as a few extra options available.

➤ **-A**   Walks through the /etc/fstab file and tries to check all filesystems at once.

➤ **-R**   Skips the root filesystem when you are checking all filesystems with the **-A** flag.

➤ **-V**   Produces verbose output.

➤ **-s**   Serializes fsck operations.

➤ **-t fstype**   Specifies the type of filesystem to be checked. If the **-A** flag is specified, only filesystems that match fstype are checked.

➤ **fs-options**

  ➤ **-a**   Repairs the filesystem automatically without any questions (use this option with caution).

  ➤ **-r**   Repairs the filesystem interactively (Will ask for confirmations).

  ➤ **filesys**   Indicates either the device name or mount point.

Basic Shell Configuration

When you are using the bash shell, two files are located in your /home directory: .bash_profile and .bashrc. The .bash_profile file contains initialization scripts that are executed at login. Here is an example of a generic .bash_profile file:

```
# .bash_profile

# Get the aliases and functions
if [ -f ~/.bashrc ]; then
            . ~/.bashrc
fi

# User specific environment and startup programs

PATH=$PATH:$HOME/bin
BASH_ENV=$HOME/.bashrc
USERNAME=""

export USERNAME BASH_ENV PATH
```

The .bashrc file contains execution scripts that are run each time a new shell is opened. Here is an example of a generic .bashrc file:

```
# .bashrc
# User specific aliases and functions

alias rm='rm -i'
alias cp='cp -i'
alias mv='mv -i'

# Source global definitions
if [ -f /etc/bashrc ]; then
        . /etc/bashrc
fi
```

Basic File Operations

For obvious reasons, you must be skilled at using basic Unix commands and filters to be a Unix administrator. Table 3.1 lists several basic commands, gives an example of the context to use each command, and explains what each command does.

Table 3.1	Basic Unix commands.	
Command	**Example**	**Explanation**
cp	cp file1 file2	Is the Unix command to copy a file. The example copies file1 to file2.
mv	mv file1 file2	Is the Unix command to move a file. The example moves file1 and renamed it to file2.
ls	ls	Prints the directory listing. You can run **ls** directly from the directory from which you want a file listing. Some special options for **ls** include **-l** (include details) and **-a** (show hidden files).
more	ls -a lmore	Prints the output of a file or command page by page. The example prints the file, listing one page at a time.
less	ls -la lless	Is similar to **more** (but **less** allows for backward movement in a file); prints the output from a command page by page.
cd	cd /etc	Is the Unix command to change a directory. The example changes into the /etc directory.
pwd	pwd	Prints the full name of the current directory you are in.
tar	tar -xvf filename.tar	Is a Unix compression utility. The example gives the appropriate options to extract verbosely the filename.tar file.
rm	rm dead.letter	Deletes a file. The example deletes the dead.letter file.

Filters

Some of Unix's most popular filters manipulate files into specific output. They include **cat, grep, wc, tail, head,** and **sort**. Using **cat** on a file concatenates the contents of the file into standard output. Here's an example of using **cat**:

```
cat filename
```

The **grep** tool is very popular to search files for a specific term or string. The output of **grep** displays only the lines that contain the term or string that was grepped. The **grep** tool can be used by itself, or to filter the output of another filter, such as **cat**. For example, both

```
cat filename | grep error
```

and

```
grep error filename
```

would search the contents of the filename for the word "error".

The **wc** filter is helpful when you need to count the number of bytes (-c), words (-w), or lines (-l) from the output of a file. The following snippet of code **cat**s the filename, pipes it through **grep,** and prints the lines that contain the term "error", and counts the number of lines of output by piping the output through **wc -l**:

```
cat filename | grep error |wc -1
```

The **tail** filter is commonly used to print logs and other large files. Simply running a

```
tail /var/log/messages
```

prints the last 10 lines of /var/log/messages. However, to run a continuous output of a log, you use the **-f** option. For instance, running

```
tail -f /var/log/messages
```

prints a running log of the /var/log/messages file.

The opposite of **tail,** called **head**, prints the first part of a message file. To print the first 10 lines of a log, for instance, type "head -n 10 /var/log/messages".

Filename Wildcards

When you are using the commands and filters discussed so far, it is often useful to implement wildcards. Wildcards—such as *, ?, [ ] , and { }—are useful to select or work with multiple files that contain similar characteristics in their file names.

 Wildcards are commonly refered to as "file globs," as "globs," or by the verb "globbing." For more information about globbing, read the man page (man 7 glob).

For the examples in the rest of this section, I will use the list of files shown here:

```
$ls
file          file3          12file
```

```
1file          file4          file34
2file          file5file
```

The asterisk (*) character is used to represent any number of characters in a file name. **file*** returns all files with file names that begin with "file" and end with any character sequence. On the other hand, *****file** returns any file name that ends in "file". Here is **file*** in action:

```
$ls file*
file3          file34
file4          file5file
```

The question mark (?) character is used to represent a single character. **file?** requests any file name that starts with "file" and ends with any other single character. On the other hand, **??file** requests any file name with two random characters that are followed by "file". Here is how to use **file?**:

```
$ls file?
file3
file4
```

Closed brackets ([ ]) are used to specify a range of characters. **file[abc]** requests the file names filea, fileb, and filec. Another example, **[169]file**, requests the file names 1file, 6file, and 9file. This example, shows the use of square brackets:

```
$ls file[123]
file3
```

You'll notice that **file[123]** yields only file3. In our original list, file1 and file2 do not exist.

Curly brackets ({ }) are used to specify a range of characters, much like closed brackets; however, when you use curly brackets, multiple character strings can be separated by commas. For instance, **file{1,34,ab}** returns file names file1, file34, and fileab. Another example, **file{ab,s,ing}34**, requests fileab34, files34, and fileing34. The use of curly brackets in a string is shown here:

```
$ls file{1,2,3,34}
file3
file34
```

Basic **vi** Usage

Text editing is one of the most popular uses of any operating system. **vi** happens to be one of the most useful and popular text editors for Unix. With **vi**, you can create and edit any text file.

vi uses different modes to assist you in editing files. When you open or create a file with **vi** (by entering **vi filename**), you are in command mode. In command mode, single keys on your keyboard have special commands. For example, pressing "i", "a", or "o" drops you into insert mode. In insert mode, you can directly insert text into the file. To return to command mode, press the Esc key.

In command mode, you can also quickly move around in your document without using the cursor keys, allowing you to keep your hands on the home row, and speeding your editing time. The j key acts as your down cursor and jumps a line. The k key acts as your up cursor and jumps up one line. The b and l keys act as your left and right cursor keys, respectively. These movement commands are subject to quantity commands. For instance, 10j jumps your cursor down 10 lines, and 5l moves the cursor right 5 characters. Other helpful moving characters are w (next word), G (end of file), $ (end of line), and 0 (beginning of line).

Command mode also offers you the opportunity to write (save), abandon (without save), and exit **vi**. To enter these commands, you always begin by pressing the colon key (:) to enter command line mode. Pressing :w + <Enter> writes your changes to the file. Pressing :q + <Enter> will quit. You can execute these commands at the same time by pressing :wq + <Enter>. In addition, you can use the exclamation point key (!) to force the command you are using. The :w! sequence writes to a read-only file, and :q! quits without saving changes.

Actual text editing uses both command and insert modes. To be efficient while using **vi**, remember that you can combine all commands with quantity, movement, and other action commands to raise productivity and simplify editing.

Table 3.2 shows some basic **vi** editing commands.

> *Note: Remember that commands are case sensitive! Lowercase l may mean move the cursor right one character, but capital L moves the curser to the last position in the window! In addition, most are subject to movement and quantity commands.*

Here are some commands and their meanings:

➤ **w**   Jumps a word.

➤ **dw**   Deletes a word.

➤ **cw**   Changes a word.

➤ **10w**   Jumps 10 words.

➤ **10W**   Jumps 10 words and ignores all punctuation.

Table 3.2	vi editing commands.
Command	Description
a	Appends text after the cursor
A	Appends text at the end of the line
c	Changes the command (for example, **cw** - changes the word)
C	Changes to the end of the line
d	Deletes the command (for example, **dw** - deletes the word)
D	Deletes to the end of the line
dd	Deletes the whole line
o	Opens the line below the current line and inserts text
O	Opens the line above the current line and inserts text
p	Puts yanked or deleted text after the cursor
P	Puts yanked or deleted text before the cursor
r	Replaces the character with the next character typed
s	Deletes the current character and inserts unlimited text
u	Undoes the last change
x	Deletes the character at the cursor

➤ **/**   Invokes a search.

➤ **/word**   Searches for the word "word" in a document.

➤ **n**   Finds the next occurrence of "word" in the document.

➤ **:s**   Invokes a search and replace for the current line.

➤ **:s/word/newword/**   Replaces every occurrence of "word" with "newword" in the current line.

➤ **:%s/word/newword/**   Replaces every occurrence of "word" with "newword" in the entire document.

Kernel Basics

Basic kernel configuration and rebuilding knowledge is essential to becoming an RHCE. You should be extremely familiar with the tools and files required to rebuild your kernel. The kernel is the most rapidly changing part of any Linux distribution. One of the reasons for the rapid development of the Linux kernel is the "two track" development system that Linux has used since kernel version 1. The version number of the Linux kernel is always in the form *major.minor.patchlevel*, where the *minor* number indicates whether the kernel is stable or in development. Stable kernels are indicated by an even *minor* number. For example, 1.0.9, 1.2.13, 2.0.36, and 2.2.5 are all stable kernels, whereas 1.1.12 and 2.3.8 are both development kernels. Stable kernels are updated less frequently and are tested before they are released; development kernels are released as frequently as possible to allow testing and to allow all developers to "sync-up" their kernel source tree with Linux's official tree.

 Development kernels are not guaranteed to compile, much less work properly. They usually do work well, so many sites that need one or more not-quite-perfect features in the development kernels will use them for production systems. (For example, many sites with SMP systems ran the 2.1.x kernels for greatly improved performance.) Real work is often being done with systems that run development kernels, so the kernel developers tend to receive excellent bug reports, which fuels the fast development cycle.

You can always retrieve the Linux kernel source via anonymous FTP from **ftp://ftp.kernel.org/pub/linux/kernel/** or from one of its many mirrors. There are directories for each kernel *major.minor* version. Each directory contains a file that indicates the latest release of that version. For example, a directory listing of the v1.2 directory shows the following:

```
-r--r--r--   1 502      101        0 Mar  29  1999 LATEST-IS-2.2.5
```

Another quick way to determine the latest kernel version is to run the **finger @linux.kernel.org** command. Doing so should give you output like that shown here:

```
[linux.kernel.org]
     The latest stable version of the Linux kernel is:     2.2.11
     The latest beta version of the Linux kernel is:       2.3.14
     The latest prepatch (alpha) version *appears* to be:  2.3.15-3
```

Once you have determined the version of the kernel source that you need, get the file linux-*x.y.z*.tar.gz or linux-*x.y.z*.tar.bz2 (where *x.y.z* is the version number). The file with the .bz2 extension is compressed with bzip2, and the file with the .gz extension is compressed with gzip. Generally, the bzip2-compressed file is much smaller (usually around 15 to 20 percent smaller) than the gzip-compressed file.

If you already have a version of the kernel source available, you may prefer to retrieve all the patch-*x.y.z*.gz or patch-*x.y.z*.bz2 files from the versions between your current kernel version and your goal kernel version. (For example, if you already have source for kernel 2.0.34 and want to install 2.0.36, you'll need patch-2.0.35.bz2 and patch-2.0.36.bz2, or the equivalent gzip-compressed patches.)

Unpacking The Kernel Source

Once you have the kernel source tar file, you need to unpack it. The canonical location for the kernel source is /usr/src/linux, and many programs expect the kernel source to be there. (For example, /usr/include/linux is a symbolic link to /usr/src/linux/include/linux.) To keep track of what kernel versions you have installed, it is best to create a directory for the kernel called /usr/src/linux-*x.y.z* (where *x.y.z* is the version number), and make /usr/src/linux a symbolic link to that directory. For example, to prepare to unpack the Linux 2.2.5 kernel source, use the commands shown here:

```
cd /usr/src
mkdir linux-2.2.5
rm -f linux
ln -s linux-2.2.5 linux
```

> *Note:*   *This example assumes that /usr/src/linux either does not exist or is a symbolic link. If it is a directory, you should move it to somewhere like /usr/src/linux.old.*

Then, to install the sources, execute

```
bzip2 -cd linux-2.2.5.tar.bz2 | tar -xvf -
```

for the bzip2-compressed version, or

```
gzip -cd linux-2.2.5.tar.gz | tar xvf -
```

for the gzip-compressed version. With GNU tar, which is the default tar supplied on Linux, the equivalent command is:

```
tar -zxvf linux-2.2.5.tar.gz
```

Patching A Kernel

If you have any patches to apply, the standard procedure is to change directories into your kernel source directory (usually by typing "cd /usr/src/linux"). Then, run the command

```
bzcat patchfile.bz2 | patch -p1 -E -s
```

for patches compressed by bzip2, or

```
zcat patchfile.gz | patch -p1 -E -s
```

for patches compressed with gzip.

The -**p1** option tells the patch to ignore the top-level directory referenced by the patch (usually "linux", but it could be anything in unofficial patches). The -**E** tells the patch to remove any files that are zero length ("empty", hence the "-E") after the patch is applied. The -**s** tells the patch to produce output only if an error occurs. Normally, the patch is rather verbose, so to see exactly what file is being updated, leave off the -**s**. With some versions of GNU patch, you can get even more information with the --**verbose** command-line option.

Building The Kernel

After the kernel source is unpacked, change directories into the kernel source directory, and then run one of these commands: **make config, make menuconfig,** or **make xconfig**. The **config** target presents you with a list of options for the kernel in the form of questions. The **menuconfig** and **xconfig** targets are menu-driven interfaces for the configuration process, the former with a text interface and the latter with an X interface. The **menuconfig** and **xconfig** options are certainly easier than the simple **config** options, but they do not always work properly. The **config** option is considered the standard way to configure the kernel because it has been available since the beginning of Linux kernel development.

Assuming you choose the **make config** route, you are presented with a series of questions, one for each of the kernel configuration options. The possible answers are generally "y" to turn the item on (or include the driver), "n" to turn the item off (or skip the driver), "m" to make the driver as a kernel module, or "?" to get help on that option.

After running **make config,** you must prepare to compile the source code using **make dep,** followed by **make clean**.

Next, you need to compile your kernel. To compile, you have two options: **make zImage** and **make bzImage**. As **make zImage** limits the kernel to botting within the first 640K of disk, we recommend you use the **make bzImage** to allow for larger kernels. With either of these commands, you can then manually add your kernel to LILO within the etc/lilo.conf and have the option to boot your old kernel, in case your new one doesn't work properly.

The methods for **make zImage** and **make bzImage** are x86 only based commands. On other architectures (such as Alpha), you can use **make boot**, which works on the x86 platform as well.

After successfully building your kernel, you must run **make modules** and **make modules_install**. Doing so builds and installs the loadable modules that you configured for your kernel. Once these commands have finished successfully, copy your new image to the /boot directory and then add the appropriate lines to lilo.conf. An example of lilo.conf is shown here:

```
boot=/dev/hda
map=/boot/map
install=/boot/boot.b
prompt
timeout=50
image=/boot/vmlinuz-2.2.5
        label=linux
        root=/dev/hda2
        read-only
other=/dev/hda1
        label=dos
        table=/dev/hda
image=/boot/vmlinuz-2.0.36-3
        label=linux-2.0.36
        root=/dev/hda2
        read-only
```

This lilo.conf example is set to boot two separate Linux images and one other. The first image is the default boot that points to the new kernel image (renamed to vmlinuz-2.2.5). The "other" section points to the first partition, which happens to be a DOS partition. The third boot option is the old kernel image.

Note: *Systems that use SCSI drives to boot also require an initrd image specified in the lilo.conf file. This option will be discussed further in Chapter 8.*

When you're finished properly editing your lilo.conf, run the **lilo** command to load and save your changes. Then, reboot and enjoy your new kernel.

Understanding Bourne Shell Scripts

Shell scripts are a set of commands, either in a file or typed in at the command line, that perform multiple operations on a file or files (which must be executable to run). To make a file executable, you can use chmod +x or chmod 755 filename.

The kernel uses specific "signature" bytes, called *magic*, of an executable file to determine how to execute that file. For example, if the first two bytes of an executable file are "#!", the kernel knows that the file is a script. The kernel then reads to the first new-line character in the file, and uses the line as the name of the script interpreter to run. If the kernel sees

```
#!/bin/sh
```

as the first line of a script, it runs /bin/sh with the script name as an argument. The kernel also knows the file magic for various other types of binary executable files (ELF, various forms of a.out, COFF from various other Unix systems, and so on). This functionality can be further extended using the binfmt_misc module in the 2.2.x kernels.

If you scan an existing shell script, you typically find comments, which help to explain what a command or section of the script is doing. All comments written within a shell script are noted with a hash mark (#) at the beginning of a line, as shown here:

```
#!/bin/sh
# This is a sample comment for a shell script.
if [ -x file ]; then echo foo; fi
```

When you are doing any sort of programming or scripting, it is a good habit to supply comments. A few months, or in some cases just a few days, after you have written your code, comments will help you (and others who need to read it) decipher what you've written.

Using Constructs

Typical scripts contain **if**, **else**, **elif**, **case**, and **for** constructs. The **if** construct supplies a conditional argument. All **if** constructs are closed with a **fi**, as shown here:

```
if foo ; then
    do something
fi
```

The **else** construct is used in conjunction with **if**. **else** gives an alternate outcome in case the first **if** isn't true, as shown here:

```
if foo ; then
      do something
else
      echo "It's not foo."
fi
```

The **elif** construct, shown here, offers the script a choice of conditions and responses:

```
if foo; then
      do something
elif bar ; then
      do somethingelse
else
      echo "sorry, can't do that"
fi
```

The **case** construct allows the script to switch between statements depending on a pattern match. **case** constructs are ended with an **esac**. Unlike **elif**, **case** requires a pattern match. In some **init** scripts, such as the **init** scripts in /etc/rc.d/init.d, **case** is used heavily. Here's an example from /etc/rc.d/init.d/named:

```
# See how we were called.
case "$1" in
  start)
          # Start daemons.
          echo -n "Starting named: "
          daemon named
          echo
          touch /var/lock/subsys/named
          ;;
  stop)
          # Stop daemons.
          echo -n "Shutting down named: "
          killproc named
          echo "done"
          rm -f /var/lock/subsys/named
          ;;
  status)
          status named
          exit $?
          ;;
  restart)
          /usr/sbin/ndc restart
```

```
            exit $?
            ;;
   *)
            echo "Usage: named {start|stop|status|restart}"
            exit 1
esac
```

The **for** construct allows for loop iteration. The **for** construct is ended with a **done**, as shown here:

```
for foo in start stop
do /etc/rc.d/init.d/named $foo
done
```

Using Variables

Shell scripts, much like programs, use *variables* for argument communication. Variables are sequences of letters, digits, or underscores that must begin with either a letter or underscore. To retrieve the contents of the variable, you must prepend a $ to the variable name, as shown here:

```
for foo in one two three; do
       echo $foo
done
```

You can also export variables to be used in child processes within the script. You do so with the **export** keyword. Essentially, **export** tells the shell to make this variable an environment variable. The environment is passed to each child process of the script.

Using The **test** Command

One of the most powerful commands in shell scripting is **test(1)**. The **test** command is an external command that is called by the shell, as shown here:

```
if test expression ; then
       do something
fi
```

On newer filesystems, **test** is symlinked to [. When [is used in a script, it has to be closed with a] to be valid, as shown here:

```
if [ expression ] ; then
       do something
fi
```

Using the end bracket was implemented to instill good programming habits.

The **test** command uses some special options to make various types of tests, as shown in Table 3.3.

You can also use **test** to compare numbers or strings, as shown in Table 3.4.

Administration Basics

As a Linux administrator, you should be familiar not only with using Unix, shell, and kernel basics, but also other tools and programs. Home directories, file default directories, daemons, logging, and backing up and restoring files are all terms you should be familiar with.

Home Directories

When a user is created, he automatically has a home directory assigned. This directory is /home/*username*. In /home/username, there are default files, such as .Xdefaults, .bashrc, and .bash_profile. These files are copies from a default file location, typically found at /etc/skel (skeleton files).

Table 3.3   test options.

Option	Explanation
[-w filename]	Is the filename writeable?
[-r filename]	Is the filename readable?
[-x filename]	Is the filename executable?
[-s filename]	Is the filename empty?

Table 3.4   test usage.

test string	Description
test n1 -eq n2	Are the numbers equal?
test n1 -ne n2	Are the numbers not equal?
test n1 -gt n2	Is the first number greater than the second?
test s1 = s2	Is the first string equal to the second?
test s1 != s2	Is the first string not equal to the second?

Superusers are users that have increased file access and control. The standard superuser is root, where user id (UID) is set to 0. However, programs such as sudo can also provide limited superuser privileges to other users.

Daemons

A *daemon* process is one whose parent process is process ID 1 (for example, the init process). Linux uses daemons to perform routine tasks, such as monitoring system resources.

For a list of what daemons you are running, you can type "ps", which reports a process status. To see what daemons are being loaded at boot, you can type "ntsysv". The daemons that are checked with an asterisk (*) are being loaded at boot. The init scripts for these daemons are located under /etc/rc.d/init.d/. You can use the init scripts to start, stop, or restart your daemons.

Managing these daemons, as well as managing networking services, is simplified by using the ntsysv program to select which daemons to start at bootup. In addition, you can use **inetd**, the "Internet super-server" daemon. **inetd** uses /etc/inet.conf. This file consists of networking services that are listening to incoming connections on specific ports. A sample section of an inetd.conf follow:

```
# These are standard services.
#
ftp       stream  tcp nowait  root   /usr/sbin/tcpd  in.ftpd -l -a
telnet    stream  tcp nowait  root   /usr/sbin/tcpd  in.telnetd
gopher    stream  tcp nowait  root   /usr/sbin/tcpd  gn
```

Services that aren't to be used are simply commented out of the inetd.conf, as shown here:

```
#cfinger stream    tcp    nowait root   /usr/sbin/tcpd      in.cfingerd
```

The format of these lines uses service stream versus dgram, the tcp versus udp, the wait versus nowait[.max], and the user[.group] program arguments.

Cron

Cron is a program that allows you to run jobs at specific intervals. Cron uses your crontab file to configure what programs to run, and when. To set up a crontab for an individual user, the user types "crontab -e" to edit the crontab file. The user crontab is automatically placed in /var/spool/cron/crontabs/. An example crontab entry looks like this:

```
# run example cron job
01 2 3 4 5  $HOME/bin/daily.job
```

Lines in the crontab file have six fields. The first field specifies the minute of the hour that the indicated executable is to be run (0 through 59). The second specifies the hour of the day to be run (0 through 23). The third specifies the day of the month to be run (0 through 31). The fourth specifies the month of the year to be run (0 through 12). The fifth specifies the day of the week (0 through 7). The final field specifies the program to be run.

In addition to individual user crontabs, there is a system crontab. It is found in /etc/crontab. An example of a system crontab looks like this:

```
SHELL=/bin/bash
PATH=/sbin:/bin:/usr/sbin:/usr/bin
MAILTO=root

# run-parts
01 * * * * root run-parts /etc/cron.hourly
02 4 * * * root run-parts /etc/cron.daily
22 4 * * 0 root run-parts /etc/cron.weekly
42 4 1 * * root run-parts /etc/cron.monthly
```

With the default root crontab setup, the crontab points to a directory in each line. When each line is run, every script in the directory is run. For instance, the first entry runs every script in /etc/cron.hourly at the first minute of every hour, and the second entry runs every script in /etc/cron.daily every day at 4:02 A.M. The third entry runs every script in /etc/cron.weekly every Sunday at 4:22 A.M., and the fourth entry runs every script in /etc/cron.monthly the first day of each month at 4:42 A.M.

 The most important information you have to evaluate services, connections, and problems with your Linux box is your system logs. The daemon that logs these messages is called syslogd. To view your logs, you can **cat** the files, or even better, **tail** them. You can find most of your log files under /var/log/. Important system messages can be found in the file /var/log/messages, whereas logs containing mail information are at /var/log/maillog.

Backing Up And Restoring Files

To be a safe Unix administrator, you should be in the habit of backing up important files regularly. Some typical programs that are used to make archives of a system are **tar** and **cpio**. **tar** is the tape archive utility. It stores and retrieves data from an archive. To make an archive with **tar**, use

```
tar -cvf filename.tar file
```

You can save this outputfile (filename.tar in the example to floppy, tape, writable CD, or even another hard drive). To restore or extract the files using **tar**, use

```
tar -xvf filename.tar
```

cpio is the "copy in-out" program. It's similar to tar; however, it can use archives in a number of different formats, including the tar format. When extracting files from an archive, **cpio** reads the archive as standard output.

Practice Questions

Question 1

Which is a valid format for mounting a CD-ROM after a typical Red Hat installation using **mount**?

  ◯ a. mount /dev/cdrom

  ◯ b. mount /mnt/cdrom

  ◯ c. mount –t iso9660 /dev/cdrom /mnt/cdrom

  ◯ d. All of the above

Answer d is correct. A default Red Hat Linux installation automatically sets
up your /etc/fstab to include the default settings for your CD-ROM drive by
mounting /dev/cdrom (shown in answer a) to the mount point /mnt/cdrom
(shown in answer b) with the is 0 9660 filesystem type (shown in answer c).
Therefore, answers a, b, and c mount your cdrom device to the /mnt/cdrom
mount point.

Question 2

What are the appropriate Hex codes for setting Linux swap and Linux native
partition types in fdisk?

  ◯ a. 82 and 85

  ◯ b. 83 and 85

  ◯ c. 82 and 83

  ◯ d. 84 and 85

Answer c is correct. When setting partition types, don't randomly guess. Simply type "l" at the command prompt and you can see a list of Hex codes that
fdisk supports.

Question 3

What command do you use to rename a file?

- ○ a. **rename**
- ○ b. **mv**
- ○ c. **nn**
- ○ d. **cp**

Answer b is correct. The **mv** command allows you to move a file from one place to another, which allows you to move it from its current name to a new name as well. Answers a, c, and d are incorrect because rename and nn are not real Unix commands, and although answer d can copy a command to a new name, it leaves the old name. While this choice would work, it isn't the best answer.

Question 4

What is the difference between mkfs and fsck?

Both mkfs and fsck are filesystem tools. The command mkfs is used to create Linux filesystems, whereas the fsck tool is used to check and repair Linux filesystems.

Question 5

What can you execute to count the number of lines in a file?

- ○ a. **lc**
- ○ b. **wc -l**
- ○ c. **cl**
- ○ d. None of the above

Answer b is correct. The **wc** command is the word count command. The -l option tells it to count the lines. Answers a and c are incorrect because they are not valid commands.

Question 6

What's the difference between the **less** and **more** commands?

The **less** and **more** commands are both filters. If you pipe the output of a file or a command through either of these filters, you get the output one page at a time. The difference, however, lies in their functionality. For example, **less** is a more powerful tool than **more**, allowing you to not only view the output one page at a time, but to scroll up and down through the file. **less** also allows you to search through the file using standard vi manipulation.

Question 7

What command lists the last 10 lines of a file?

○ a. **grep**

○ b. **cat**

○ c. **head**

○ d. **tail**

Answer d is correct. The **tail** command lists the last 10 lines of a file. Answer a is incorrect because grep is a filter. Answers b and c display the contents of a file; however, **cat** lists all contents of the file and **head** lists the first 10 lines. Therefore, they are incorrect.

Question 8

Entering the command **ls foobar?** could give you which output? [Check all correct answers]

❏ a. foobarbaz

❏ b. foobazbar

❏ c. foobar?

❏ d. foobarz

Answers c and d are correct. The ? wildcard means that the missing character is a single-character wildcard. Using a ? in a file name is valid, so the ? wildcard found both foobar? and foobarz to be valid. Answers a and b are incorrect because they have more than one character after the requested filename.

Question 9

Where can system and mail logs be found on Linux?

O a. /log

O b. /logs

O c. /var/adm/syslogs

O d. /var/log

Answer d is correct. On some systems that were set up by an expert, or by administrators accustomed to another flavor of Unix, you may find symlinks from some of the other options to /var/log.

Question 10

Which **vi** commands could be used to move you into insert mode? [Check all correct answers]

❑ a. I, i, A

❑ b. a, i, O

❑ c. 0, a, i

❑ d. I, A, O

Answers a, b, and d are correct. I and i are used to insert text at the beginning of the line and at the cursor, respectively. A and a are used to append at the end of the line and append after the next letter, respectively. O and o are used to open the line above the current line and open the line below the current line, respectively. Answer c is incorrect because a zero (0) is used instead of the letter O. Although you may not encounter the 0 vs. O trick on your RHCE exam, it can easily play tricks on you when you are trying to administer a console where 0 and O appear to be the same character.

Need To Know More?

 Frisch, Æleen. *Essential System Administration*, O'Reilly & Associates, Sebastopol, CA, 1995. ISBN 1-56592-127-5. This book gives you many of the basics required for using Unix style operating systems, commands, filesystems, and so forth.

 Lamb, Linda and Arnold Robbins. *Learning the vi Editor*, O'Reilly & Associates, Sebastopol, CA, 1998. ISBN 1-56592-426-6. This book is an excellent learning aid for learning all the capabilities and methods for using **vi**.

 Siever, Ellen. *Linux In A Nutshell*, O'Reilly & Associates, Sebastopol, CA, 1997. ISBN 1-56592-167-4. This book gives you a general look at Linux, with a focus for globbing in Chapter 6, **vi** in Chapter 8, and general commands in Chapters 12 and 13.

 http://metalab.unc.edu/LDP
The Linux Documentation Project. This site links to many Linux-related FAQs and HOWTOs.

 http://www.samba.org
For more information about current development and documentation regarding Samba, visit Samba's Web site.

 http://www.sendmail.org
For more information about current development and documentation on Sendmail, visit Sendmail's Web site.

Red Hat Advanced Prerequisites

4

Terms you'll need to understand:

√ Queue

√ Daemon

√ Protocol

√ Octet

√ Supernetting

√ Routing

√ Permissions

Techniques you'll need to master:

√ Partitioning disks

√ Printing with Unix

√ Networking with TCP/IP

√ Routing with TCP/IP

√ Configuring network services

The RHCE 300 exam is designed to certify the advanced Linux or Unix engineer and system administrator of Red Hat Linux. Anyone who participates in the program should have intermediate to advanced working knowledge of the principles of computer hardware, printing, networking basics, basic TCP/IP networking, networking services, and security basics.

In this chapter, I'll explain what to expect and what is expected out of you when you take your certification exam, as well as the simple Linux basics. This chapter will outline many of the basics and give you additional resources to aid in your preparation.

Hardware Basics

The RHCE 300 certification exam is based on Red Hat 6.0 running on Intel hardware. You should be aware that Red Hat also runs on a number of other hardware platforms such as Alpha and Sparc. For this exam, you should be well versed in Intel and Intel clone architectures. A firm knowledge of Interrupt Request (IRQ) settings, hard disk subsystems, and basic disk partitioning is a must.

Intel Architectures

Intel and known compatibles (also known as *IBM compatibles*) are based on Complex Instruction Set Computing (CISC) central processing units (CPUs). CPUs process low-level commands called *instruction sets*. The time required to carry out these instruction sets is based on the CPU's speed and architecture. When compared to RISC CPUs, CISC CPUs use more complex instruction sets and have fewer registers with which to execute them, making them less efficient. Some RISC processors are used in the popular (formerly Compaq's DEC) Alpha, Hewlett-Packard's PA-RISC, Sun's SPARC, SGI's MIPS, and IBM's PowerPC. Over the years, Intel and Intel clones have become the industry standard for computing hardware. Many once-proprietary hardware vendors are adapting the Intel architecture in their systems, allowing for greater compatibility and affordability.

The base of the Intel personal computer (PC) is the *motherboard*. Motherboards typically have sockets and slots integrated directly on the board for the CPU, the random access memory (RAM), and the Peripheral Component Interconnect (PCI) and Industry Standard Architecture (ISA) buses. Unlike older x86 boards, the serial (communication) and parallel ports, along with the Integrated Drive Electronics (IDE) and floppy controllers, are also integrated on board.

IRQ Settings

Currently, the most popular card bus used in PC hardware today is PCI. Most Intel motherboards have both ISA and PCI bus slots available. The differences between ISA and PCI buses are the way they handle IRQ and input/output (I/O) addressing, and their data transfer speed. The ISA bus's settings, such as IRQ and I/O, are hard-wired directly on the card. This arrangement does not allow the operating system to query the bus itself, or change the settings without jumpering the card itself. Plug-and-play ISA cards are an exception, but require special configuration tools. The ISA bus has these characteristics:

➤ It is limited by the maximum clock setting of approximately 8MHz.

➤ Its maximum data transfer rate is 8Mbps.

➤ It is limited by the 16-bit data width and 20-bit address width.

The PCI bus, however, allows the BIOS to control IRQ and I/O addressing. The operating system can directly query the PCI bus, so the settings can be controlled from within the operating system. The PCI bus has these characteristics:

➤ It is faster than the ISA bus, allowing for a maximum clock of 33MHz.

➤ Its maximum data transfer rate is 132Mbps.

➤ It has a 32-bit data width and a 32-bit address width.

Serial ports on Intel and Intel clone computers generally have standard I/O and IRQ settings. Table 4.1 lists the standard settings for serial ports.

Hard Disk Subsystems

Two of the most common hard disk subsystems used in current Intel hardware are IDE and Small Computer Systems Interconnect (SCSI). IDE drives have the controller located directly on the piece of hardware and use an IDE bus that is typically integrated on the motherboard. Most Intel motherboards have two IDE buses. Each bus supports one master and one slave drive, limiting the number of IDE devices to four.

Table 4.1 Standard serial ports.			
Linux Serial Port	**DOS COM Port**	**I/O**	**IRQ**
ttyS0	com 1	3F8	4
ttyS1	com 2	2F8	3
ttyS2	com 3	3E8	4
ttyS3	com 4	2E8	3

SCSI devices use a controller that is separate from the drive itself. These controllers are run on SCSI cards (also called *SCSI adapters*) and are connected to the computer through the ISA or PCI slots. SCSI devices are not limited to master and slave drives as are IDE devices. SCSI devices are limited only by the number of devices the SCSI card supports. Typical cards can support anywhere from 7 through 30 devices; however, higher-quality cards are reported to support over 100 devices! Performance factors differentiate the qualities of IDE and SCSI devices. Typical SCSI devices can transfer data from a range of 10Mbps through 80Mbps, whereas typical IDE devices are limited to a range of 8Mbps through 33Mbps. Both systems' speed rates depend on the device and the controller card.

Disk Partitioning

Another must for understanding Linux and its basics is hard drive partitioning. *Partitioning*, which we briefly looked at in Chapter 2, is a mechanism to segment a single physical disk into multiple logical disks. These logical disks appear as a contiguous section of physical blocks.

An entire hard disk does not have to be partitioned completely. You can save the remaining space for future allocation, or use it as a gap to allow for resizing partitions.

 Moving and resizing partitions is tricky, and can easily corrupt your filesystem. Before altering your partition table, always back up your data!

The number of partitions created on a drive is typically set by the particular machine's needs. Separate partitions are suggested for separate operating systems to use, and in Linux's case, for Linux Swap. However, you should also opt to assign separate partitions for mounting separate filesystems, such as /home, /var, /log, and /root for large-disk installations or active workstations.

Printing

Linux uses the printer spooling systems that were originally developed for BSD (Berkeley Systems Distribution) Unix. Linux can maintain multiple printers at multiple sites as well as multiple print queues. Some basic printing commands you will use include **lpr, lpq, lprm, lpd,** and **lpc,** described in Table 4.2.

Table 4.2	Basic printing commands.
Command	**Description**
lpr	Adds jobs to the print queue
lpq	Lists jobs currently in print queues
lprm	Removes jobs from the print queue
lpd	Is the printer daemon that sends data from the spool to the printer
lpc	Is the administrative interface for printing

To add a printer to your system via direct parallel connection, first ensure the printer is physically connected properly. Make sure that the lpd server is started at boot-time (check by running **ntsysv**). Edit /etc/printcap, and add an entry for the new printer. Create your spooling directory on mkdir /var/spool/newps. Make sure your print spool's permissions are set to 755 (we will go into more detail on permissions later in this chapter). Create the printer's accounting file with the **touch** command. You can then start the printer in its queue using the **lpc** command, as shown here:

```
#touch /var/adm/lp_acct/ps3
#chown daemon /var/adm/lp_acct/ps3
#chmod 755 /var/adm/lp_acct/ps3
#lpc up ps3
```

The spooling system on Linux also can print to remote printers. To add a remote printer, simply edit /etc/printcap, adding lines similar to those shown in the following:

```
#remote printer setup
remlp|print on remote line printer:\
        :lp=:rm=remote:rp=lp2:sd=/var/spool/remlp
```

> *Note:* *Notice the above /etc/printcap entry has no references about the details of the printer itself. This is because the host will manage the job after it's sent.*

This entry sets up the remote printer named remlp. Not specifying the **lp=** field tells us that this entry is for a remote printer. The **rm=** field points us to the destination system (here, we've named it "remote"). The **rp=** field holds the name of the target printer. The **sd=** field selects the spool directory the printer will use.

Networking Basics

A Linux box without a network is like a typist without hands. Therefore, a Linux administrator who wishes to obtain his RHCE must have a good understanding of networking basics such as Transmission Control Protocol/Internet Protocol (TCP/IP) fundamentals, network ports, and networking services.

TCP/IP Fundamentals

The most important networking protocol used in today's networks is TCP/IP. It is the fundamental protocol used to establish the Internet, as well as the majority of the world's wide area networks. Networking is one of Linux's star features, making it more popular every day for business networks, Internet Service Providers (ISPs), manufacturing facilities, network companies, and others to use.

TCP/IP And The Open Systems Interconnection (OSI) Layer Model

The TCP/IP Layer model is based on the OSI layer model. The OSI model consists of seven layers, whereas the TCP/IP model has only four. Here is a list of the OSI model layers:

➤ Application Layer

➤ Presentation Layer

➤ Session Layer

➤ Transport Layer

➤ Network Layer

➤ Data Link Layer

➤ Physical Layer

Compare those with the TCP/IP model layers:

➤ **Application Layer** Handles TCP/IP network daemons and applications. This layer performs the jobs of the OSI's Presentation Layer and its Session Layer in addition to OSI's basic Application Layer.

➤ **Transport Layer** Handles all the data routing and delivery issues, including session initiation, error control, and sequence checking. This layer covers OSI's Transport Layer and part of the Network Layer.

➤ **Internet Layer** Handles all the data addressing, transmission, and the IP. This layer covers part of the OSI Network Layer.

➤ **Network Access Layer** Specifies the procedures for transmitting data over the network, including how to access the physical medium (this is used for many protocols, including Ethernet and FDDI, the Fibre Distributed Data Interface).

TCP And User Datagram Protocol (UDP) Protocols

TCP is not the only protocol used in TCP/IP networking. Some applications, such as NFS, use a sibling protocol called UDP. Both protocols allow the application to contact a service on a specific port. However, UDP doesn't establish a connection; rather, it sends single packets to the service.

Internet Control Message Protocol (ICMP) Packet Types

ICMP is used by the kernel code to send error messages to other hosts. There are several ICMP packet types, and some can carry multiple messages. Some valid types are echo-reply, destination-unreachable, source-quench (deprecated, but NT still sends them for some reason), redirect, echo-request, router-advertisement, router-solicitation, time-exceeded, parameter-problem, timestamp-request, timestamp-reply, address-mask-request, and address-mask-reply.

The destination-unreachable packet can carry one of 14 different messages. These include network-unreachable, host-unreachable, protocol-unreachable, port-unreachable, fragmentation-needed, source-route-failed, network-unknown, host-unknown, network-prohibited, host-prohibited, TOS-network-unreachable, TOS-host-unreachable, communication-prohibited, and host-precedence-cutoff.

The redirect packet can carry one of four messages: network-redirect, host-redirect, TOS-network redirect, and TOS-host-redirect.

The time-exceeded packet (also known as ttl-exceeded) can carry one of two messages: ttl-zero-during-transit and ttl-zero-during-reassembly.

The parameter-problem packet can carry one of these two messages: ip-header-bad and required-option-missing.

Understanding Ports

Network services are each assigned (or bound to) a port. Ports are TCP's and UDP's abstraction of a service endpoint. There are 64k (or 65,536) possible ports available for use. All ports under 1024 (low-number ports) are considered *privileged* ports. This means that only the root can bind to them. However, 1024 and above are *unprivileged* ports, meaning that any user can bind to them.

Every networking program should look into /etc/services to get the port number (and protocol) for its service. /etc/services is a text file that provides a mapping between names for Internet services and their underlying assigned port numbers and protocol types. Table 4.3 lists some standard services from a sample /etc/services file (the table does not list all the services found in /etc/services).

Table 4.3	Some of the services in the /etc/services file.		
Service	**Port/Protocol**	**Alias**	**Comments**
echo	7/tcp	N/A	N/A
echo	7/udp	N/A	N/A
netstat	15/tcp	N/A	N/A
ftp	21/tcp	N/A	N/A
ssh	22/tcp	N/A	N/A
telnet	23/tcp	N/A	N/A
smtp	25/tcp	mail	N/A
name	42/udp	nameserver	N/A
whois	43/tcp	nicname	# usually to sri-nic
finger	79/tcp	N/A	N/A
http	80/tcp	N/A	# www is used by some # broken progs, http is more # correct
www	80/tcp	N/A	
pop-3	110/tcp	N/A	# PostOffice V.3
auth	113/tcp	ident	# User Verification
nntp	119/tcp	usenet	# Network News Transfer
imap	143/tcp	N/A	# imap network mail protocol
exec	512/tcp	N/A	# BSD rexecd(8)
login	513/tcp	N/A	# BSD rlogind(8)
who	513/udp	whod	# BSD rwhod(8)
printer	515/tcp	spooler	# BSD lpd(8)
route	520/udp	router routed	# 521/udp too
mount	635/udp	N/A	# NFS Mount Service
nfs	2049/udp	N/A	# NFS File Service
irc	6667/tcp	N/A	# Internet Relay Chat

Basic TCP/IP Networking

The most important concept to understand with TCP/IP networking is IP addressing. An *IP address* is a numeric identifier assigned to each machine on an IP network. An IP address is a software address, not a hardware address (hardware addresses are hardcoded into the machine or network interface card).

IP Numbers

An IP address is made of up 32 bits. These bits are separated into four sections called *octets*. (Each octet contains 4 bytes of information and specifies either the network or the machine node.) Every machine on a subnet has the same network address but individual node addresses. You can display an IP address in three ways. The first and most common method is dotted decimal. An example of the dotted decimal method is 130.57.30.56. The second way is using the binary system. If you convert 130.57.30.56 in binary, it is 10000010.00111001 .00011110.00111000. The third way is the hexadecimal system. If you notate 130.57.30.56 using Hexadecimal, it is 82 39 1E 38.

> *Note: Throughout this section—and the entire book—IP addresses are notated using the dotted decimal format.*

IP Classes

There are three classes of IP networks: Class A, Class B, and Class C. Different classes are used depending on network size. The Class A network is used for a small number of networks with a large number of nodes. The Class B network is rarely used in a network, but could be used in a large network where numerous Class C networks were unmanageable and a Class A network is too large. The Class C network is used for a very large number of networks that have few nodes.

A Class A network uses the addressing format Net.Node.Node.Node, allowing you to have up to 127 networks and 16,777,216 nodes per network. The Class A networks range from 1.0.0.0 to 127.0.0.0.

> *Note: Class A networks are no longer being assigned because none is available to assign. In fact, some Class A networks are already being carved up into smaller networks.*

Being assigned a Class A network gives you all network addresses under the Net address. For instance, a company that owns the 12.0.0.0 Class A set of IP addresses has every IP address from 12.0.0.0 to 12.255.255.255.

A Class B network uses the addressing format Net.Net.Node.Node. This allows you to have up to 16,384 networks and 65,534 nodes per network. The Class B networks range from 128.0.0.0 to 191.0.0.0. Being assigned a Class B network gives you all network addresses under the Net.Net. assignment. For instance, a company that owns the 130.1.0.0 Class B network owns every IP address from 130.1.0.0 to 130.1.255.255.

The Class C networks are the most common network class used today. They allow you to have up to 2,097,152 networks, but you are limited to having only 254 nodes per network. Class C networks range from 192.0.0.0 to 223.0.0.0. Being assigned a Class C network gives you all network addresses under the assigned Net.Net.Net.Node address. For instance, an administrator or company who owns the 200.0.2.0 Class C network owns every IP address from 200.0.2.0 to 200.0.2.255.

You may be wondering what happens with network addresses above 223.255.255.255. Well, there are other classes of networks: Class D and Class E. Class D is used for multicast packets. These include the addresses from 224.0.0.0 to 239.255.255.255. A multicast transmission is used when a host wants to broadcast to multiple destinations, such as when a host is attempting to learn all the routers on its network. The Class E range of addresses is 240.0.0.0 through 255.255.255.255. These numbers are reserved for future use. You should not assign either Class D or Class E addresses to nodes on your network.

Network addresses are controlled by an official Internet organization called the Network Information Center (NIC), also referred to as InterNIC. Its Web site is at **http://www.internic.net**.

The Internet Assigned Numbers Authority (IANA) has reserved the following three blocks of the IP address space for private networks:

➤ 10.0.0.0 through 10.255.255.255

➤ 172.16.0.0 through 172.31.255.255

➤ 192.168.0.0 through 192.168.255.255

These addresses can be used on any internal private network free of charge. However, these addresses aren't publicly routable.

ᴄ ernetting IP Classes

?, a new adaptation to the IP classes was proposed. The idea was to
multiple classes and so on in order to reserve IP numbers. Otherwise,
s would be wastefully assigned (for example, a Class B address might

be assigned when only two Class Cs' worth of addresses was required), and we would run out of IP addresses quickly. Therefore, Classless InterDomain Routing (CIDR) was invented.

Using supernetting, the class subnet masks are extended so that a network address and subnet mask can, for example, specify multiple Class C subnets with one address. For example, if you need about 500 addresses, you can supernet two Class C networks together. Table 4.4 shows supernetted subnets.

It is expected that CIDR will have enough IP addresses available for the next few years, until IPv6 is implemented. IPv6 uses 128-bit addresses, which would comfortably allow over four billion unique IP addresses!

Subnets

To create a subnet, you split IP addresses into two parts: a host and a network. Typically, the destination network is derived from the network part of the IP address; therefore, hosts with identical IP network numbers should be found within the same network.

Every subnet is assigned a *netmask*, the number of bits interpreted as the subnet number. For instance, a Class C network number of 192.168.1.0 has a netmask of 255.255.255.0, whereas a Class B network number, such as 190.54.0.0, has a netmask of 255.255.0.0.

Network Configuration

Ifconfig is used to configure the kernel-resident network interfaces. It is used at boot-time to set up network interfaces as necessary. The first interface you'll have to setup is the Loopback Interface (**lo**), as shown here:

```
#ifconfig lo 127.0.0.1
```

Table 4.4 Supernetting subnets.	
Subnet/Result	**Description**
193.60.220.0	Class C subnet address
193.60.221.0	Class C subnet address
--	
193.60.220.0	Supernetted subnet address
255.255.252.0	Subnet mask
193.60.220.255	Broadcast address

To view the configuration of the interface, run **ifconfig lo**, as shown here:

```
$ ifconfig lo
lo          Link encap:Local Loopback
        inet addr:127.0.0.1 Mask:255.0.0.0
        UP LOOPBACK RUNNING MTU:3924 Metric:1
RX packets:677619 errors:0 dropped:0 overruns:0 frame:0
TX packets:677619 errors:0 dropped:0 overruns:0 carrier:0
Collisions:0
```

The loopback interface has been assigned a netmask of 255.0.0.0 because 127.0.0.1 is a Class A address.

The second interface you need to set up is the Ethernet interface. As with the loopback interface, you set this one up with **ifconfig** (and in nearly the same manner):

```
$ifconfig eth0 207.239.117.252 netmask 255.255.255.0
```

```
$ifconfig eth0
eth0        Link encap:Ethernet HWaddr 00:10:4B:63:05:94
        net addr:207.239.117.252 Bcast:207.239.117.255
        Mask:255.255.255.0
UP BROADCAST RUNNING MULTICAST MTU:1500 Metric:1
RX packets:6236605 errors:1 dropped:0 overruns:0 frame:1
TX packets:6449859 errors:0 dropped:0 overruns:0 carrier:11
Collisions:25319
Interrupt:17 Base address:0x6100
```

For the eth0 interface, the broadcast address is automatically set, in this case to 207.239.117.255. The maximum size of Ethernet frames the kernel generates for this interface (message transfer unit) has been set to 1500.

After setting up your **ifconfig**, you must add a routing entry that points to the network that it can be reached through eth0, as shown here:

```
#route add -net 207.239.117.253
```

You can use the **route** command to verify you have the correct routing entries. To check your routing table, use the **route -n** command, as shown here:

```
Kernel IP routing table
Destination     Gateway    Genmask          Flags Metric Ref Use Iface
207.239.117.254 0.0.0.0    255.255.255.255 UH    0      0   0   eth0
207.239.117.253 0.0.0.0    255.255.255.255 UH    0      0   0   eth0
207.239.117.0   0.0.0.0    255.255.255.0   U     0      0   0   eth0
```

```
127.0.0.0          0.0.0.0  255.0.0.0        U    0      0  0  lo
0.0.0.0            207.239.117.1 0.0.0.0     UG   0      0  0  eth0
```

Once establishing this route, you may wish to set up hostname resolution. To do so, use the /etc/hosts file. (If you don't use DNS or NIS for address resolution, you must put all hosts in the /etc/hosts file.) The /etc/hosts file has three fields. The first is the IP address, the second contains the fully qualified domain name, and the third hosts any aliases for the name. Table 4.5 shows a sample /etc/hosts.

Configure Domain Name Service (DNS)

To configure the use of the BIND nameservice for host lookups, you have to tell the resolver library what nameservers to use. The file to specify nameserver is called resolv.conf, as shown here:

```
search lanscape.net
nameserver 0.0.0.0
```

If the resolv.conf file is empty, the resolver assumes the nameserver is on your local host.

The **search** option specifies the local domain. Therefore, if the nameserver can't find the name "sites", it looks for "sites.lanscape.net", as specified in the /etc/hosts file printed above. The **nameserver** option specifies the IP address of the nameserver, which in this case is localhost, or 127.0.0.1.

Network Tools

Some additional tools that are helpful when working with networks and their inevitable problems are **ping** and **traceroute**. The **ping** command sends an

Table 4.5 Sample /etc/hosts.		
IP Address	**Domain**	**Alias (If Applicable)**
127.0.0.1	localhost	localhost.example.net
237.209.156.252	web1.example.net	web1
237.209.156.253	sites.example.net	sites
237.209.156.254	www.example.org	

ICMP echo request to the specified IP address. It reports the time it takes to get a response from the requested machine, as shown here:

```
#ping 237.209.156.253
PING 237.209.156.253 (237.209.156.253): 56 data bytes
64 bytes from 237.209.156.253: icmp_seq=0 ttl=255 time=0.4 ms
64 bytes from 237.209.156.253: icmp_seq=1 ttl=255 time=0.2 ms
64 bytes from 237.209.156.253: icmp_seq=2 ttl=255 time=0.2 ms
64 bytes from 237.209.156.253: icmp_seq=3 ttl=255 time=0.2 ms

-- 237.209.156.253 ping statistics --
4 packets transmitted, 4 packets received, 0% packet loss
round-trip min/avg/max = 0.2/0.2/0.4 ms
```

The **traceroute** tool is used exactly as its name implies. You use it to trace the route between you and the requested machine. The snippet shown here is an example of output of traceroute to the domain pritchard.inc.net:

```
#traceroute pritchard.example.net
traceroute to pritchard.inw.net (256.23.140.37), 30 hops max, 40 byte
packets
 1 192.168.117.1 (192.168.117.1) 1.374 ms 0.896 ms 0.834 ms
 2 10.1.1.1 (10.1.1.1) 8.552 ms 6.476 ms 6.440 ms
 3 192.168.194.33 (192.168.194.33) 18.956 ms 18.906 ms 18.837 ms
 4 ord1-core1-s5-0-0.example.net (192.168.52.41) * 26.367 ms *
 5 192.168.10.93 (192.168.10.93) 24.911 ms 24.301 ms 25.962 ms
 6 core2.example.net (192.168.4.45) 62.657 ms 54.196 ms *
 7 border7-fddi-0.example.net (192.168.98.51) 48.723 ms 219.232 ms
 8 NorthRoyalton.example.net (192.168.211.18) 36.319 ms 61.095 ms *
 9 pritchard.example.net (192.168.140.37) 63.738 ms 66.498 ms
   63.625 ms
```

IP Routing

IP routing is the process of a packet finding the appropriate host by traveling through a sequence of hosts from an original host to a destination host. The three protocols used in IP routing are:

➤ **Address Resolution Protocol (ARP)**   Used to map IP addresses to Ethernet addresses

➤ **Reverse Address Resolution Protocol (RARP)**   Used to permit hosts to find out their IP address at boot-time

➤ **Routing Information Protocol (RIP)**   Used to dynamically adjust routes inside a small network

Routes

Routes are specific paths set up for packet information to travel from the source to its destination. Routes can be established three ways via static, dynamic, and default routes.

Static routes are used for small to medium-sized networks. These networks tend to be very simple because they do not have several redundant paths to destinations. Static routes are established by issuing **route** commands at boot-time.

Dynamic routes differ from static routes; with dynamic routes, the optimal path to destinations is determined as requested, and then updated as necessary. Dynamic routing is typically used by either the routed or gated daemon.

Default routes are established between your immediate host and its host, between the host's host and its host, and so on. For instance, if a packet's destination is 204.248.89.7, and the internal router's routing table entries include 192.168.0.1 and 92.168.1.0, then the packet is sent to the default route (typically 0.0.0.0). The default route is assigned a gateway, which redirects the packet to the router's host. If the host's router doesn't have the 204.248.89.x routing table entry, the packet is forwarded to the host's host and so on. Each of these exchanges is called a *hop*. After 30 hops, if the packet hasn't reached its destination, it dies. This scenario is called a ttl-exceed.

Networking Services

After working with networks for an extended period of time, you will become familiar with a variety of networking services. Some of these popular services include network filesystem (NFS), sendmail, POP3 and IMAP, File Transfer Protocol (FTP), DNS, Dynamic Host Control Protocol (DHCP), Samba, the Hyper Text Transport Protocol Daemon (HTTPD), NIS, and inetd.

NFS

NFS allows filesystems that physically reside on one computer system to be used by other computers on the network. These connections appear as simply a local disk to remote users. NFS configuration files can be found in /etc/fstab and /etc/exports. NFS uses several daemons to handle its services. These services are started at boot-time in the /etc/rc.d/init.d/nfs scripts.

Some of these services include:

➤ **nfsd**   Handles filesystem exporting and file access requests from remote systems. This daemon gets run multiple times as more remote systems use the services.

➤ **biod**   Performs NFS block I/O operations for client processes.

➤ **rpc.mountd**   Handles mount requests from remote computers.

➤ **rpc.lockd**   Manages file locking for both client and server systems.

➤ **rpc.statd**   Handles lock crash and recovery services for both client and server systems.

➤ **portmap**   Facilitates the initial connection between local and remote servers.

sendmail

This is the most popular mail program used as a mail transport agent (MTA). It does the physical sending and receiving of user and system email. You use sendmail in conjunction with a mail delivery agent (MDA) and a mail user agent (MUA). The MDA receives the incoming mail from sendmail and delivers it to the appropriate user. A typical Red Hat Linux install uses procmail as the MDA for sendmail. Some other commonly used MDAs include mail.local and deliver. After the MDA has delivered the mail, the user uses an MUA to retrieve it. Some popular Unix MUAs include pine, elm, mutt, and mailx. Going the other direction, a user uses his MUA (pine) to send mail directly to the MTA (sendmail).

POP3 And IMAP

POP3 and IMAP are protocols that allow a user to retrieve her mail from the mail server to her mail reader. POP3 pulls mail from the mail spool one message at a time to a local spool. The user can then opt to delete all the messages on the mail spool, or leave all them there. IMAP, however, reads the mail messages directly from the spool, without copying the messages to the local spool. The user can then change, delete, and create folders, and so forth on her local mail reader. When she does so, the changes are automatically applied to the mail spool.

FTP

FTP is used to transfer files between systems over a network. To connect to a system via FTP, the user must either supply a valid username and password, or the system must be able to accept anonymous users.

DNS

DNS is used to translate between domain names, such as redhat.com to IP addresses, such as 199.183.24.134. DNS is registered with InterNIC.

DHCP

DHCP (developed by Microsoft) is a descendant of the boot protocol (bootp), which automatically assigns IP addresses to a client on a local network. DHCP uses UDP while the client sends a DHCPDISCOVER message as a broadcast packet to the network.

The DHCP server receives this packet and assigns (either statically or dynamically) an IP address to the client. The DHCP server sends to the client a DHCPOFFER packet that contains an address and the lease time, as well as other pertinent networking information (such as address, netmask, gateway, nameservers, and so on). The client then issues a DHCPREQUEST for the specified address. The server then responds to this with the DHCPACK (which agrees with the client and starts the lease time).

 This procedure differs from that used with bootp. In bootp's case, it simply sends the address without managing the lease time.

DHCP uses /etc/dhcpd.conf for configuration files and /etc/dhcpd.leases for lease information.

Samba

Samba is a server for the SMB protocol, which is the default file and printer sharing protocol that all versions of Windows, OS/2, and LanManager use. Samba allows the connectivity of these alternative operating systems to use a Unix or Linux box as a file or print server. Samba consists of two daemons: smbd (the Samba server) and nmbd (the NetBIOS nameserver). Clients use nmbd to find other hosts on the network. Configuration files are located in /etc/smb.conf.

HTTPD

HTTPD is the http (or World Wide Web) server. On Red Hat, the default httpd is Apache. Apache is a free Webserver that was originally derived from the NCSA http server. The configuration files are located in /etc/httpd/conf/.

NIS

NIS, originally called *Yellow Pages*, was developed by Sun Microsystems to simplify filesystem administration by maintaining the files in a central database.

The clients contact the database server to retrieve information. Two basic NIS utilities include **ypcat** (which displays an NIS database) and **ypmatch** (which searches an NIS database).

inetd

This is the Internet services daemon that listens for service requests on network connections and then starts up the appropriate daemon to respond to the particular request.

Security Basics

All Unix administrators should know the basics for securing their systems, including monitoring users and groups, setting file permissions properly and using umask, and using shadow passwords.

Monitoring Users And Groups

One of the most time-consuming duties of a Red Hat system administrator revolves around monitoring users and groups. Some basic administration tasks to monitor include services used, user accounts, and even software that is used.

Some typical things to watch for include unneeded services. To see what services are automatically started at boot, run ntsysv. If any services that you don't use are checked, simply uncheck them. Doing so stops them from being started at boot. You can also stop services you're currently running (for example, **nfs**) by running **/etc/rc.d/init.d/nfs stop**.

Some common sense when assigning user accounts can save you many headaches later. For instance, set up guidelines when users choose their passwords; they shouldn't be the same as their usernames, nor should they be any type of English word. It's best to have a mixture of case and numerical and alphabetical characters. Also, allow shell access only to those users who need it. For instance, if a user is simply pulling his mail from the account, set his shell access to /usr/bin/passwd (or something similar). Doing so forces him simply to change his password instead of allowing him to have shell access.

Another good area to monitor is software usage; keep an audit of the software you're running. Many times, unwanted users exploit popular software, such as sendmail or BIND, and then gain root access to your system. Keep up to date by using the most current versions of your software.

Setting File Permissions Properly And Using umask

Every file, program, and directory is set up with file permissions. Performing an ls -l in a directory prints the list of files including details, as shown here:

```
-rw-rw-r--  1 kara    kara      7688 Jan 13 14:32 pick
drwxr-xr-x  9 kara    kara      1024 Mar 27 12:15 public_html
-rw-r--r--  1 root    root    434898 May 7 1998 termcap
-rw-r--r--  1 root    root      3313 Apr 30 1998 wgetrc
```

The first group of characters represents the permissions for the file. The permissions are noted (when you are using ls -l) by a string of 10 characters, drwxrwxrwx and combinations thereof. When a particular character is replaced by a -, then the permission assigned to that character is not granted. These characters are split into four groups. The first character is represented by a "d", which stands for a directory. Therefore 'd'rwxr-xr-x indicates a directory, whereas -rw-rw-r-- implicates a filename. The remaining nine characters are split into three groups, rwx rwx rwx. The first group pertains to the owner, the second to the group, and the third to everybody else. The "r" in each case stands for readable, the "w" for writable, and the "x" for executable. Table 4.6 shows an example of permission settings.

When you are assigning or referring to permissions of a file, the r, w, and x characters are assigned numeric values of 4, 2, and 1 respectively. You then add these values together per group to get the permission values (for example, rwx = r+w+x = 4+2+1 = 7; r-x = r+0+x = 4+ 0 +1 = 5). Table 4.7 shows permission strings and their numerical values.

Therefore, a file with -rw-r--r-- file details has permissions set to '644'. By default, all files are created with file permissions of 666. These permissions are adjusted per user by their default umask. A umask sets the files permissions by subtracting the user's umask from the default 666. For example, if a umask is

Table 4.6	Permissions.
Permission String	**Explanation**
-rwx------	Readable, writable, and executable by the owner only
-rwxr-x--	Readable, writable, and executable by the owner; readable and executable by the group
-rwxr-x--x	Readable, writable, and executable by the owner; readable and executable by the group; executable by the public

Table 4.7 Permission values.

Permission String	Numerical Permission Value
-rwx------	7-0-0
-rwxr-x--	7-5-0
-rwxr-x--x	7-5-1

set to 022, the files created within that shell and its subprocesses are set to 644 (666-022).

To set the umask within a shell, use the **umask** command. Here's an example:

```
#umask 022
```

Files that need to have their permissions changed—such as to be executable or to limit access to the owner and the group—use only the **chmod** command. Here's an example:

```
#chmod 777 filename
```

This code sets the file name to have 777 permissions (-rwxrwxrwx), and the world can read, write, and execute them. However,

```
#chmod 770 filename
```

causes the owner and group—but not anyone else—to be able to read, write, and execute the file name.

By default, when a user is created, she is given her own user ID and group. To add users to other groups, edit the /etc/group file. The following is an excerpt from an /etc/group file:

```
luci::402:steve,kara,jburke
egypt::499:alan,barb
steve:x:500:
```

Files that have specified access to the group named luci give users steve, kara, and jburke access. On the other hand, alan and barb do not have access because they are assigned to the egypt group, not to luci and vice versa. To set a specific group to use a file, use the **chgrp** command. For instance

```
#chgrp luci index.html
```

sets the group ownership of index.html to the luci group. The index.html file has 664 permissions, is owned by steve, and the luci group is assigned. Therefore, steve and users in the luci group (steve, kara, and jburke) can read and write to that file, whereas everybody else can only read the file. The following shows changing the group ownership of the index.html file to luci and is verified with the **ls –l** command:

```
#chgrp luci index.html
#ls -l index.html
-rw-rw-r-- 1 steve  luci     3709 Mar 22 17:57 index.html
```

Using Shadow Passwords

Shadow passwords have several purposes. First, the password field of /etc/passwd is removed (replaced by an "x"). The file /etc/shadow then contains the password hash. The permissions on the shadow file make it unreadable by anyone but root (and, on some distributions, the shadow group). As a result, extracting password hashes to run through **crack** or any other similar password-guessing program is more difficult as compared to running the program on a system that doesn't use shadow passwords. The shadow file contains password aging information as well.

You can convert a system to shadow passwords by running the **pwconv** program. If necessary, you can later convert it back by using **pwunconv**. The change should be transparent to all programs that use Pluggable Authentication Modules (PAM). You can control password aging with the **chage** program.

Practice Questions

Question 1

What hardware architectures are currently supported by Red Hat? [Check all correct answers]

- ❑ a. Macintosh
- ❑ b. Alpha
- ❑ c. IBM compatible
- ❑ d. SPARC

Answers b, c, and d are correct. Currently, Red Hat offers official supported versions of Red Hat for the Alpha, IBM compatible, and SPARC architectures.

Question 2

What is the printing daemon?

- ○ a. **lpd**
- ○ b. **lpr**
- ○ c. **lpq**
- ○ d. **lpc**

Answer a is correct because lpd is the line printer daemon. Answer b is incorrect because **lpr** is the command that adds jobs to the queue. Answer c is incorrect because **lpq** lists the current jobs in the queue. Answer d is incorrect because **lpc** is the administrative interface for printing.

Question 3

What permission allows a file to be readable by the owner, group, and user, while only allowing write access to the owner and group?

- ○ a. 644
- ○ b. 750
- ○ c. 755
- ○ d. 774

Answer d is correct. Permissions of 774 give a file -rwxrwxr--permission attributes. This means the file is rwx by owner, rwx by group, but only r by user. Answer a is incorrect because 644 allows rw by owner, r by group, and r by user. Answer b is incorrect because 750 allows rwx by owner, r-x by group, and no access by user. Answer c is incorrect because 755 allows rwx by owner, r-x by group, and r-x by user.

Question 4

> Why do you need DNS?
>
> _____

You need DNS for domain name resolution. DNS is used to convert IP addresses to domain names, and domain names back to IP addresses. This process allows you to connect to the Internet with a domain name (such as **www.coriolis.com**) instead of having to remember 209.140.152.4.

Question 5

> NFS is used to read filesystems on a Linux server with Windows clients.
>
> ○ a. True
> ○ b. False

Answer b is correct. Although NFS is required for setting up a network file system, it isn't used to read filesystems on a Linux server from a Windows client. In fact, you must set up Samba on the Linux server to be able to read Linux filesystems from your Windows client over a network.

Question 6

> To see the route between your machine and a remote machine, which of the following could you use?
>
> ○ a. /usr/sbin/tracert
> ○ b. /usr/bin/traceroute
> ○ c. /bin/ping
> ○ d. None of the above

Answer d is correct. Answer a is incorrect because the **tracert** command is used on Windows machines to trace a network route. Although the **traceroute** command is used on Linux to trace a route, it's located in the /usr/sbin directory, not /usr/bin. Therefore, answer b is incorrect. Answer c is incorrect because **ping** is used to send ICMP echo request packets to network hosts.

Question 7

You must use a DNS server to ping **www.redhat.com**.

○ a. True

○ b. False

Answer a is correct. If you aren't using a DNS server, you have to ping the IP address of **www.redhat.com**.

Question 8

What are the three classes of IP networks and how do they differ?

The three classes of IP networks are the A, B, and C classes. These are based on 32-bit addresses, written in the xxx.xxx.xxx.xxx format. Class A networks are the largest class of network and include all addresses in a class (such as 204.0.0.0 through 204.255.255.255). Class B networks include addresses in a range such as 204.4.0.0 through 204.4.255.255. Class C is the most widely used network class. It is assigned in a 255-node range (for example, from 204.4.25.0 through 204.4.25.255).

Question 9

Which of the following is a single valid Class C private network range?

○ a. 192.168.0.0 through 192.168.255.255

○ b. 10.0.0.0 through 10.255.255.255

○ c. 192.168.0.0 through 192.168.0.255

○ d. 10.1.0.0 through 10.1.255.255

Answer c is correct.

Question 10

What are the seven layers within the OSI layer model?

_____

The seven layers are Application, Presentation, Session, Transport, Network, Data Link, and Physical.

Need To Know More?

Albitz, Paul and Cricket Liu. *DNS and BIND*, O'Reilly & Associates, Sebastopol, CA, 1998. ISBN 1-56592-512-2. This book covers implementation and usage of DNS and BIND.

Baines, Dominic. *Samba Black Book*, The Coriolis Group, Scottsdale, AZ, 1999. ISBN 1-57610-455-9. This book covers the implementation and usage of Samba.

Blair, John D. *Samba: Integrating Unix and Windows*, SSC, Inc., 1999. ISBN 1-57831-006-7. This book covers everything from a technical tutorial of Samba to a reference guide and HOWTO manual.

Costales, Bryan and Eric Allman. *Sendmail*, O'Reilly & Associates, Sebastopol, CA, 1997. ISBN 1-56592-222-0. This book covers all of the technical aspects of compiling, configuring, and using Sendmail.

Frisch, Æleen. *Essential System Administration*, O'Reilly & Associates, Sebastopol, CA, 1995. ISBN 1-56592-127-5. This book gives you many of the basics required for using Unix style operating systems, commands, filesystems and so forth.

Garfinkel, Simson and Gene Spafford. *Practical Unix and Internet Security*, O'Reilly and Associates, Sebastopol, CA, 1996. ISBN 1-56592-148-8. This book covers system security for both Unix systems and the Internet.

Hung, Craig. *TCP/IP Network Administration*, O'Reilly & Associates, Sebastopol, CA, 1998. ISBN 1-56592-322-7. This book discusses the methods and concepts of TCP/IP networking.

Kelly, Petter, P. Donham, David Collier-Brown. *Using Samba*, O'Reilly & Associates, Sebastopol, CA, 1999. ISBN 1-56592-449-5. This book covers implementation and usage of Samba.

Schmidt, Friedhelm. *The SCSI Bus and IDE Interface*, Addison Wesley Longman, Reading, MA 1997. ISBN 0-20117-514-2. This book gives you all the details relating to the IDE Interface and SCSI bus.

Siever, Ellen. *Linux In A Nutshell*, O'Reilly & Assocates, Sebastopol, CA, 1997. ISBN 1-56592-167-4. This book gives you a look at the Linux operating system and its concepts.

http://metalab.unc.edu/LDP
The Linux Documentation Project. This site links to many FAQs and HOWTOs related to Linux.

http://www.samba.org
For more information about current development and documentation regarding Samba, visit Samba's Web site.

http://www.sendmail.org
For more information about current development and documentation on Sendmail, visit Sendmail's Web site.

Installation

Terms you'll need to understand:

√ Media

√ Package

√ Autodetect

√ Boot loader

√ X Window system

Techniques you'll need to master:

√ Planning a successful installation

√ Installing a Red Hat Linux system successfully

√ Partitioning hard drives

√ Understanding install options and packages

√ Configuring install time peripherals

√ Installing boot loader successfully

√ Troubleshoot Installation

The underlying goal of becoming an RHCE is to certify your skills in the installation, configuration, and administration of a Red Hat Linux system. The first step to achieving your goals as an RHCE is to master the skills of installation. In this chapter, we will discuss the steps to successfully install a Red Hat 6.0 system.

Getting Started

Before you begin your installation of Linux, you have to decide why you are installing Linux in the first place. What are your needs? What do you want to do? Linux has a vast variety of applications, uses, and support. Deciding what you're going to do in advance will help you decide what to install or set up.

Server Vs. Workstation

You can use Linux in either a server or workstation environment. In fact, if necessary, you can use it in both. If you are just a home user, or perhaps a work-at-home user, you're probably looking to set up a workstation. On your workstation, you can set up all your dial-up applications, as well as work on your home programming projects and more. However, if you are trying to set up a router, a file server, an Internet gateway, a mail server, a Dynamic Host Control Protocol (DHCP) server, or even a Quake server, you need to evaluate your requirements for setting up a server.

Hardware Requirements

If you're simply planning on setting up an at-home or office workstation, your hardware requirements are very unlimited. Although it's doubtful you would be very happy surfing the Net—or compiling a new kernel—on a 386/16 with 8MB of RAM, it is possible. Linux can use most PC hardware, with the exception of winmodems and just-released hardware.

> *Note: Just-released hardware, if not released with a Linux driver, is typically supported within a few weeks of its release.*

Drivers are currently being developed for the winmodem family and should work with Linux in the near future. A good resource to check to see if your hardware is supported is **www.redhat.com/support/docs/hardware.html**.

If you want to set up a router or a firewall, you can use any basic hardware setup. In fact, using as either a router or a firewall isn't CPU- or memory-intensive. You can therefore set up a very adequate router on a 486 with 16MB of memory and a 250MB hard disk. Other hardware you may have to introduce to your system, depending on your setup, includes networking hardware such as network interface cards (NICs), modems, ISDN adapters, or even frame relay cards.

If you want to set up a network file server, your hardware requirements will be different than those when you are setting up a simple workstation, or even a router. NFS servers are not CPU bound, so a slower system such as a 486 is adequate. However, you should evaluate your speed and size requirements. If you will be serving a large number of files, or large files, you must keep ample hard disk space. If your machine will be serving a large number of users, or will be kept under high load, you should consider hard disk speed as well. You may opt to use SCSI disks, which have faster access times than IDE disks. Using SCSI disks, however, requires that you use an SCSI adapter. Memory is used on an NFS server for cache. Larger amounts of memory allow for faster write and accessibility on commonly used files.

If you are planning to set up a database server, you should evaluate all your input/output (I/O) needs. Database servers are very CPU intensive, so you need a CPU that can handle the amount of users using the system. As when implementing an NFS server, you need ample amounts of disk space and memory. The speed of your hardware (hard disk and memory) may also be a large factor when you choose hardware.

Pre-Installation

To make your Red Hat 6.0 install go smoothly, you should plan and be prepared for as much of the install as possible before beginning. Most importantly, you should have several documentation and information resources available for quick reference during the install, or for troubleshooting afterward. An excellent resource for this is the Red Hat 6.0 Installation Guide. This guide is included with the retail version of Red Hat, which you can purchase directly from Red Hat (http://www.redhat.com/), or from a reseller such as Best Buy or Fry's. A hard copy of the manual only is also available from Red Hat. In addition, you can view or download the manual for free from Red Hat's Web site at http://www.redhat.com/corp/support/manuals/RHL-6.0-Manual/install-guide/manual/. In addition, other great documents can be found on Red Hat's Web site at http://www.redhat.com/docs/.

Installation Method Preparation

After you have gathered the necessary installation materials, it's very important to make sure you have all the necessary media—such as your install CD and boot disks—prepared. With Red Hat 6.0, different media can be used—or in some cases, are required—depending on what method you decide to use to boot the installation program.

You should also have access to any peripherals you want to set up during the installation, as well as all the technical information for any hardware connected to, or installed inside, the machine. If you are planning to install over a network, you should ensure that you are properly connected to your network and that you have located a stable server to install from.

Using A CD-ROM

If you have a bootable CD-ROM, you can start your installation by bootinf from the Red Hat 6.0 distribution CD. Make sure your BIOS is set to boot from the CD-ROM first. If you are planning to set up a dual-boot system (discussed in Chapter 7) and already have a DOS partition on the drive, you can choose to use the autoboot feature, located under the directory /dosutils on the Red Hat 6.0 CD. However, if you don't have a bootable DOS partition or a bootable CD-ROM, you must use a boot floppy.

Using A Boot Floppy

If the boot floppy is not included with your installation media, you can create it by using either **rawrite** (on DOS) or **dd** (on a Unix machine). Using either of these writes the boot image to a floppy. You can run **rawrite** directly from the Red Hat 6.0 CD by following these steps:

1. Load the CD and change into the \dosutils directory.

2. Run **rawrite**. You are asked to supply the path to the boot directory that you want to load. For instance, for boot.img, enter "\images\boot.img". You are then asked to provide your target. You are using a floppy, so choose "A:".

3. You are next prompted to put a floppy disk and hit Enter. The process takes a few minutes, but when it is finished, you then have a working boot disk.

To use **dd** on a Unix system to create a boot disk from the CD, first mount the CD-ROM. Next, type the command "dd if=/mnt/cdrom/images/boot.img of=/dev/fd0", replacing /mnt/cdrom with the mount directory of your CD-ROM. You may also need to replace /dev/fd0 with the appropriate mount point of your floppy. The boot image, named boot.img, is on the Red Hat 6.0 CD under the /images directory. You can also download the boot.img file from one of Red Hat's FTP mirrors. A list of mirrors can be found at **http://www.redhat.com/mirrors.html**.

Special boot floppies are required in these situations:

➤ If you are planning to install Red Hat Linux by using a PCMCIA network card or CD-ROM drive

➤ If you are planning to install Red Hat Linux via network file system (NFS) or FTP

When you need one of the special boot disks listed above, you can create it using the same method as creating a regular boot disk as discussed earlier in this section. As we discussed for creating a regular boot disk, you can use **rawrite** (DOS) or **dd** (Unix) to write the special boot image to a floppy. The image required to use PCMCIA devices during the installation is called **pcmcia.img**. The image required to install via NFS or FTP is called **bootnet.img**.

Planning Your Configuration

During the installation, you are prompted for several configuration, setting, and installation options (including network settings, host and domain information, root password, and hardware specifications). Before actually beginning your install, you should have all this information prepared, to save you from having to find it—or figure it out—during the installation process.

One of the most important configuration issues deals with the physical hard drive installation. You should know exactly what drive you plan to install on, and on exactly what partition. Knowing this information is especially important if you have multiple drives, or existing partitions from a previous Linux install or other operating system. Specifying the wrong drive or partition during the install will destroy any information on the drive, and you will not be able to recover it.

You should also plan your partition layout. If you're installing on a small drive, or setting up a long-term dedicated service machine, you may opt simply to install all the packages and directories in one partition (in addition to your swap partition). For installations on machines with multiple operating systems, existing partitions, or simply very large drives, it's best to create multiple partitions. The most common dedicated partitions are set up for the following filesystems:

➤ /

➤ /home

➤ /var

➤ /tmp

➤ /boot

➤ /usr/local

Setting up separate filesystems is helpful when you are managing large filesystems. Splitting filesystems amongst separate partitions saves rebuild time if one filesystem becomes corrupted, as well as sets up better security when other users attempt to access the system. In addition, setting up these separate filesystems makes system upgrades easier. For example, creating a separate file system for users' home directories allows you to upgrade the entire system without damaging user data.

 In addition to planning your physical installation, you should have the information prepared for configuration settings and installation options when prompted. Some of this information will include network settings, host and domain information, root password, hardware specifications, and more.

Installation Process

To simplify explaining the installation process, and to allow for quicker reference, this section is divided into six sections. The first describes how to begin your installation and discusses how to install from CD-ROM, over NFS, and more. The second section discusses the first stage of the installation process. It describes the configuration options for the actual installation process. The third section covers the second stage of the installation process. The fourth section discusses hard drive options. The fifth section discusses installing packages. It explains how to select individual packages and describes some of the most commonly used packages. The last section details the installation's third stage, during which you configure peripherals, network settings, and more.

Beginning Your Installation

As mentioned earlier in this chapter, you begin your installation in different ways, depending on your method of installation. The most standard installation type simply uses a boot floppy and the Red Hat 6.0 CD-ROM. Some options don't require a boot floppy at all. Others don't require the CD, but require special boot floppies. The most common types of installations include DOS autoboot, boot floppy/CD combination, NFS, FTP, and hard drive installations.

DOS Autoboot Install

To begin your install without using a boot floppy, you should have a bootable DOS partition on your machine. Boot to the DOS partition. Next, insert your Red Hat CD and change into the /dosutils directory. Under the /dosutils directory is a tool named autoboot.exe, which automatically boots from a DOS machine into the Linux installation. At the first welcome screen, hit Enter at the boot: prompt to choose "Install or Upgrade" a Red Hat machine. When prompted, choose to install with the CD media.

  The commercial Red Hat 6.0 CD is bootable. Therefore, for a system whose bios can support booting from CD-ROM, simply enable this option in your bios and boot directly from the CD-ROM.

Standard Boot Floppy Install

To begin your install using the standard boot floppy and the CD-ROM, simply power on the machine with the boot floppy in the floppy drive. At the welcome screen, hit Enter at the boot: prompt. Doing so enables you to "Install or Upgrade" a Red Hat machine. If you are using a PCMCIA CD-ROM for the installation, you must use the special PCMCIA boot floppy that contains the pcmcia.img boot image. When prompted, choose to install with the CD media.

NFS Install

To begin your install using NFS, you need to use the special NFS boot disk that contains the bootnet.img boot image. At the welcome screen, hit Enter at the boot: prompt. Doing so enables you to "Install or Upgrade" a Red hat machine. Next, you are asked to select between an NFS or FTP install. Choose the NFS option. You are then asked to set up the NFS settings. Enter your NFS server name and the directory on the NFS server where the Red Hat directory tree is located. See Figure 5.1.

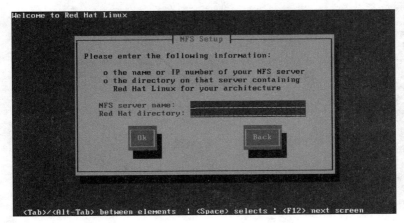

Figure 5.1   NFS setup.

FTP Install

To begin your install using FTP, you will also need to use the special FTP boot disk that contains the bootnet.img boot image. At the welcome screen, hit enter at the boot: prompt to enable you to "Install or Upgrade" a Red Hat machine. You will then be asked to select between an NFS or FTP install. Choose the FTP option. Next, you are asked to set up the FTP settings. Enter your FTP site name and the directory on the FTP server where the Red Hat directory tree is located. If the FTP server is non-anonymous, or you are planning to install via a proxy server, check the appropriate box at the bottom of the FTP setupscreen. See Figure 5.2.

Hard Drive Install

To begin your install after downloading or copying the Red Hat directory tree to a local hard drive, use the standard boot floppy with the boot.img boot image. At the welcome screen, hit Enter at the boot: prompt to allow you to "Install or Upgrade" your Red Hat system. When prompted, choose the "Install from hard-drive" option. You are next prompted to select the partition that currently holds the Red Hat directory tree. You must also enter the path to the Red Hat tree, if it is located anywhere other than the root (/) directory.

Installing Red Hat: The First Stage

The first step of the install is actually to configure the installation process itself. It asks for your native language, your keyboard style, and even what type of install you plan to use. The installation process opens with a welcome screen that asks you to select in what native language you want to install Red Hat.

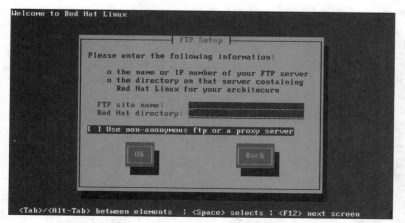

Figure 5.2 FTP setup.

Figure 5.3   Choose a language.

Red Hat 6.0 supports most languages, including English, German, Icelandic, and more (see Figure 5.3).

You are then asked to select what type of keyboard you have, such as U.S., French, and so on. Next, you are given the option of what install medium you are using (such as CD-ROM versus hard disk, or FTP versus NFS, depending on your boot floppy). The install then advances to the second stage.

Installing Red Hat: The Second Stage

The first steps during the second stage of your install decide the overall plan for your installation. From this stage, you can decide to simply upgrade from an existing Red Hat version or to start a fresh install. You also are given the option of selecting pre-set configurations (such as workstation or server) or installing with a custom configuration. Figure 5.4 shows the window that prompts you to choose the preconfigured server, preconfigured workstation, or custom configuration options for installation.

The Workstation Configuration

Choosing the Workstation configuration automatically installs the most common packages used on a personal workstation. In addition to the base Red Hat install, some of the workstation features include many of the development packages, such as the development libraries like libtiff-devel-3.4-6. The workstation configuration also installs a more advanced X windowing system and X applications such as desktop backgrounds, enlightenment, gnome, gimp, multimedia packages, and xscreensavers. The partition layout of a Workstation configuration is very simple. It creates a swap, /boot, and /root partition. With the default

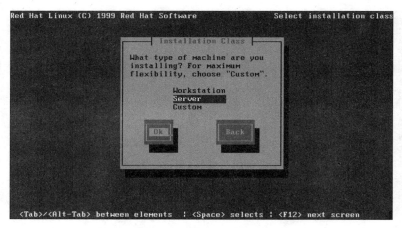

Figure 5.4 Selecting the installation class.

workstation install, you install around 350 packages, 80 of which are different than those installed when you choose the Server configuration.

The Server Configuration

Choosing the Server configuration automatically installs many of the most common packages used on a networked server. Unlike the workstation install, the server configuration chooses the majority of the most stable packages. Eliminating the development packages and extra X windows tools, the number of packages installed is smaller, limited to around 275 packages, and only 12 of them are different than those installed with the workstation configuration. However, these 12 unique packages are all very significant, and some are quite large. Some of the features installed with these packages include:

➤ Anonymous FTP

➤ Caching nameserver

➤ bind

➤ Advanced Perl

➤ postgresql

➤ Samba

The automatic partitioning scheme is a little more complex for the server configuration than for the workstation configuration. The server partitioning is set for a 256MB / (root) partition, a 512MB /usr partition, a 512MB /home partition, a 16MB /boot partition, a 64MB swap partition, and a 256MB /var partition.

Choosing the automatic server configuration destroys any existing partitions on your machine. Do not choose the server option if you have an existing partition, such as another operating system, that you do not want to irreversibly lose.

The Custom Configuration

Choosing the Custom configuration allows you to set up any particular configuration you want. You are given two ways to select your packages: You can select either a feature that automatically selects the necessary packages or one that selects individual packages manually. You are even given the option to install everything, which is simple for new users.

Examining Hard Disk Options

After you choose your configuration method, the installation moves on to begin setting up the physical hard drive. First, Linux scans the system to autodetect whether you have any SCSI adapters installed. If none is found, you are asked if you have one installed. If you answer yes, you are prompted to select your adapter from a device listing.

Next, you must specify exactly where you want the Linux install to be physically placed. You do this by partitioning, formatting, and setting up mount points. First, you are asked to select a disk-editing tool. You are given the option of Disk Druid or fdisk. Disk Druid is Red Hat's install-time disk management utility. It can create and delete disk partitions according to user-supplied requirements as well as manage mount points for each partition. The traditional Linux disk partitioning tool is fdisk, introduced in Chapter 3. The program fdisk is a bit more flexible than Disk Druid, but it requires you to have some experience with disk partitioning and to be accustomed to using a text interface.

Disk Druid

Selecting Disk Druid presents you with a graphical user interface to help partition and select mount points on your drive. Disk Druid is available only when you are installing Red Hat Linux. The first screen is the Current Disk Partitions screen, shown in Figure 5.5. This screen shows all currently establish partitions and disk drive summaries.

Each line in the Current Disk Partitions section represents a disk partition. Each line has five fields:

➤ **Mount point** This indicates where the partition will be mounted when Red Hat is installed.

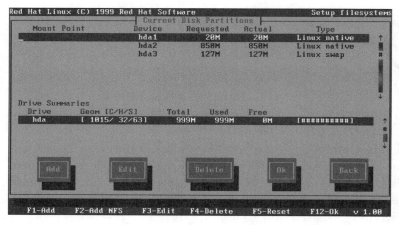

Figure 5.5 The Current Disk Partitions screen of Disk Druid.

➤ **Device** This displays the partition's device name.

➤ **Requested** This specifies the minimum size requested when the partition was created.

➤ **Actual** This shows the space that is currently assigned to the partition.

➤ **Type** This shows the partition's type, such as Linux Native, Linux Swap, or other type.

Each line in the Drive Summaries section represents a hard disk on your system. Each line has six fields:

➤ **Drive** This shows the hard disk's device name.

➤ **Geom[C/H/S]** This shows the hard disk's geometry, which consists of three numbers that represent the number of cylinders, heads, and sectors. The hard disk geometry is reported by the hard disk itself.

➤ **Total** This shows the total space available on the hard disk.

➤ **Used** This shows how much of the hard disk space is currently assigned to partitions.

➤ **Free** This shows how much of the hard disk space is still available.

➤ **Used** This is a bar graph that is a visual representation of the space currently used on the hard disk.

The buttons located at the bottom of the screen are what makes Disk Druid a popular tool. With the Add button, you can add partitions to a drive. With Edit, you can modify attributes of the partition selected under the Current

Disk Partitions section. With Delete, you can delete current partitions. The OK and Back buttons allow you to navigate backward and forward as well as through the install, depending on whether you are finished or need to return to the first step.

 If you are setting up different partitions for separate filesystems, you must mount each partition to the particular filesystem. For instance, if you are setting up a partition for /var, set the mount point to /var (as opposed to /).

fdisk

The traditional Linux partitioning tool is fdisk. It is available both during and after installation. After installation, you can use fdisk when repartitioning, adding additional drives, and so on. It is a text-based tool, and not considered very user-friendly.

Note: You should be familiar with disk partitioning before using fdisk.

When you select fdisk to edit partitions, you see the Partition Disks dialog box (shown in Figure 5.6), which lists every disk on your computer. To edit a specific disk, highlight the disk you'd like to partition and then select Edit. Next, you enter fdisk and can partition the disk you selected. (You can repeat this process for each disk you want to partition.) When you are finished, select Done.

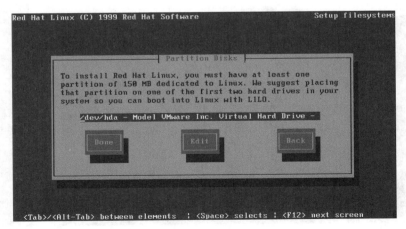

Figure 5.6   fdisk Select Drive.

After selecting a drive, you are dropped into a command line mode program to edit the selected drive. At the command (m for help): prompt, type "m" and then press Enter. Doing so gives you a list of all available commands (as discussed in Chapter 3). First, type "p" to print the current partition table. You can then add and delete partitions as needed, change their type, and more. Figure 5.7 shows the text-based interface of fdisk.

After setting up all the appropriate partitions, enter "w" to write to table and exit. You are then returned to Current Disk Partitions screen (refer back to Figure 5.5), where you can assign the mount points to each partition.

Partition Schemes

In addition to setting partitions for filesystems or operating systems, you must dedicate a partition to Linux Swap. The Linux Swap partition is used as virtual random access memory (RAM), which is typically set anywhere from 32- through 128MB, depending on the amount of installed RAM in the system and the size of your hard drive; however, the size is limited to 2GB. After you select the partitions for your drive and set them to be the proper partition types, the Red Hat installation formats the swap space and then the separate partitions. The following is an example of a partitioning scheme for a Red Hat Linux server:

➤ 300MB / (root) (this size may vary)

➤ 16MB /boot

➤ 300 through 700MB /usr

➤ 512MB /home (minimum)

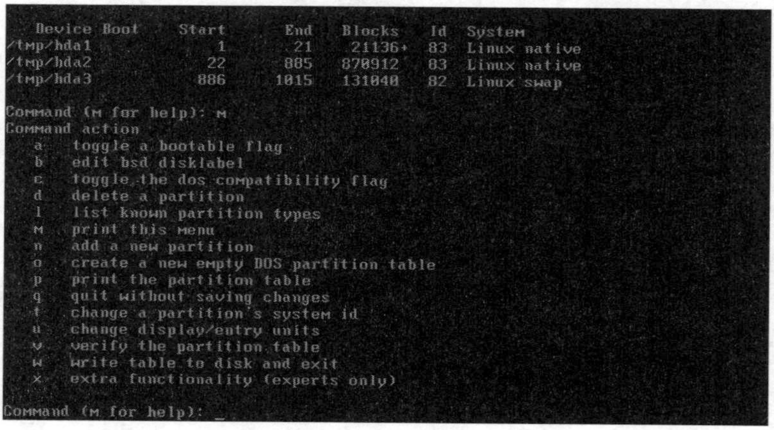

Figure 5.7   The fdisk interface.

➤ swap partition with a maximum of 2GB

➤ The sizes of /tmp and /var vary, depending on the number of users and the size of your system

 A typical Red Hat Linux installation uses the DOS style partition table, which recognizes only four primary partitions. To resolve this problem, create extended partitions that hold logical partitions. An extended partition can hold up to 12 partitions, allowing for a maximum of 16 partitions on one drive. Regardless of the number of primary partitions, the first logical partition always has a device number of 5. For example, the first logical partition on the first IDE hard drive would be named hda5.

Installing Packages

During the Custom configuration install, you are first given the option to select package groups to install. You can choose among 31 features, listed and described in Table 5.1, in addition to simply installing everything.

Table 5.1 Installation package groups.	
Package Group	**Description**
Printer Support	Installs printer support to a local or network printer
X Window System	Installs graphical user interface support
GNOME	Installs tools within the X window system
KDE	Installs the X window environment KDE
Mail/WWW/News Tools	Enables your machine to manage and use mail and Internet services
DOS/Windows Connectivity	Allows connections to and from DOS and Windows clients
File Manager	Enables your machine to support services for file management
Graphics Manipulation	Installs packages to read, create, and alter graphics files
Console Games	Installs console games for entertainment
Console Multimedia	Installs multimedia support for the console
X Multimedia Support	Installs packages that allow multimedia use within the X window system

(continued)

Table 5.1 Installation package groups (continued).

Package Group	Description
Networked Workstation	Enables the machine to communicate with other machines on a network
Dial-up workstation	Enables the machine to communicate with other machines via a modem
News Server	Sets up the machine to be used as a news server
NFS Server	Allows the machine to serve as a network file server
SMB (Samba) Connectivity	Enables the machine to communicate with Windows clients
IPX/NetWare Connectivity	Installs the capability to communicate with or as NetWare clients
Anonymous FTP Server	Installs the packages necessary to allow anonymous file transfer service
DNS Name Server	Sets up the machine to serve as a domain name server
Postgres (SQL) Server	Enables the machine to host a SQL database server
Network Management Workstation	Allows the machine to manage networks remotely
Tex document formatting	Enables the machine to handle Tex documents
Emacs	Installs the popular text editing tool
Emacs with X windows	Installs the graphical text editing tool for X window system
C Development	Allows the machine to be used to program C
Development Libraries	Installs development and new libraries
C++ Development	Enables the machine to be used for C++ development programming
X development	Installs packages necessary for use with programming for the X environment
GNOME development	Allows for programming for GNOME
Kernel Development	Installs packages necessary for programming kernel code
Extra Documentation	Installs additional documentation that is helpful for new users

Selecting Individual Packages

Choosing the option "select individual packages" (as shown in Figure 5.8) at the bottom of the screen allows you to select or deselect all the packages manually. Unlike some early distributions, these packages are now sorted into a directory tree, arranged within 29 categories.

 To learn more about what a certain package is, press F1 while selecting it.

The first two categories list the Amusements/Games and Amusements/Graphics packages. These packages are used simply for entertainment. Many of these packages require the X window system to be installed, or a specific desktop environment, such as KDE. These packages are typically noted by starting with the environment name, such as

```
kdegames
```

or by beginning with an x, such as

```
xbill
```

Some of the most popular packages under these headings are **fortune-mod, gnuchess, xbill, xearth,** and **xscreensaver.**

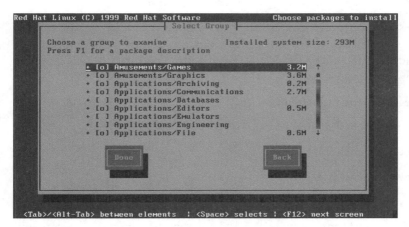

Figure 5.8   Choose the "select individual packages" option.

The next 12 categories list all the applications available for initial installation. The applications are divided into application type groups, including archiving, communications, databases, editors, emulators, engineering, internet, multimedia, productivity, publishing, system, and text. Manually selecting these packages is helpful when you are budgeting disk space or if you don't want a lot of programs you'll never use.

Some of the most used applications on Linux can be found in these groups:

➤ **Applications/Communications**   Within this group, you can find programs such as **mgetty, sendfax, minicom**, and **dip** for use with fax, modem, and serial console connectivity.

➤ **Applications/Editors**   Within this category, you can choose **Emacs, jed**, and **vim** text editors.

➤ **Applications/Emulators**   Under Emulators is the **dosemu** program.

➤ **Applications/Internet**   Within this category, you can find mail readers, newsreaders, Web browsers, chat clients, and even compression tools.

➤ **Applications/Multimedia**   Under this category, you can find tools such as the Gimp (for graphic manipulation) and programs such as **rhsound** and **mpg123** (for use with audio and other multimedia projects).

➤ **Applications/Publishing**   Under this directory, you can find tools required for manipulating text, such as **ghostscript, groff**, and **pdf**.

➤ **Applications/System**   Under this group, you can find many of your system-specific tools. Some of the most used packages in this group are the mtools and the **netcfg, pciutils, screen**, and **rdate** tools.

The next five categories contain all the Development packages. You can use Development packages for debugging programs, programming and compiling, and even including the latest features of a specific program. The five Development groups are:

➤ Development/Debugging

➤ Development/Languages

➤ Development Libraries

➤ Development/System

➤ Development/Tools

Some of the most commonly used packages within these groups are egcs within the languages group, which is used when compiling new kernels, and the kernel source, which can be found in the system group. In addition, some development tools can be found under the tools group, such as **autoconf, cvs, make,** and **patch**.

The largest group of packages (in install size) is the Documentation group. Within this group you can:

➤ Select individual documentation packages for specific programs, such as sendmail, XFree86, or gimp.

➤ Select the linux man-pages and faq (frequently asked questions).

➤ Install Linux HOWTOs in multiple languages ranging from Chinese to English to Polish.

The next five groups include packages to set up your system environment. The very heart of the Linux install is found within these groups. They are:

➤ System Environment/Space

➤ System Environment/Daemons

➤ System Environment/Kernel

➤ System Environment/Libraries

➤ System Environment/Shells

Within the space group you can select programs such as **ipchains, controlpanel,** and **shapecfg**. All program daemons for both workstations and servers can be found within the daemon group. Some of these include apache, bind, ppp, squid, lpr, samba, and sendmail. The kernel group contains the packages for the kernel-BOOT, kernel-ibcs, and kernel-smp. The libraries used amongst many of your programs, compilers, and within your X system are found under the Libraries group. Some of these packages include gnome-libs, ncurses3, kdesupport, qt, libpng, and xpm. Some of your optional shells for use with linux, such as bash and ksh, are found under the group shells.

The three final groups from which you can select individual packages are the User Interface groups. These packages are used, and in some cases required, for setting up your X window graphical user interface. The groups are:

➤ **User Interface/Desktops**   In this group, you can select from among the multiple desktop environments that you can use with Linux. Some of these include AfterStep, fvwm, kde, and WindowMaker.

➤ **User Interface/X**   Here, you can find X tools and fonts.

➤ **User Interface/X Hardware Support**   Here, you can find configuration tools, video hardware drivers, and support.

After selecting all the packages you plan to install on the system, you will be notified if there are any package dependency requirements that need to be met. This means that if you select one package that requires another package to run appropriately and you didn't select the required package, you are notified and prompted to install the dependency requirements. Once all the dependency requirements are met, Red Hat begins the physical install process. It creates the physical filesystem on the drive you are installing to, checks to see that you have adequate disk space, and finally begins physically installing the chosen packages. In addition, Red Hat 6.0 automatically detects the type of CPU you have installed, and optimizes the installed kernel. The autodetected types of CPUs include Pentium Pro, PII/PIII, and AMD's K5 and K6. All other CPUs are set up with the default 386 settings.

 During the installation process, you can view install messages and other information on the first five virtual consoles. Pressing Alt+F1 displays the installer. Pressing Alt+F2 presents a bash shell. Pressing Alt+F3 displays an Installer message log. Pressing Alt+F4 shows all of your kernel messages. Pressing Alt+F5 displays the standard output of mke2fs.

Installing Red Hat: The Third Stage

After installing all the packages you have chosen, you are prompted to begin setting up the initial configuration, for specific selected packages. During the initial configuration process, you are asked to set up several system, software, and hardware settings. You are prompted to select simple settings for things such as your time zone and are asked to choose a unique root password for superuser login access. You are also prompted to set up items such as your mouse, printer, networking, boot services, and X windows.

Configuring Peripherals

Red Hat 6.0 incorporates an autodetect feature, which probes for attached hardware to detect what type of hardware you will configure. For standard mouse and peripheral types, Red Hat will automatically detect its type during the installation process. You are given the option to configure your mouse and select its exact model. For two-button mouse types, you are given the option to "Emulate Three Buttons", as shown in Figure 5.9.

 If you are using a trackball or other unlisted mouse type, select the type "Generic" for the type of mouse you are using. For example, choose Generic Serial for serial connected mice or Generic PS/2 for ps/2-style mice.

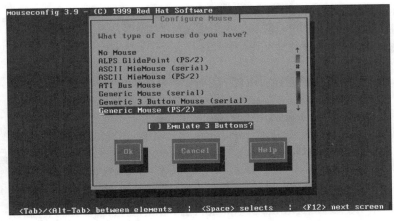

Figure 5.9 Mouseconfig.

If printer support was selected and installed, you are automatically prompted to set up your printer. You are first asked to select how the printer is connected. You can set up a printer that's connected locally, remotely via samba (Windows 95/98/NT), or via NetWare.

To connect a local printer, you will be presented a screen, shown in Figure 5.10, to select the name of the printing queue and the spool directory.

Red Hat then scans for detected ports and asks for your printing device.

Note: When setting up your printer device, keep in mind that /dev/lp0 in Linux is the equivalent to LPT1 under DOS.

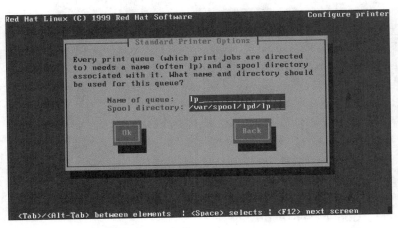

Figure 5.10 Configuring printing.

The next screen prompts you for your printer model. When prompted, select the "fix stair stepping while printing" option, which aligns all the text to the left margin (instead of printing the margin in a stair stepping pattern).

Configuring Network Settings

If you selected and installed networking support, you are automatically prompted to enter your local networking information. (You are not prompted during installation to set up dial-up information—you must configure dial-up after you have installed Red Hat Linux.) To set up networking, you are given the option of using Static IP address, BOOTP, or DHCP, as shown in Figure 5.11.

When you set up a system for use with a static IP address, you are requested to provide standard local network information. You must enter a unique local IP address for your machine. This number could be part of a private non-routeable network and use a 192.168.x.x IP or 10.x.x.x IP number. You may opt to give your machine a routable IP, which your network administrator or Internet provider assigns. You are then asked to provide your netmask, gateway, and primary name server settings for the system. Next , you are prompted for your DNS information, such as domain name, host name, and back-up name server locations.

Configuring Boot Settings And LILO

In addition to your networking services, you can set up many of your boot settings and preferences for boot processes. During this stage, you can create an individual boot disk for your system, which allows you to boot Linux if your Linux loader or install becomes corrupted.

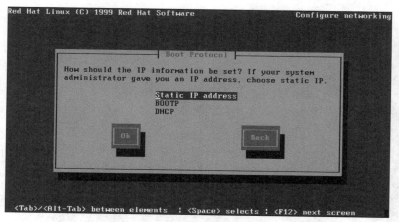

Figure 5.11 Configure networking.

You are first prompted to select what packages you want to automatically run at boot-time. These options vary depending on the packages you installed. However, some typical packages you'll find include apmd, crond, gpm, linuxconf, sendmail, and sound. The ntsysv program is called to select what packages you want to run at boot-time. See Figure 5.12.

To change these settings after initial setup, run **ntsysv** as root from the console or as an xterm.

LILO is the Linux bootloader. During the initial configuration, you are prompted for where you want to either install the bootloader to the master boot record (MBR) or the first sector of the boot partition. Typical Linux systems use LILO as their chosen bootloader and install the bootloader in the MBR. Installing it here is especially important if you want the bootloader to manage multiple operating systems installed on the same system. However, if you plan to use another bootloader, such as the NT bootloader or OS/2 bootloader, you should install the Linux boot loader on the first sector of the boot partition and point your existing boot loader to the boot partition. See Figure 5.13.

After determining where to install the boot loader, you are given the opportunity to set up LILO. You are first be prompted to specify any special options you need to run LILO. Next, you can set up your bootable partitions. Some bootable

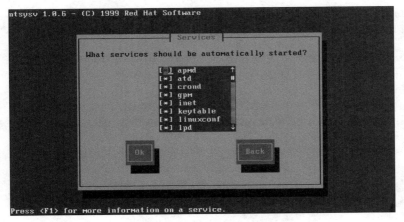

Figure 5.12   Services started at boot-time.

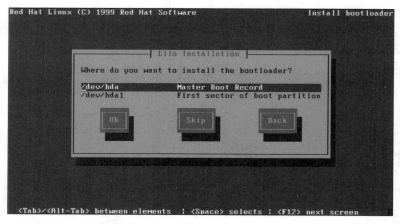

Figure 5.13 Installing bootloader.

partitions include the Linux boot partition, as well as bootable partitions set aside for other operating systems (such as DOS, Windows 3.x/95/98/NT, OS/2, and other Unix operating systems). You'll know if you have set up LILO properly whenever you reboot. Especially if you're booting multiple operating systems, you must hit the Tab at the LILO: prompt. Hitting the Tab key again shows you your boot options. Next, enter your preference or allow the system to boot into its default.

Configuring X Window System

During the final step of your Red Hat install, you install and configure your video, monitor, and X Window System options, among others. Linux automatically probes for your video card. You are then prompted to select your video card from a list. If your video card isn't listed, simply select the Unlisted Card option. Red Hat then installs the appropriate X server for your video card.

You are next asked to set up your monitor. Many popular monitor types are already listed and pre-configured with standard vertical and horizontal refresh rates and frequencies. If your monitor isn't listed, choose the "custom" option, and find the horizontal and vertical frequency and refresh rates in your owner's manual. If you can't locate your owner's manual, another place to try is the manufacturer's Web site.

 Setting a frequency or refresh rate higher than what your monitor can support may cause damage to your monitor.

After you select your monitor, X runs an auto test. Your screen may flash, and you are then prompted to confirm if your screen appears to be running properly and at your selected resolution. To complete the setup of the X window system under Red Hat 6.0, you can select a new feature to automatically start X at boot-time.

Verifying Your New Installation

After completing your installation, the first thing you will do is restart your machine. When your machine successfully boots, log in as "root" with your root password you selected during the installation. Before trying to use programs or services on the newly installed Linux machine, view your dmesg log file by entering "cat /var/log/dmesg" at the prompt. The output of dmesg is a log of the messages that you see during boot time. Within dmesg, you can look for the kernel that initializes your partitions, your ethernet card, and more. Listing 5.1 shows a sample section of dmesg output.

Listing 5.1   Snippet from /var/log/dmesg.

```
................................. done.
PCI: PCI BIOS revision 2.10 entry at 0xfb5a0
PCI: Probing PCI hardware
PCI->APIC IRQ transform: (B0,I19,P0) -> 17
PCI->APIC IRQ transform: (B0,I20,P0) -> 16
Swansea University Computer Society NET3.039 for Linux 2.1
NET3: Unix domain sockets 0.16 for Linux NET3.038.
Swansea University Computer Society TCP/IP for NET3.037
IP Protocols: ICMP, UDP, TCP, IGMP
Starting kswapd v 1.5
pty: 256 Unix98 ptys configured
Real Time Clock Driver v1.09
PIIX3: IDE controller on PCI bus 00 dev 39
PIIX3: not 100% native mode: will probe irqs later
    ide0: BM-DMA at 0xf000-0xf007, BIOS settings: hda:pio, hdb:pio
    ide1: BM-DMA at 0xf008-0xf00f, BIOS settings: hdc:pio, hdd:pio
hda: IBM-DHEA-36480, ATA DISK drive
ide0 at 0x1f0-0x1f7,0x3f6 on irq 14
hda: IBM-DHEA-36480, 6197MB w/476kB Cache, CHS=790/255/63, (U)DMA
eth0: 3Com 3c905 100baseTx at 0x6100, 00:10:4b:63:05:94, IRQ 17
```

After viewing the dmesg file, log in as root and check to see that things are working properly. Take a look at your /var/log/messages file to see if any processes have any errors. In addition, examine your installation process in /tmp/install.log.

Troubleshooting Your Installation

After viewing the dmesg logs, you may notice that specific pieces of hardware may not be loading properly. If you think a piece of hardware has a compatibility issue—or perhaps the driver for your hardware was not available during installation—check out the "Hardware Compatibility HOWTO" on the Linux Documentation Project at **http://metalab.unc.edu/LDP/HOWTO/Hardware-HOWTO.html**.

Another troubleshooting source is Red Hat, which offers a hardware guide for the Red Hat-specific distribution. Red Hat also offers version-specific lists for older versions of Red Hat. These lists can be found at **http://www.redhat.com/support/docs/hardware.html**. Although both the Red Hat and the Linux Documentation Project list much of the same information, the Red Hat list is most often more accurate and current because Red Hat follows the support for each individual version.

One of the most common installation problems outside of hardware support relates to LILO. Occasionally, a disk sector is bad and LILO doesn't install to it properly. Other times, it doesn't work because it was misconfigured. One of the best ways to troubleshoot your LILO problems is to watch the output of LILO itself.

Watch for your LILO prompt. If you don't get any part of the LILO prompt, LILO didn't load. If you get an L, the first-stage boot loader is loaded and started. If you get an LI, the second-stage boot loader is loaded. If you get an LIL, the second-stage boot loader is started. If you get an LIL?, the second-stage boot loader was loaded at an incorrect address. If you get an LIL-, the descriptor table is corrupt. If you get LILO, all of LILO has been loaded correctly.

Practice Questions

Question 1

> What command(s) can you use to create a Linux installation boot floppy?
>
> ○ a. **bb** and **rawwrite**
>
> ○ b. **dd** and **rawrite**
>
> ○ c. **vi** and **pico**
>
> ○ d. **mkboot disk**

Answer b is correct. The **dd** and **rawrite** tools are the Unix and DOS tools used to create an installation boot disk. The **mkbootdisk** command (answer d) is used to create after-installation boot disks, such as those used in Rescue boot disk sets.

Question 2

> What types of installs require a special boot disk? [Check all correct answers]
>
> ❑ a. PCMCIA
>
> ❑ b. FTP
>
> ❑ c. NFS
>
> ❑ d. HTTP
>
> ❑ e. Samba

Answers a, b, c, and d are correct. An installation that requires a PCMCIA device (answer a)—such as a CD-ROM or network card—during installation needs a boot disk made with the pcmcia.img image. FTP (answer b), NFS (answer c), and HTTP (answer d) all require a boot disk made with the bootnet.img. Answer e is incorrect because Samba is no longer supported as of Red Hat 6.0.

Question 3

How can you troubleshoot LILO problems after installation?

You can troubleshoot LILO problems by examining how LILO responds during iboot-time. If you don't get the LILO prompt and don't boot, you should use the boot disk to see that LILO was installed and to check that it will be loaded. If you receive a part of the LILO command, such as L or LIL?, you can tell what happened (not all of the bootloader was loaded or started, or the address or descriptor table is corrupt, for example).

Question 4

Where can you find out about hardware compatibility issues?

Several online resources are available to help you learn about current hardware compatibility and other hardware issues. You can find the Red Hat-specific site at **http://www.redhat.com/support/docs/hardware.html**. The Linux Documentation Project, a general Linux hardware compatibility resource, is located at **http://www.metalab.unc.edu/LDP/HOWTO/Hardware-HOWTO.html**.

Question 5

What logs should you view after an installation to ensure proper installation as well as to troubleshoot installation problems? [Check all correct answers]

❑ a. /var/log/messages

❑ b. /var/log/maillog

❑ c. /tmp/install.log

❑ d. /bin/dmesg

Answers a, c, and d are correct. You should read /var/log/messages, /tmp/install.log, and the output of /bin/dmesg after installation. Answer b is incorrect because /var/log/maillog is used to log mail transactions sent by Sendmail.

Question 6

> What is a bootloader?

A bootloader is a program used to manage the boot process of an operating system. Many bootloaders, such as LILO, can manage multiple operating system boot processes, allowing a machine to have the option of booting more than one operating system from separate partitions on the same machine. At this time, however, you cannot boot multiple operating systems simultaneously.

Question 7

> What network setting options are you given during the installation process?
>
> ○ a. static, bootp, dhcp
>
> ○ b. dynamic, static, dhcp
>
> ○ c. dhcp, NIS, dial-up
>
> ○ d. kickstart, routeable, assigned

Answer a is correct. Although you can choose to install NIS and ppp support, you aren't given the option to configure them during installation. Also the dynamic, routeable, and assigned options listed in answers b and d are incorrect as they are not valid options related to a Red Hat Linux installation.

Question 8

> What is the Linux equivalent to LPT1 that is used in DOS?
>
> ○ a. LPT1
>
> ○ b. lp
>
> ○ c. lp0
>
> ○ d. pt0

Answer c is correct. It then follows in order, LPT2 equals lp1, LPT3 equals lp2, and so on.

Question 9

> Why do you use the "emulate three buttons" option during mouse configuration?

You use this option when you are installing a two-button mouse. Generally, the third button is used in some applications for special purposes. It is most commonly used to aid in the copy and paste feature of Linux (highlight the appropriate text with the left mouse button to copy and then click on the appropriate place with the middle mouse button to paste the text). You then have this functionality by clicking on both buttons simultaneously. If you have a three-button mouse, don't select that option.

Question 10

> What services can't be configured during installation? [Check all correct answers]
>
> ❑ a. PPP
> ❑ b. Sound
> ❑ c. Video
> ❑ d. Scanner
> ❑ e. Apache
> ❑ f. Trackball

Answers a, b, d, and e are correct. Although you can install Apache during installation, you can't configure it. Answer c is incorrect because video is configured during the X Window system installation. Answer f is incorrect because the trackball is configured during mouse installation.

Task 1

> Practice installing the Red Hat Linux 6 distribution on the Intel platform. Try the different workstation, server, and custom installations and see how they are different. Read through and install different packages to learn how they interrelate. Use the different types of installation media, and try the installation via NFS, HTTP, FTP, and more. Become comfortable with maneuvering through the different installation prompts, options, and programs.

Need To Know More?

Red Hat Linux 6.0: Operating System Installation Guide. Red Hat Software, Inc., Durham, NC, 1999. ISBN 1-888172-28-2. Chapters 3 through 6 discuss in depth the installation steps of Red Hat 6.0.

http://redhat.com/knowledgebase/rhlinuxdocs.html/

Within the documentation portion of www.redhat.com, Red Hat's Web site, you can find links to postscript versions of the previously mentioned *Red Hat 6.0 Installation Guide* that you can download and print, as well as HTML versions that you can search on-line.

Basic Configuration And Administration

6

The development of Red Hat 6.0 saw a large increase of amount of services and programs you were able to automatically install and configure during the installation progress. As with most operating systems, you still have some configuration to do after your installation. To be a successful RHCE, you must know how to configure packages, programs, and peripherals that aren't installed during installation, as well as be able to perform system administration tasks.

System Configuration Tools

One of the most common myths about using Linux is that it is hard to configure and customize a system after the initial installation. Although this statement was true in the early years of Linux, you no longer have to configure, install, or upgrade system components by hand. Today, Red Hat includes several tools that make the configuration of your Linux system much simpler. Two of these tools are **linuxconf** and Red Hat's **control-panel**. In addition to these configuration management tools, you can run many configuration programs manually, such as **kbdconfig**, **timeconfig**, and **mouseconfig**.

Using **linuxconf**

This popular tool allows you to configure and control many parts of your system. In addition, **linuxconf** can manage a wide range of programs and tasks, such as adding new users (described here) and getting connected to a network (discussed later in this chapter).

To run **linuxconf**, you must be the *superuser*, also known as root, on your system. At the root prompt, simply type "linuxconf" to invoke the program **linuxconf**, which is located in the /bin directory.

The **linuxconf** program offers you four types of interfaces. You can use the command line mode to configure your system by using scripts. You can use the character-cell mode, which, like the Red Hat installation program, allows you to use an easy-to-follow graphical user interface, without the use of X. You can also use an X window-based mode, which uses a point-and-click tree menu-type interface. The last interface is a Web interface, which uses all the advantages of the Web for remote administration tasks. It even works well with text-based browsers, such as lynx. By default, **linuxconf** runs in either character-cell or X mode.

Administering Users

To add users when you're in X Window mode, follow these steps:

1. Invoke the **linuxconf** program by typing "linuxconf" at the root prompt.

2. To open the Users accounts tab, shown in Figure 6.1, select Config then Users Accounts, then Normal, then User accounts.

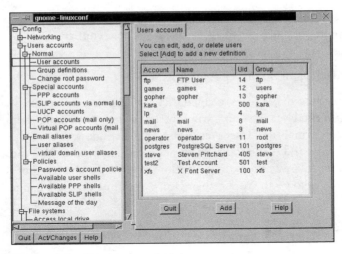

Figure 6.1   User Accounts tab.

3. If you have more than 15 accounts on the system, **linuxconf** provides you with a filter screen, where you can select a smaller range of accounts. To get the full list, select Accept without changing any of the parameters.

4. The Add button will open the User account creation dialog box, in which you enter all the information for a new account. You are then presented with seven fields in which to supply information for the account:

➤ **Login Name**   This is the only required field.

➤ **Full Name**   This is for the user's full name.

➤ **Group**   This allows you to specify any specific group that should be assigned to the account. By default, **linuxconf** assigns a group that is equivalent to the login name.

➤ **Supplementary Groups**   This is where you can add the user to supplementary groups, in addition to a single group. To specify more than one group, simply leave a space between each group name.

➤ **Home**   This gives you the option of specifying a specific home directory. The default is /home/*$user*, where *$user* is the user's login name.

➤ **Shells**   This allows you to specify the location of the shells. This field has a drop-down box that displays the default shell.

➤ **User ID**   This is the number associated with individual user accounts. The system automatically sets this when the account is created.

5. When all the appropriate fields are filled, click on the Accept button. You are then prompted to enter the user's password and confirm it. Passwords must have at least six characters.

6. When finished, click on the Accept button.

After creating a user account, you can change the user's information or password by returning to the User Accounts window. To do so, open config then Users accounts then normal then User Accounts. At the window, choose the user you want to change and then modify the user's entries as needed. You can edit all user accounts this way with the exception of root. To change root's password, use the menu to go to Config then Users Accounts then to change root's password.

Red Hat's Control Panel

Red Hat's Control Panel, shown in Figure 6.2, is an X application that serves as a launching pad for several configuration tools. To start Red Hat's Control Panel, start up an xterm as root while in X, and then type "control-panel". Next, simply select the button for whichever tool you want to run.

> *Note:* *When running control-panel, you should not run or edit any configuration files that it may use.*

Some Control Panel tools are Users and Groups, printer configuration (printtool), and network setup (netcfg). You can also configure extras using the kbdconfig, timeconfig, mouseconfig, and sndconfig tools, discussed later in this chapter.

User And Group Configuration

The Users and Groups configuration tool allows you to add, delete, and edit user and group settings. To list current system users, click on the Users button. Use the Add, View/Edit, and Remove buttons to add, edit, or delete user files. When you add or edit user files, you can set up the username, the password,

Figure 6.2 Red Hat Control Panel.

the user and group ID, the user's full name, the home directory, and the shell. You can also set up users' private information such as office address, office phone number, and home phone number.

To list all current groups listed on the server, click on the Groups button. You will get a list of all current groups listed on the server. You are then given the option of adding, editing, and removing groups with buttons listed at the bottom of the screen. When adding or editing group files, you can give information including the group name, the group password, the group ID, and the list of users that belong in the group.

Printer Configuration

The printer configuration tool is called printtool. It edits the /etc/printcap file, which is used to configure your printers. Running printtool will open a screen, which displays any current printer queues that are listed in /etc/printcap. The buttons along the bottom allow you to edit, add, or delete printer queues. In addition, you can reload your printers, reload the lpd print daemon, or print test pages to your selected printers in the Tests menu. Adding a printer is simple. You are asked for your printer name, the spool directory, and printer device. You can then select your printer type from a list, and select some options, if necessary, such as page size.

Network Configuration

Choosing the network configuration tool runs the netcfg program. The first screen lists your machine hostname and domain, and allows you to search for hostnames under additional domains. Here, you also list your current name servers. If you make any changes to the list, you must save your information and reactivate your network device.

By choosing the Hosts button, you can add, edit, and delete different hosts to which your machine can connect, as well as add, edit, and delete aliases for these hosts. Adding or editing your hosts simply requires the IP for the host machine, the full name of the host, and a nickname for it. When you edit these hosts, you are actually editing your /etc/hosts file.

Choosing the Interfaces button lists all current interfaces installed on your machine. Some typical interfaces include lo (for local host), eth0 (for ethernet), and ppp0 (for ppp) connections. From this screen, you can add, edit, copy, alias, delete, and turn on and off different interfaces. When you add an interface, you're given the option of ppp, slip, plip, ethernet, arcnet, token ring, or pocket ATP. Depending on the type, you're asked to provide options such as authentication type, addresses, and protocols.

If you choose the Routing button, you see a list of any special routing rules you have set up. You can also set up your network gateway here. From this window, you can add, edit, and delete routing options. To edit a static route, click on the Add button. Here you can enter a device, the network, netmask, and gateway options.

Configuring Extras With Linux Administration Tools

Many system administrators enjoy being able to configure, reconfigure, or simply fix their extra settings and peripherals, including keyboards, the clock, a mouse, and sound cards. There are several administration tools available on Linux to do these tasks. Some of the most commonly used ones include kbdconfig, timeconfig, mouseconfig, and sndconfig. Each of these configuration programs is run in console menu mode (this mode is also used during the installation process). In fact, kbdconfig, timeconfig, and mouseconfig are actually used in the installation process!

If you get a new type of keyboard, or are experimenting with keyboards in other languages, you may wish to use the **kbdconfig** tool. To invoke the **kbdconfig** tool, simply type "kbdconfig" at the root prompt. You are then prompted with a blue, red, and yellow screen that asks you to select what type of keyboard you have. When you have selected your keyboard, use the Tab key to select the OK button and then press Enter. It's that simple.

You can just as easily adjust your time settings. To do so, use the **timeconfig** tool by typing "timeconfig" at the root prompt. You can then select what time zone you are in and Tab to select OK. This utility is a favorite for administrators who travel amongst several time zones.

To install a new mouse or trackball, use the **mouseconfig** tool. To do so, simply type "mouseconfig" at the root prompt. Choose your appropriate mouse from the list and then use the Tab key to select OK when you are finished.

A little more involved, albeit not much, is the sound configuration tool. To set up sound on your system, use the **sndconfig** tool by typing "sndconfig" at the root prompt. The screen first prompts you to autoprobe for PnP soundcards that can automatically be configured. If no card was automatically found, you are prompted to select your soundcard from a list. After you have the appropriate sound device selected, or detected, your system runs a few test sounds to verify that your card is working. If you hear the appropriate sounds, use the Tab key to select OK and you will then be finished.

Unlike some of the other configuration tools, the **sndconfig** tool adds entries into your /etc/conf.modules file. The **sndconfig** tool sets the driver, IRQ and IO settings—as well as any aliases that may be needed—in this file.

Filesystem And Mount Configuration

In order to read, write, or otherwise use additional filesystems and devices, you must be able to mount them. To do so, use the **mount** command. Along with the **mount** command, you must supply information such as the device, the filesystem type, and the mount point. Several types of filesystem types are available:

➤ **vfat**   Used to mount Windows partitions and filesystems

➤ **msdos**   Used to mount MS-DOS filesystems and devices

➤ **ext2**   Used for Linux filesystems

➤ **iso9660**   Used for CD-ROM devices

The syntax for using the **mount** command for a device is:

```
mount -t type /dev/device /mnt/mountpoint
```

Replace *type* for the filesystem type, *device* for the device or partition to be mounted, and *mountpoint* for the mount directory you want to use. For example, to mount an iso9660 filesystem of a CD-ROM to /mnt/cdrom, first make sure the /mnt/cdrom mount point is created and then issue this command:

```
mount -t iso9660 /dev/cdrom /mnt/cdrom
```

Many times, you can eliminate the filesystem type and mount point, allowing for easier mount procedures. For instance, rather than issuing the command, you could simply enter "mount /dev/cdrom". You can do this because of the entries in the /etc/fstab file, discussed in Chapter 3. Entries in the /etc/fstab file set up default settings for mount options. Each entry sets default settings such as the mount point, the type of filesystem, how it should be mounted, if it is to be dumped, and in what order it should be mounted. Here is an example of an /etc/fstab file:

```
/dev/hda3       /               ext2      defaults          1  1
/dev/hda1       /boot           ext2      defaults          1  2
/dev/hda4       swap            swap      defaults          0  0
/dev/fd0        /mnt/floppy     ext2      noauto            0  0
/dev/cdrom      /mnt/cdrom      iso9660   noauto,ro,user    0  0
```

The first entry specifies that /dev/hda3 should be mounted to / (root) as an ext2 filesystem with default mount options. It should be dumped and mounted first. The second line specifies that /dev/hda1 be mounted as /boot as an ext2 filesystem. It should be mounted with the default mount options, should be dumped, and should be mounted second. The third line specifies that /dev/hda4 be mounted as swap as a swap filesystem with default mount options, but not be dumped or mounted in any order. The fourth line specifies that /dev/fd0 be mounted as /mnt/floppy with an ext2 filesystem with no automatic mount options, and so on.

 When reading the /etc/fstab file, make note of the different device naming conventions. For instance, /dev/hda1 is the first master hard drive. The h specifies that it's an IDE drive, and the 1 specifies it is the first partition on the drive. However, /dev/sdb3 indicates that it's the second (slave) SCSI drive. The 3 indicates it is the third partition on that drive.

Adding entries to /etc/fstab (or changing them if necessary) doesn't require you to restart any services to make the changes go into effect. In fact, after changing the /etc/fstab file, you can mount the devices in several manners, for example:

```
mount /mnt/mountpoint
```

or

```
mount /dev/device
```

The unsupplied information, such as type, *mountpoint*, or *device* (as needed) are automatically assigned. You can use this convention unless you decide to read from a device with other filesystems and so on that are specified in the file. For instance, if your floppy has a msdos filesystem, specify the –t **msdos** for the type options. To unmount any filesystem or device, use the **umount** command as you would use the **mount** command, as in

```
umount /mnt/cdrom
```

Managing Packages With RPM

RPM, which you use to manage packages, is open source and can be used on several other Linux distributions and even commercial Unix systems other than Red Hat. RPM can run in many modes. Some of these include being able to install, query, verify, check signature, uninstall, build, and rebuild databases; fix file permissions; and set owner and group settings. RPM files are notated with the .rpm extension.

Getting To Know RPM

Much like Linux, RPM didn't just magically appear and work. It was developed over time, based on several other package-management projects. The first development of today's RPM was found in RPP. RPP was actually used in the first Red Hat Linux distributions. In fact, its first features are still the foundation for the purpose and features of RPM today. RPP is credited with being the initial source for the simple one-line commands used to install and uninstall packages. RPP also introduced the scripts that are run before and after packages are installed and uninstalled. The initial query and verify features were also introduced with RPP. Unfortunately, the features available with RPP just were not enough.

The need for more led the Red Hat software developers to peer in on the projects for package management that the developers of the BOGUS distribution were developing. The BOGUS developers, led by Rik Faith, were working on a project for package management called PMS (Package Management System). The feature that RPP was lacking that PMS had mastered was the concept of *pristine sources*. Pristine sources allowed the packager to release versions of software and to track the changes made to the previous version.

Three more steps were taken before we had the RPM we all know and love today. Interestingly enough, Red Hat software itself supported and/or developed all three steps. The first step was when Faith and Doug Hoffman were contracted by Red Hat Software to produce PM, the new updated Package Manager that incorporated the features of RPP with the pristine source feature of PMS. Although PM's functionality was close to that of the RPM we have today, it still lacked good database design and had no multiple architecture support. PM was never used in a commercially available product.

Red Hat developers Marc Ewing and Erik Troan completed the last two steps for developing RPM. The first of these two steps introduced the first version of the official RPM, which was developed in Perl. The last step rewrote RPM in the C development language to increase the program's speed.

Installing, Uninstalling, And Upgrading With RPM

The fundamental job of RPM is to add and remove components from your system. An rpm file is actually a type of compressed archive. Using the **rpm** tool, you can install, delete, and upgrade these RPM-archived packages.

To install an RPM file, use the command line option -i (for install). For example, to install an RPM file for sendmail (such as sendmail-8.9.1-2.i386.rpm), enter

```
rpm -i sendmail-8.9.1-2.i386.rpm
```

To uninstall a package, use the command line option -e (for erase). To uninstall the sendmail-8.9.1-2.i386.rpm sendmail package, enter

```
rpm -e sendmail-8.9.1-2.i386.rpm
```

Another task that you can perform with RPM is to upgrade individual components or packages on your system without having to completely reinstall them. Unlike tar files or gzip packages, the configuration files of RPM packages are preserved when you upgrade. Therefore, you won't lose your configuration. To upgrade a package, simply use the -U option (for upgrade). To upgrade to the sendmail-8.9.1-2.i386.rpm sendmail package, enter

```
rpm -U sendmail-8.9.1-2.i386.rpm
```

 When you are installing or upgrading a package, it is helpful to use the -v and -h options. The -v option (for verbose) prints out the name of the file within the package it is installing. The -h option (for hash mark, #) prints hash marks to show how far the installation has progressed. An example of using both these options is:

```
rpm -ivh sendmail-8.9.1-2.i386.rpm
```

Another helpful RPM install option is –F (for freshen). Freshen allows you to automatically compare a list of rpm files against the rpm files already installed on your system. If an rpm within the list of rpms is newer than the one on your system, it is automatically upgraded. If an rpm within the list is not newer than the one on your system (or it is not even installed on your system), it is ignored. To use the –F option, simply run

```
rpm -F *.rpm
```

from the directory that contains the list of rpm files you want to compare. Note that *.rpm refers to every rpm file in that directory. You can also use other wildcards, filenames, or combinations thereof to get whatever result you are looking for.

Querying With RPM

RPM was designed to have querying capabilities. The RPM archives have custom binary headers that contain data about the package and its contents, allowing you to query individual packages very easily. You can search through your system database for packages and files, find out to which package a file belongs, and so on.

To query for a specific package, use the -q option (for query). Using the **rpm –q** option requires an argument that specifies the package name, such as libc. However, passing an –a option (for all) to the –q option such as

```
rpm -qa
```

queries and prints all installed rpm files on your system. Here's an example output of querying specifically for all the libc packages you have installed on a system:

```
# rpm -q libc
   libc-5.3.12-31
   libc-5.3.12-28
```

This output shows that this particular system has two libc packages installed: libc-5.3.12-31 and libc-5.3.12-28. To get information about those specific packages, you can use the –i option with the query. The format for this is

```
rpm -qi packagename
```

The output of this gives you information such as the name of the package, any relocations (if applicable), the version, the vendor that distributed it, the release number, the build date, the install date, and the source rpm and more. In addition, it gives you a summary of the package and a description that gives some details of the package and what it is used for.

Additional options used with the rpm query function are the –l (for list) and the –f (for file) options. The –l option queries for the contents of an RPM file. The –f function queries files of an rpm. The **rpm –ql** command is used against an existing rpm file. It lists all the files and directories that are contained within the rpm. For instance,

```
rpm -ql libc
```

lists all the files and directories of the libc package. The **rpm –qf** command is used against an existing file; using this command on a file queries for the package that owns the specific file. For instance, doing an

```
rpm -qf xbill
```

while you're in the /usr/lib directory yields

```
xbill-2.0-6
```

which means that the xbill-2.0-6 RPM file installed the /usr/lib/xbill file.

 You aren't always expected to use the package name. If you are using Linux's tab completion feature, it's especially useful to use the **–p** option. Doing so specifies that you are using the full package filename, not just the package name. For instance, using **rpm –qi libc** gets the same results as using **rpm –qip libc-5.3.12-31.src.rpm**.

Verifying With RPM

In addition to using RPM to query for specific files you have already installed on your system, you can verify packages that you have installed against the original package stored in an RPM database. You verify a package when you want to check for problems, such as corrupted or missing files, within it. After verifying a package, you can reinstall the package because any current configurations you have set for the package are preserved.

To verify a package, you use the -**V** option (for verify). The output of the -**V** option is a string of eight characters, possibly followed by a **c** (which notes that it is a configuration file) and then followed by the path and filename. The most important information in the output is the eight-character string, where each character displays the result of the comparison between one attribute of the file compared to the value of the same attribute recorded in the RPM database. Seeing single periods (.) for a specific character means that the attribute matched.

Table 6.1 lists the eight characters and their attributes.

To give you an idea of what verifying a package looks like, here an example of verifying the sendmail package:

```
$rpm -V sendmail
      G.    /etc/aliases.db
S.5   .T  /var/log/sendmail.st
```

The output shows two files with differences, the aliases.db, and the sendmail.st files. The aliases.db file has different Group attributes; the sendmail.st file has different file sizes, MD5 sums, and Mtimes.

Table 6.1	RPM—Verify characters and attributes.
Character	**Attribute**
5	MD5 sum
S	File size
L	Symlink
T	Mtime
D	Device
U	User
G	Group
M	Mode (includes permissions and file type)

Using RPM's GnoRPM Tool

RPM offers a graphical administration tool, GnoRPM, which is a GUI tool that replaces glint as the package management tool. To invoke GnoRPM, simply type "gnorpm" from the root prompt. Once GnoRPM is running, you are presented with a browser style window (shown in Figure 6.3). In the left window is a directory tree available for packages. The packages are split amongst several directories such as Amusements, Applications, and Development. The right window lists the files in that directory. Some of the buttons along the top are Install, Upgrade, Uninstall, and Query, and they are all options available with the manual RPM tools.

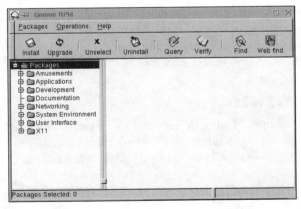

Figure 6.3   GnoRPM.

Building RPMs

RPM would not be nearly as effective if you could not build your own RPM packages. Using the -b option (for build) with rpm allows you to build your own package. In addition to the -b option, you can use the -t option (for tar files) to look inside tar files for the spec file to use.

After specifying the first argument, you must specify the stage of building and packaging that is to be done. Here are some options and what they do:

➤ -bp   Executes the "%prep" stage from the spec file. It typically unpacks the source and applies any needed patches.

➤ -bl   Tells rpm to do a "list check". The "%files" section from the spec file is macro expanded, and the rpm checks to make sure the files actually exist.

➤ -bc   Tells rpm to do the "%build" stage from the spec file, following the prep stage. Essentially, it is the equivalent of a "make install".

➤ -bb   Has rpm build a binary package. This build is done after the prep, build, and install stages.

➤ -ba   Builds both binary and source packages. This option is also done after the prep, build, and install stages.

After making changes to rpm files, including patches and updates, you may opt to rebuild the rpm to include the new changes. There are two ways to use rpm in this manner: you can use the --**recompile** option or the --**rebuild** option. When you run rpm with either option, rpm installs the named source package and then automatically does a prep, compile, and install. In addition, the --**rebuild** option builds a new binary package. After the build has completed, the build directory is automatically removed (by using --**clean**), and the source and spec files for the package are removed.

Basic Networking

The number one favorite features of Linux are centered around its networking capabilities. Red Hat Linux supports a number of network interfaces and protocols ranging from modem to network interface card and TCP/IP to IPX.

Exploring /etc/sysconfig

The files found under the /etc/sysconfig are files that scripts use to execute during boot-time. These files are named by the devices that they configure, such as clock, mouse, and network.

Beneath the /etc/sysconfig directory is a directory that contains network script files. These are located under /etc/sysconfig/network-scripts. The network-scripts directory contains files such as ifcfg-etho, ifup, ifdown, and ifup-ppp. The "if" in these scripts stands for interface. The rest of the naming convention is self-explanatory. The ifcfg script configures the named device, and ifcfg-ppp configures the ppp interface. The most common networking tools and scripts that you will use are **netcfg** and **ifconfig**; and **ifup**, **ifdown**, and **netstat**.

Using The netcfg Tool

The network configurator tool is a graphical tool that you use to add, delete, and configure network interfaces, devices, and more. To start the **netcfg** tool, simply type "netcfg" at the root prompt. Figure 6.4 shows the interface of netcfg.

With network configurator, you can configure name services, network hosts, network interfaces, and even routing. Several buttons allow you to perform various tasks:

➤ **Names**   Here, you can set up your system hostname and domain. In addition, you can set up hostnames that are searchable as well as your preferred nameservers.

➤ **Hosts**   Here, you can directly edit the /etc/hosts file. You can also add, edit, or remove hosts entries, such as machine alias settings.

➤ **Interfaces**   This is a little more interesting. Here, you can add, edit, clone, alias, remove, activate, and deactivate your network interfaces. Some interfaces that you can see here are your loopback, ethernet, and ppp interfaces. You can assign IP addresses to each as well as set their protocol configuration type (such as dhcp or none). You can also specify

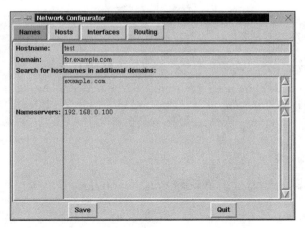

Figure 6.4   Network configurator.

to activate the interface at boot-time as well as change the state that the interface is currently in (active or inactive).

➤ **Routing** This allows you to set up routing options. The basic routing options that you can set up here include your default gateway and default gateway device. If you have more than one interface for which you want to set routing rules, you can also add them here.

Using The ifconfig Tool

You use the **ifconfig** tool to print your current network setup. The output includes settings for your loopback, ethernet, ppp, and other interfaces if they are active. Listing 6.1 shows sample output of **ifconfig** on a system with an Ethernet connection to a network. The active interfaces are identified by **eth0** and **lo** on the left. Within each section, you see the hardware address, inet address, broadcast address, netmask address, I/O settings, and more.

Listing 6.1 Sample output of **ifconfig**.

```
eth0     Link encap:Ethernet  HWaddr 00:80:C8:42:73:E3
         inet addr:192.168.0.15 Bcast:192.168.0.255
         Mask:255.255.255.0
         UP BROADCAST RUNNING  MTU:1500  Metric:1
         RX packets:104 errors:0 dropped:0 overruns:0 frame:0
         TX packets:97 errors:0 dropped:0 overruns:0 carrier:0
         collisions:0 txqueuelen:100
         Interrupt:3 Base address:0x300

lo       Link encap:Local Loopback
         inet addr:127.0.0.1  Mask:255.0.0.0
         UP LOOPBACK RUNNING  MTU:3924  Metric:1
         RX packets:48 errors:0 dropped:0 overruns:0 frame:0
         TX packets:48 errors:0 dropped:0 overruns:0 carrier:0
         collisions:0 txqueuelen:0
```

Using The ifup, ifdown, And netstat Commands

The **ifup** and **ifdown** commands are used to administer the network connections manually. You can **ifup** *(interface)* to activate the interface and **ifdown** *(interface)* to deactivate an interface. For example, to bring up the eth0 interface, type "ifup eth0".

Using the **ifup** command does not bring the interface up after you reboot!

Once you have a routing table established, or a network connection, you can monitor your routing table using the **netstat** command. In addition to printing your routing table, it displays your network connections, interface statistics, masquerade connection, netlink messages, and more.

To view the different information, you pass the specific options to **netstat**. To view the routing table, enter "netstat –r". To view the interface information, enter "netstat –i". To view any of your masqueraded connections, enter "netstat –M".

User Administration

For most Linux administrators, the most time consuming and important job is user administration. User administration can involve everything from adding and deleting users, modifying user information, setting up basic user shell settings, to setting up user window managers.

Adding Users

There are about four different ways to add new users to your system.. You used to have to add users manually, but you can now also use tools such as **useradd**, **linuxconf**, and **userconf** to set up user accounts, passwords, home directories, shells, and more.

Adding users manually can be a very tedious task. You first have to edit the user and groups files to add the user information at /etc/passwd and /etc/group, respectively. Next, you must create the user's home directory and copy the default files and user directories from /etc/skel. Finally, you have to change the ownership of the new home directory so that it is owned by the new user.

The most popular Linux (and Unix) user addition tool is **useradd**, which is the same as **adduser**. To add a new user using **adduser**, as root, enter "adduser *newuser*", where *newuser* is the new user's username. Next, enter "passwd user" to set the user's password. You are prompted to enter the user's password and then confirm it. The **adduser** (and **useradd**) command automatically sets up the user's home directory by automatically copying the files located in /etc/skel.

As mentioned earlier in this chapter, **linuxconf** a graphical user interface tool used to set up many things under Linux, including new users. To invoke **linuxconf**, enter "linuxconf" at the root prompt. Then, move through the directory tree in the left screen to go through Config, then Normal, then User accounts. Next, click on the Add button. You are next prompted for information such as the login name, the user's full name, his group (optional), any additional groups, and special permissions. After hitting Accept, you are asked to enter a user password and confirm it.

You can use another graphical user interface tool, **userconf**, to add users. The **userconf** tool, which is a little more user-friendly than **linuxconf,** has buttons and self-explanatory tabs (rather than the directory tree). To invoke **userconf,** enter "userconf" at the root prompt. To add a user, click on User Accounts and then the Add button. You can then add the user information exactly as you do when you use **linuxconf.**

Deleting Users

A good system administrator keeps a good audit on the users on her machine. The main thing to keep track of is which users are active and which are not. You should remove accounts that are no longer being used, such as those for employees no longer working there. Leaving old accounts on your system is a security risk.

You can remove users from your system in four main ways: You can remove them manually, remove them within a group (with **groupdel**), or use the friendly interfaced tools such as **userdel** or **linuxconf**. Each tool differs, and which one you use is simply a preference.

If you do not like to trust automatic programs, or if for some reason your tool is not functioning or is not available, you can remove the user manually. First you will want to edit your password file and remove the line assigned to the user. Next, remove the user's entry in the /etc/group file. Finally, rename, move, or delete the user's home directory, including the .login and .profile files within the user's home directory.

System administrators who are accustomed to administering a large group of users, or users for a large corporation, may wish to set up their users by group. For instance, they may have set up all users in the Sales department in the group named Sales. They may also have set up their temporary contractor users in the group named contractor. Using **groupdel** *contractor* removes all system entries referring to that group. Keep in mind, however, you must manually search your filesystems for remaining files. Another problem with using **groupdel** is that you can't remove a primary group for an existing user.

The most popular Unix user deletion tool is **userdel**. To delete a user with it, enter "userdel *username*" from the root prompt. The **userdel** tool automatically removes the user's entries in both the /etc/passwd and /etc/group files. Simply using the **userdel** tool without any options removes these two entries, but not the user's home directory and files. To remove these, pass **userdel** the –r option. For example,

```
userdel -r username
```

removes *username*'s entries in the /etc/passwd and /etc/group files as well as *username*'s home directory.

As you've seen, **linuxconf** is a very useful tool, and you can use it to delete your users. To do so, you are given a few options that are unavailable when you use other deletion methods. After starting **linuxconf** from the root prompt, you are again presented with the directory tree in the left window of the screen. Select through the tree options from Config to Users accounts to Normal, and then User accounts. Select the user you want to delete by double-clicking on the username. Then, click on the Delete button. You are then prompted to choose to archive the account's data, delete the account's data, or leave it alone. Lastly, choose Quit and then Activate changes.

Modifying User Information

A time will come when you need to modify a user's information. Perhaps your user gets married and has a new last name. Maybe you just need to change the user's password, or change his permissions. For whatever reason, there are ways to simply modify the user's account without having to recreate it.

To change a user's password, you can manually edit the user's /etc/passwd entry, run the **passwd** command, use **linuxconf**, or even assign a random password using **mkpasswd**. In addition, some **useradd** command options allow you to specify such information during creation. For a complete list of options available, use **man useradd**. I'll discuss the two most commonly used ways: **passwd** and **linuxconf**.

Running the **passwd** command from the root prompt prompts you to change the root password. To change a user's password using **passwd**, run

```
passwd username
```

You are then prompted to change and verify the *username*'s new password. This command is also made available to users for their own password. However, only root can use the **passwd** command to change other users' passwords.

Understanding The Basic User Environment

Any time a user is created, either manually or with a user administration tool, a certain number of default files and directories are created in the user's home directory (located at /home/*username*). By default, the files that are copied into the user's home directory include .Xdefaults, .bash_logout, .bash_profile, and .bashrc, which we will discuss more fully in the next section.

These default files are copied from the /etc/skel directory, which contains "skeleton" files that are used by default when a new user is created. Anything found in this directory is automatically copied to a user's directory when the directory is created. For instance, when KDE is installed, two files are copied automatically to the /etc/skel directory. They include .kde and .kderc, which are configuration files for the KDE window manager. You should put anything else you would like to have copied into a user's home directory in /etc/skel as well.

Adding files to /etc/skel affects only new users created on the system. You must manually copy any additional files you want existing users to have.

The /etc/skel Files

The .Xdefaults file is the basic X Windowing system resources file. Users use this file when they start up their X session. The .Xdefaults file is used by every different type of Window Manager, including KDE, Window Maker, Enlightenment, AfterStep, and fvwm. You will find the following within the .Xdefaults file:

➤ Settings for basic X window applications. For instance, it contains the defaults (such as color, size, and font options) for the emacs and xemacs editor.

➤ Settings (such as color, highlight options, and scrolling) for Xterm.

➤ Other system options for X, such as scrolling and the visual bell.

The .bash_logout file is a bash shell logout script. A default Red Hat 6.0 .bash_logout script is very simple, as you can see in the following example:

```
# ~/.bash_logout

clear
```

The default .bash_logout script simply tells the shell to clear the screen after logout. You can set bash to do a number of other things in the .bash_logout file. For instance, you can have the shell execute the fortune program, sleep for five seconds, and then clear. To do so, simply add the path and executable for the fortune program and then add a "sleep 5" line within the script.

A bit more complex, the .bash_profile is the script used to run the bash shell, briefly discussed in Chapter 3. Some options that are set in .bash_profile include alias settings, path settings, and startup programs. In fact, the alias settings aren't supplied within the .bash_profile file itself. Instead, it calls the .bashrc file and executes the alias settings there. Listing 6.2 shows a sample .bash_profile file.

Listing 6.2 Sample .bash_profile.

```
# .bash_profile
# Get the aliases and functions
if [ -f ~/.bashrc ]; then
      .~/.bashrc
fi

# User specific environment and startup programs

PATH=$PATH:$HOME/bin
BASH_ENV=$HOME/.bashrc
USERNAME=""

export USERNAME BASH_ENV PATH
```

The .bashrc file is executed when called by the .bash_profile script. The .bashrc contains any alias and function settings. Therefore (customizable for each individual user), you can set aliases for commands, such as alias "ls –l" to "ls", so that each time you run "ls", you get "ls –l". Here's a sample .bashrc file (keep in mind that the .bashrc isn't required to run bash):

```
# .bashrc

# User specific aliases and functions

alias rm='rm -i'
alias cp='cp -i'
alias mv='mv -i'

# Source global definitions
if [ -f /etc/bashrc ]' then
      ./etc/bashrc
fi
```

 If you ever have to create a user manually, be sure to copy all the files from the /etc/skel directory!

Virtual Consoles

Virtual consoles are a feature of Linux that is most coveted by many other operating systems. Virtual consoles allow you to have multiple text-based logins on separate virtual screens on your system.

To access separate virtual consoles on your system from a console screen, simply use the key combination Alt+F (numeric key, as in F1 and F2). For instance, Alt+F1, Alt+F2, and so on. (Note: The + does not mean press the plus sign key. It means to press the Alt key plus the Function key.) To navigate between an X session and a virtual console, use Ctrl+Alt+F1 to leave your X session and return to the first console; then, use Alt+F7 to return to your X session.

By default, six virtual consoles are available after installation, Alt+F1 through Alt+F6. However, you can change your console settings and the number of consoles available on your system in your /etc/inittab file. Listing 6.3 is a sample excerpt of your /etc/inittab file where you specify virtual console settings.

Listing 6.3 Snippet of /etc/inittab file.

```
#
# inittab    This file describes how the INIT process should set up
#            the system in a certain run-level.
#
# Author:    Miquel van Smoorenburg, <miquels@drinkel.nl.mugnet.org>
#            Modified for RHS Linux by Marc Ewing and Donnie Barnes

# Run gettys in standard runlevels
1:2345:respawn:/sbin/mingetty tty1
2:2345:respawn:/sbin/mingetty tty2
3:2345:respawn:/sbin/mingetty tty3
4:2345:respawn:/sbin/mingetty tty4
5:2345:respawn:/sbin/mingetty tty5
6:2345:respawn:/sbin/mingetty tty6
```

Adding additional lines to the section of your /etc/inittab shown in Listing 6.3, such as

```
7:2345:respawn:/sbin/mingetty tty7
```

enables your seventh virtual console.

You can also set console settings in your /etc/security/console.perms file. This file controls the options (such as privileges that are set during login) for your console user group. Permissions for the console user group typically include shutdown, halt, and reboot.

Practice Questions

Question1

Where can you enable or disable virtual consoles?

- ○ a. /etc/inittab
- ○ b. /etc/consoles.conf
- ○ c. /etc/virtual.consoles
- ○ d. /etc/X11/consoles.conf

Answer a is correct. In the/etc/inittab file, there is a section that allows you to specify virtual console settings. They are in a format similar to **1:2345:respawn:/ sbin/mingetty tty1**. To add an additional virtual console, simply replicate the line in numerical order at the end of the list, where the numerical order represents the **1:** and the **tty1** is equal to your virtual console number (,8: and **tty8**, for example). To disable them, simply delete the corresponding line.

Question 2

How can you navigate around virtual consoles (*x* means console number)?

- ○ a. Ctrl+w*x*
- ○ b. Alt+w*x*
- ○ c. Alt+F*x*
- ○ d. Alt+a+*x*

Answer c is correct. Alt+Fx, where Fx is a function key, is used to navigate between virtual consoles. Answers a, b and d are incorrect, because control, a, and w are not valid virtual console options.

Question 3

How could you unmount a device? [Check all correct answers]

❑ a. #unmount /dev/device

❑ b. #umount /mnt/device

❑ c. #umount /device

❑ d. #umount /root

Answers b, c, and d are correct. This is true when the device's mount point is equal to either /mnt/device (as listed in choice b) or simply /device (as listed in choice c). Answer d unmounts the /root filesystem. This option is valid if /root is mounted on a separate hdax device. Answer a is incorrect because it would be possible only if **unmount** was aliased to the **umount** command because **unmount** is not a valid command.

Question 4

Where are default user directories kept?

○ a. /etc/user.defaults

○ b. /usr/user.defaults

○ c. /usr/skel

○ d. /etc/skel

Answer d is correct. The /etc/skel directory contains all "skeleton" directories and files that are automatically installed into a user's home directory, when they are created with tools such as **useradd, userconf,** or **linuxconf.**

Question 5

How can you add Mary, a new user, to your system?

○ a. Add Mary to the /etc/passwd, /etc/group, and create her home
       directory in /home (copying files from /etc/skel)

○ b. **useradd**

○ c. **adduser**

○ d. **linuxconf**

○ e. All of the above

Answer e is correct. You can add Mary manually (answer a) if you want or need
to. The tools in answers b, c, and d are also available.

Question 6

Which of the following can you use for multiple administration and configuration tasks? [Check all correct answers]

❏ a. linuxconf

❏ b. control-panel

❏ c. Xconfigurator

❏ d. XF86Setup

Answers a and b are correct. Both of these tools can perform, or are linked to,
multiple configuration tasks. Although answers c and d are also configuration
tools, they are limited to simply X setup and don't configure administration or
other tasks.

Question 7

How can you print your active network interfaces?

○ a. **netstat −r**

○ b. **ifconfig**

○ c. **netcfg**

○ d. **cat /net.status**

Answer b is correct. Answer a is incorrect because it is used to print your current routing table, not network interfaces. Answer c is incorrect because although it is used to configure your network, it doesn't simply report the active interfaces. Answer d is incorrect because there is no such thing as **cat /net.status**.

Question 8

> What commands can you use to rebuild a source RPM file? [Check all correct answers]
>
> ○ a. **--rebuild**
>
> ○ b. **--rbld**
>
> ○ c. **--recompile**
>
> ○ d. **--rb**

Answers a and c are correct as those options are used by RPM to rebuild an RPM source file. Answers b and d are not valid options.

Question 9

> What is RPM?
>
> _____

RPM is the Red Hat Package Manager. It is used to install, uninstall, and manage packages that are installed on a Red Hat Linux system.

Question 10

> What tool can you use to set up a printer?
>
> ○ a. lpr
>
> ○ b. lpd
>
> ○ c. printtool
>
> ○ d. vi /etc/printcap

Answer c is correct. Answers a and b are incorrect because they are the tool and daemon used for printing, respectively. It is possible to manually set up your printer by editing the /etc/printcap file, but it is more easily done with a configuration tool. Therefore, answer d is incorrect.

Task 1

After installing your fresh Red Hat Linux system, go back through and configure your peripherals again. Change your mouse settings. What does that do?

Task 2

If a network is available, configure your machine for one. Set up your machine for a static IP address. Change it to use a DHCP server (if available).

Task 3

Browse your Red Hat CD (or installation download) or the Internet for RPM files that aren't already installed on your system. Perhaps install an additional Window Manager. Try upgrading to a new version of RPM (if available). How do you go about doing that? Switch to virtual console 10. What do you mean it doesn't work? Fix that!

Need To Know More?

 Baily, Edward C. *Maximum RPM*, Sams Publishing, Indianapolis, IN, 1997. ISBN 0-672-31105-4. The first section of this book, including Chapters 1 through 8, covers all aspects of using RPM to manage RPM packages.

 Frisch, Æleen. *Essential System Administration*, O'Reilly & Associates, Sebastopol, CA, 1995. ISBN 1-56592-127-5. Chapters 2, 5, 9, and 12 cover Unix essentials to filesystems, user accounts, disks, and printing. Linux methods were modeled after these.

 Heckman, Jessica Perry. *Linux In A Nutshell*, O'Reilly & Associates, Sebastopol, CA, 1997. ISBN 1-56592-167-4. Chapters 4, 13, and 14 are an excellent reference for the Linux Bourne Shell (see Chapter 4) and Linux system and network administration commands (Chapters 13 and 14).

 http://metalab.unc.edu/LDP

The Linux Documentation Project contains a section with various Linux HOWTOs, including installation, networking, RPM, and more discussed in this chapter. Follow the link from HOWTOs listed on the site, or visit http://metalab.unc .edu/ LDP/HOWTO/HOWTO-INDEX-3.html.

 http://www.rpm.org/

Under the Documentation portion of the RPM Web site, you can get HOWTOs and other information references regarding using RPM. In addition, development information can be located under the Resources section of the site.

 http://www.solucorp.qc.ca/linuxconf/

For latest downloads, patches, HOWTOs, and such for using **linuxconf**, be sure to visit the Linuxconf Home Page, found at this address.

Advanced Installation

. . . .

Terms you'll need to understand:

√ Dual boot

√ Boot manager

√ Clone

√ Prototype

Techniques you'll need to master:

√ Installing a multi-boot system

√ Implementing an automatic installation system

In addition to standard Red Hat Linux installation, several other installation methods and options are available. These options allow you to boot multiple operating systems, or even automate the install. You may even need to install a system that is to be run *headless*, meaning without a monitor and keyboard. Your typical Red Hat Linux user probably does not even know that most of these options exist. However, becoming an RHCE means that you do know about them and that you can set up and configure them properly.

Dual Booting Linux

Administrators often like to dual boot their systems. This means that the administrator installs more than one operating system and then chooses which one to run.

> *Note: Currently, running more than one operating system simultaneously is possible only by using software packages such as VMware.*

You can set up your machine to give you the option of which OS you want to run at boot-time. In this section, we'll discuss setting up your machine with the option to boot either Linux or Microsoft Windows.

Disk Partitioning

To dual boot your machine between Linux and Windows properly, you must create separate partitions on your hard drive for each operating system. It is typically best to create at least four partitions for this—or more, if you decide to create separate partitions for the /home, /var, and other directories on your Linux filesystem.

The four primary partitions are for Linux /boot, for Windows, for Linux Native, and for Linux Swap. Creating the first (50MB or fewer) partition for Linux /boot allows the system to more easily boot properly. This is especially useful on large disks with more than 1024 sectors, or disks that require LBA mode. The following is an example of a partition table on a system with four partitions:

```
Disk /dev/hda: 240 heads, 63 sectors, 839 cylinders
Units = cylinders of 15120 * 512 bytes

    Device Boot    Start      End    Blocks   Id  System
/dev/hda1             1        7     52888+  83  Linux
/dev/hda2     *       8       75    514080    b  Win95 FAT32
/dev/hda3            76      813   5579280   83  Linux
/dev/hda4           814      839    196560   82  Linux swap
```

The first is a boot partition for Linux. It is a Linux Native-type partition and is mounted to /boot. The second is a DOS partition, which is used for an installation of Windows 98. The third and fourth partitions are also for Linux. The third is the root partition, which is a Linux Native-type partition and mounted to /. The fourth is a Linux Swap-type partition and is not mounted to any filesystem.

Sometimes, you may wish to dual boot a system after you already have an initial operating system, such as Windows, installed. To dual boot the Windows system with Linux, you must resize or shrink your current Windows partition. One helpful commercial program that allows you to do so is Partition Magic by Power Quest. It is a DOS program that can resize many types of partitions safely without destroying data. As of Partition Magic's version 4, you can also resize Linux partitions. After you resize a partition, you can then restart your computer into the Linux installation, and create a Linux partition with the newly freed space.

Installing Both Operating Systems

Setting up a dual boot system from scratch is much easier to configure properly, and will most likely have fewer errors. By default, you should always install your alternate (not Linux) operating system first. Doing so allows you to set up the Linux bootloader to boot both operating systems during installation. In addition, some other operating systems format the entire disk during their default installations. By installing the non-Linux operating system first, you eliminate the risk of the other operating system deleting your Linux installation.

If you use the other operating system to partition your disk, simply leave the unpartitioned space available for Linux. Red Hat Linux can format and partition the unallocated space during installation. Some administrators find it helpful to partially begin the Red Hat Linux install before installing the guest operating system. By this, I mean you can start the Red Hat Linux installation to the point where you format the drive and then stop the Red Hat Linux install to install the guest operating system. You can then use Disk Druid (discussed in Chapter 5) or fdisk (discussed in Chapters 3 and 5) during the Red Hat Linux installation to set up all your partitions. Make sure to create your DOS or guest operating system partition and set it to the appropriate type (for Windows, this is type b). You can then write the partition table and when it begins the next step of the Red Hat Linux installation, you can reboot the system and begin your guest operating system installation.

Boot Managers

Several boot managers can boot Linux as well as manage other operating systems to boot on the same system. Some of the popular ones include:

➤ **LILO** Discussed in Chapters 3 and 5, and short for Linux Loader, this is the default bootloader used with Linux. Red Hat Linux, as well as most Linux vendors, recommends that you use it as your default boot manager.

➤ **System Commander** This is a commercial product that you can purchase from a local software vendor.

➤ **SysLinux** This executes the Linux boot from a DOS filesystem.

Even if you decide not to use LILO as your boot manager, you still need LILO to manage your Linux boot. You decide where to install LILO based on the default boot manager you decide to use. If you are using LILO, choose to install LILO in the master boot record (MBR) on your system. If you choose to use another boot manager, such as System Commander, install LILO to the first partition of the /boot partition.

Using LILO

If you are using LILO as your default boot manager, you can select the operating system to boot during the installation process. After your system performs its default BIOS checks and detection, you see the LILO: prompt. If you leave this prompt alone, whatever operating system is chosen as default boot simply boots.

To interrupt the automatic process and specify which operating system to boot, hit the Shift key as soon as you see the LILO: prompt. To see what boot options are available, hit Tab. You can then specify which operating system to boot, as well as any options that you may require. These options—as well as the default boot operating system, the delay of the LILO: prompt, and more—are specified in the /etc/lilo.conf file. The following is an example of an /etc/lilo.conf file on a system that is dual booted with Red Hat Linux 6.0 and Windows 98:

```
boot=/dev/hda
map=/boot/map
install=/boot/boot.b
#prompt
delay=20
timeout=2400
root=/dev/hda3
read-only
image=/boot/vmlinuz-2.2.10
     label=2.2.10
     vga=0x317
image=/boot/vmlinuz-2.2.5-15
     label=linux
```

```
other=/dev/hda2
   label=dos
   table=/dev/hda
```

The first line (boot=/dev/hda) specifies the boot device and specifies where LILO is to be installed. In this case, it specifies to install LILO to the super-block of /dev/hda. If the first line had been

```
boot=/dev/hda1
```

it would have specified to install LILO to the first partition of the /dev/hda1 partition. Likewise,

```
boot=/dev/sda
```

would have specified to install LILO to the superblock of the SCSI device.

The second line specifies the path to the system map file. This line is indicated by the map=/boot/map. The /boot/map file contains the names and locations of the kernel or kernels to boot. The third line indicates the location of the boot sector. This is indicated by the install=/boot/boot.b.

The rest of the /etc/lilo.conf file specifies settings and arguments that go into effect at the LILO: prompt. The **delay** option sets the amount of time you have to hit the Shift key at the LILO: prompt (to interrupt the default boot process and specify any other options or boot operating systems). The **timeout** option is used to specify the amount of time that the system continues to boot by default if a key has been pressed but nothing was manually executed at the LILO: prompt.

The next two lines are related to the /root directory. The **root=/dev/hda3** speci-fies to mount the root directory on /dev/hda3. The **read-only** option specifies to mount the /root filesystem as read only, allowing you to check the /root filesystem with fsck. Default Red Hat Linux 6.0 systems specify the **read-only** option after each image entry in /etc/lilo.conf. You can specify **read-only** be-fore the **image** entries, making it a global setting, which does not require you to set it for each entry.

The last lines of code are grouped into sections to indicate the bootable sys-tems on the machine. The first two sections, named **image**, specify different Linux kernels that are installed and configured on the machine. The first line in each section indicates where the kernel image is located (for example: image= /boot/vmlinuz-2.2.5-15). The second line in each **image** section specifies the label that is to be associated with the kernel image (for example: lable=linux).

The **label** setting is the name associated with the kernel image you are prompted to choose from at the LILO: prompt. For instance, on this system, hitting the Tab key at the LILO: prompt reads **2.2.10**, **linux**, and **dos**, which are the labels set within the /etc/lilo.conf file.

The third section following the **image** sections mimics the Linux **image=** lines, but it has different boot images and label names. This section is labeled as an **other** entry. The **other** entrytells LILO that there is a bootable system on another partition—for example, the entry other=/dev/hda2 tells LILO that a bootable system resides on the second partition of the first hard-drive (hda2). The remaining options under the **other=** entry specify options used to boot the system. In this case, the **other=** entry specifies booting the DOS partition, which happens to be Windows 98.

After making any changes to the /etc/lilo.conf file, always be sure to rerun LILO to activate your changes. To do this, simply type "lilo" at the root prompt.

Installing Red Hat Linux Automatically

Many large companies, or even hardware resellers, often need to configure Red Hat Linux on many machines. If all the machines have the exact same hardware configuration and need the exact same software configuration, you can automate the installation by using a program called **kickstart**.

The program **kickstart** automates your installation by automatically answering the questions that the install program asks. The **kickstart** utility works with an ASCII-based instruction file that can be supplied from a boot floppy installation disk, or even from an NFS server.

The **kickstart** program automatically installs Red Hat Linux using several methods. The two main supported methods are CD-ROM- and NFS-based installations. FTP and HTTP installations, though not commonly advertised, are supported as well.

The **kickstart** program uses a kickstart configuration file called ks.cfg. The ks.cfg file contains all the configuration answers to all the questions that are prompted during an installation. If an answer is not provided in the ks.cfg file, the installation pauses and prompts you to answer the question. Once you answer the question, the automatic installation resumes. A sample ks.cfg file follows:

```
lang en
network --bootproto dhcp
cdrom
device ethernet
keyboard "us"
zerombr yes
clearpart --linux
part /boot --size 16
part / --size 250
part swap --size 128
install
mouse ps/2 --emulthree
timezone --utc US/Central
xconfig --server "FBDev" --monitor "lcd panel 1024x768"
rootpw redhat
auth --useshadow --enablemd5
#lilo --append 'anything-needed'
%packages
@ Workstation
%post
```

This shows a very simple and very basic ks.cfg file. The first line specifies that English is the selected language. The second line specifies your network configuration, which in this case is DHCP. The third line specifies the installation medium. This reads either **cdrom** or **nfs** *–server name.of.server –dir /pathtoimage/ imagefile* and so on. The next two lines configure any devices such as ethernet and keyboard.

The next five lines in this file relate to the hard disk and its partitioning. The first option, **zerombr**, instructs Red Hat Linux to clear the current partition information. The **clearpart** option specifies to clear all the Linux partitions on the disk. The three **part** options specify the partitions to be created on the disk, including partition type, mount point, and size. By default, creating the ks.cfg file from your main computer sets the size options to 1. Therefore, you must edit the ks.cfg file to set the appropriate disk size in megabytes. We will discuss these changes to the ks.cfg file in more detail later in the "Using Diskette-based Kickstart" section later in this chapter.

The next option, **install**, is a required parameter that states you will do a fresh install of Red Hat Linux. The next three options in this sample ks.cfg file are additional configuration settings. The **mouse** option allows you to set the mouse type, in addition to any options you need, such as emulating three buttons. The **timezone** option specifies what time zone to set on your machine. The **xconfig** line specifies what X server to install and what type of monitor you are using.

The final options set system information and installation information. The **rootpw** line allows you to specify the root password. If you have the encrypted version of your root password, you can use the option line

```
rootpw -iscrypted $whatever%the?scheme*is
```

The **auth** line allows you to permit the use of shadow passwords and MD5 use. In addition, if your systems are going to use LILO, you can install and configure LILO using the **lilo** option. You can also append any information that LILO needs by using the **−append** option.

The next section specifies the packages you want to install. Under the **%packages** line, you can specify individual names of packages to be installed. This is used if the system is to be configured custom, or if you are going to install additional packages. In addition, you can specify to install the default configuration (such as workstation or server). To do so, use **@ Workstation** or **@ Server** as needed. Make sure that if you use this option, you place a space between the @ sign and the setting.

The final option is called **%post**. This section runs any special commands after the system has been installed. For example, you may wish to run a command in the **%post** section that sets up your name server. To do so, type

```
echo "nameserver 192.168.0.254">>/etc/resolv.conf
```

where *192.168.0.254* is your specified nameserver.

Using Diskette-Based Kickstart

The most common type of kickstart installation uses a kickstart boot floppy and CD-ROM. The required boot floppy uses a ks.cfg configuration file. The ks.cfg file is created based on the install information on your prototype machine. This means that in order to have a successful ks.cfg bootdisk, you must manually set up one identical machine with the specific settings that you need on the system. After installing the system with everything you want, you can create the ks.cfg file. To do this, simply run the **mkkickstart** command and redirect the output to the ks.cfg file. For example,

```
mkkickstart >ks.cfg
```

can be run only as root. The **mkkickstart** utility then probes your prototype system for its configuration. Whenever it is finished, view the ks.cfg file to ensure that everything was detected properly.

The **mkkickstart** does not properly report the partition sizes to the ks.cfg file. You must correct this manually. The lines you must correct are those that start with the **part** option (for partition). By default, the partition sizes are set to 1, which means 1MB. You must adjust these numbers according to the partition sizes you want to set up.

After you have created the ks.cfg file, copy it to your boot disk. The appropriate boot disk for this system uses the standard boot.img boot image. Simply copy the ks.cfg file to the boot diskette's top-level or root directory.

To start your kickstart installation, boot your system with the boot floppy, and have the Red Hat Linux CD-ROM in the cdrom drive. At the boot prompt, enter "linux ks=floppy". Your installation should go automatically from that point.

Using Network-Based Kickstart

To use the network-based kickstart, you must have an NFS server available on your network to service the installations. In addition, you have to use the StaticIP, bootp, or DHCP scheme for your system. To use a DHCP server, you should have the configuration information for the newly installed system, the location of the kickstart file to be used, and the location of the NFS server available on the DHCP server. The NFS server is used to supply the installation files; however, the DHCP server is set to supply the network information as well as individual ks.cfg files for the installed machines, if necessary.

To start a network-based kickstart install, you simply need a Red Hat Linux boot disk created with the bootnet.img boot image. At the boot: prompt, type "linux ks". This looks for the NFS and DHCP servers automatically and obtaining all the necessary information.

Setting up network-based kickstart network installs are a bit complex and differ from network setup to network setup. Therefore, documentation for this process is limited. Although network kickstart procedures will be helpful to your career if you work in a large company, extensive knowledge of this process is unnecessary for your RHCE certification. However, you should have a good working knowledge of it.

Practice Questions

Question 1

> What type of boot image is required to use kickstart using a CD-ROM?
>
> ○ a. bootnet.img
>
> ○ b. boot.img
>
> ○ c. ks.cfg
>
> ○ d. ks.img

Answer b is correct. Answer a is incorrect because the bootnet.img image file is used when doing network installations. Answer c is incorrect because ks.cfg is a configuration file used with kickstart, not a boot image. Answer d is incorrect because ks.img isn't a valid option.

Question 2

> You must have a DHCP server in order to use kickstart.
>
> ○ a. True
>
> ○ b. False

Answer b is correct. A DHCP server is not required with either type of kickstart installation. The CD-ROM doesn't require the DHCP server during installation, even if you are planning on using DHCP for the systems! In addition, with network installs, DHCP servers are required only if you need the DHCP server to assign individual ks.cfg files for each machine (to assign individual static IP addresses) and so on.

Question 3

> How do you create a kickstart boot floppy?
>
> _____

To create a kickstart boot floppy, you first need to create the boot floppy with the appropriate boot image. When you use a CD-ROM, you create the boot image with the boot.img file. For network installations, you use the bootnet.img files. To create the boot disk, use the **dd** command on Linux (as described in Chapter 5). Next, you must create your kickstart configuration file named ks.cfg by running **mkkickstart** on the machine prototype that you want to clone. Write the output of **mkkickstart** to the file ks.cfg by typing "mkkickstart >ks.cfg". Finally, copy the ks.cfg file to your boot floppy.

Question 4

What are the **%post** entries in the ks.cfg file used for?

- ○ a. Logging entries
- ○ b. Scripts run during installation
- ○ c. Configuration options
- ○ d. None of the above

Answer d is correct. The **%post** entries are scripts or commands that are run after the installation. Although these scripts may indicate some logging, or configuration options, they can be set up only with the scripts that are run there.

Question 5

How do you force kickstart to prompt you for information during an installation? Why would you want to do this?

To force kickstart to prompt you for an answer or setting during installation, simply do not provide the setting in the ks.cfg file. This is helpful if you want to specify IP addresses without using a DHCP server, or if peripherals such as video or mouse differ on various machines.

Question 6

> Why do you need to run **lilo** after editing lilo.conf?
>
> ○ a. To rerun configuration settings and apply them to the appropriate lilo files, such as boot.b
>
> ○ b. To add new operating systems or kernels installed on the system to lilo boot manager
>
> ○ c. To save your changes made to lilo.conf
>
> ○ d. To check for errors made when editing lilo.conf
>
> ○ e. All of the above

Answer e is correct. Running **lilo** after editing lilo.conf allows **lilo** to update its files, such as /boot/boot.b, to add new volumes and so on (answer a). Adding new boot partitions, kernel images, and so on (answer b) also requires running **lilo** so that they will be recognized during boot-time as options. Answer c is questionable as correct because writing to the /etc/lilo.conf is saved when writing the physical file, but running LILO would save the changes to your boot configuration. Answer d is true as well; running **lilo** finds settings within the file that are duplicated labels or invalid boot images.

Question 7

> Why is the root filesystem mounted read-only during the LILO execution but then remounted read/write later during the boot process?
>
> ○ a. So crackers cannot get root information during the boot process with boot sniffers
>
> ○ b. So if system tasks fail during boot, you can run **fsck** on the filesystem without risking damage
>
> ○ c. So you cannot write to the root filesystem without root's password
>
> ○ d. So that other operating systems, like Windows, can't overwrite your root partition

Answer b is correct. If your boot fails when checking filesystems or other LILO boot options, the filesystem can be dropped to a shell and you can manually check the filesystem without risking damage to the filesystem. Answer b is incorrect because you can't run **fsck** on a mounted filesystem. Answers a and d are incorrect because those options are impossible to do, therefore invalid.

Question 8

How can you interrupt the boot process to boot a different operating system if one is already installed?

○ a. Press Ctrl+Alt+Delete after the Loading MS Windows prompt

○ b. Press Shift after the boot: prompt

○ c. Press Tab after the LILO: prompt

○ d. Press Enter at the LILO: prompt

Answer c is correct. You can also press the Shift key at the LILO: prompt. Answer a is incorrect because pressing Ctrl+Alt+Delete while loading Windows or Linux reboots the system. Answer b is incorrect because if you are getting a boot: prompt, you are booting with an installation disk. In addition, the Shift key won't help you with that option. Answer d is incorrect because pressing Enter at the LILO: prompt automatically boots the default set operation system or kernel image.

Question 9

If you are installing Windows on a dual-boot system with Linux, why should you install Windows first?

You aren't required to install Windows first on a dual boot system, but if you plan to use LILO as your default boot manager, it is recommended to do so. By installing Windows first, you save the risk of overwriting your master boot record where LILO is installed, or destroying your Linux partitions altogether.

Question 10

Linux allows you to run Windows and Linux at the same time.

○ a. True

○ b. False

Answer b is correct. At the current time, Linux does not allow you to boot multiple operating systems simultaneously. There are commercial products available that enable you to run other operating systems on virtual machines on Linux, such as VMware, but not co-existing on a machine.

Task 1

One of the most repeated special installation options you will use is Linux's ability to multi-boot systems for free. Partition a system with the recommended partition methods and layouts (or even better for partition-crazy zealots) and install Windows, or other available operating system on one partition.

Task 2

For those needing a little more challenge, figure out how to dual boot different Linux distributions! Successfully configure a machine to boot Linux by default, but give yourself the option of booting one or more operating systems.

Task 3

Pretend you have 500 machines just like yours on which to install Red Hat Linux. Use kickstart and develop a boot disk that sets up all 500 machines just like yours. What if 250 of them have larger hard drives? Change the ks.cfg file to reflect this change for the other boot disks. Set them up to prompt you when it is time to set up your X configuration.

Need To Know More?

Red Hat Linux 6.0: Operating System Installation Guide. Red Hat Software, Inc., Durham, NC, 1999. Index H from page 379-381 covers the **kickstart** installation processes.

http://metalab.unc.edu/LDP

The Linux Documentation Project contains links to HOWTOs available for Linux based operations. Following the HOWTO links to the Kickstart HOWTO (**http://metalab.unc.edu/LDP/HOWTO/KickStart-HOWTO**), and more.

Advanced Configuration

8

Terms you'll need to understand:

√ Quota

√ Runlevel

√ Initialization script

√ Kernel module

√ **make**

√ cron

Techniques you'll need to master:

√ Setting up user quotas

√ Understanding runlevels

√ Understanding System Initialization Scripts

√ Understanding the Linux kernel

√ Compiling a Linux kernel

√ Configuring a Linux kernel

√ Setting up cron jobs

√ Configuring bash

The objective of the RHCE program is to promote advanced skills amongst its participants. Although one of the goals of Red Hat software is to package a product that an average skilled Linux user can use easily, the goals for an RHCE are set higher. An RHCE should be skilled not only in installation methods, but in configuration methods as well. An RHCE should also be able to customize all parts of the system—from the kernel to the bash shell. This chapter will discuss many types of advanced configuration methods.

Understanding Quotas

Quotas are essential to system administrators who are administering the data, Web servers, and so on of many users. The quota system is much like setting up a budget for how much disk space a user or group can use on a system.

In order to use system quotas, your Red Hat Linux kernel must be configured to use quotas. By default, the installed Red Hat Linux kernel already has quota support compiled in; however, if you are using a custom or recompiled kernel, you must ensure that quota support is compiled.

Once kernel quota support is compiled, you need to see if the quota rpm is installed. To do so, enter "rpm –q quota". If installed from a Red Hat Linux 6.0 system and the quota rpm is installed,

```
quota-1.66-6
```

is returned to you. If you do not have the quota rpm installed, you can either obtain the rpm files from your favorite Red Hat FTP site, or install them from CD-ROM. To install, simply run

```
rpm –Uvh quota*
```

from the directory that contains your quota rpm files.

The necessary quota files are started in the startup script, located in /etc/rc.d/rc.sysinit. When executed, the scripts look to see if the appropriate scripts are available and then runs **/sbin/quotaon** to turn on quotas. Here are a few snippets of code from the rc.sysinit script that is required to run quotas. This should automatically be placed in your rc.sysinit file when installing the rpm:

```
# Update quotas if fsck was run on /.
if [ X"$_RUN_QUOTACHECK" = X1 -a -x /sbin/quotacheck ]; then
    action "Checking root filesystem quotas" /sbin/quotacheck -v /
fi
if [ -x /sbin/quotaon ]; then
```

```
     action "Turning on user and group quotas for root filesystem"
     /sbin/quotaon /
fi
```

In addition to the script being started in the rc.sysinit file, you must have the quota options set in the /etc/fstab files. Editing the /etc/fstab files allows you to enforce the quota system on specific partitions. The following example shows how **usrquota** and **grpquota** must be added to the /etc/fstab files to enable quotas on two partitions:

```
/dev/hda2     /            ext2    defaults                     1 1
/dev/hda7     /home        ext2    defaults,usrquota,grpquota   1 2
/dev/hda5     /var         ext2    defaults,grpquota            1 2
/dev/hda6     /var/spool   ext2    defaults                     1 2
```

From the above example, you notice that the /home partition is **usrquota**- and **grpquota**-enabled, but the /var partition has only **grpquota** enabled.

To set the quotas for specific users and groups, you would use **edquota**. Edquota is the quota editor. The **edquota** tool allows you to set up disk limits per user, using the quota.user file.

 You can use a prototype to help set up user and group quotas by invoking the –p option with **edquota**.

Red Hat Linux also offers a few utilities to help you manage your quota system:

➤ **/sbin/quotaon**   Running this as root turns on the quota system.

➤ **/sbin/quotaoff**   Running this disables the quota system.

➤ **/sbin/quotastats, /sbin/quotacheck, /usr/sbin/repquota**   Running these generates some reports for **quota systems**.

Understanding The /etc/inittab File

The /etc/inittab file describes what processes are started at boot-time and during normal operation. In addition, this file contains the settings for the virtual consoles and such. The /etc/inittab file is documented very well, explaining what each section of the file is for.

The first section is simply for information only. It states the use and author of the file. The second section discusses the seven *runlevels*, which are the different states of where or how the system is running. Runlevel 0 is the halt state. Runlevel 1 indicates that the system is running in single-user mode. Runlevel 1 allows you to administer your system without multi-user support.

 Did you forget your root password? You can boot into runlevel 1, into single-user mode, and change the password.

Runlevel 2 is multi-user mode, but it has no networking support. Runlevel 3 is full multi-user mode and does offer full networking support. Runlevel 4 isn't used. Runlevel 5 on Red Hat Linux is full multi-user mode and boots into an X-based login screen. Runlevel 6 is for rebooting. Following the runlevel descriptions is a line that starts with "id:". This line specifies the default runlevel to boot into. After your system is booted into a particular runlevel, you can access other runlevels using the **init** or **telinit** commands. By issuing an **init 6** at the root prompt, you can command the system to reboot. However, issuing an **init 1** commands the system to boot into single-user mode. These commands can only be issued by root. Here is an example of an /etc/inittab file:

```
#
# inittab     This file describes how the INIT process should set up
#             the system in a certain run-level.
#
# Author:     Miquel van Smoorenburg, <miquels@drinkel.nl.mugnet.org>
#             Modified for RHS Linux by Marc Ewing and Donnie Barnes

# Default runlevel. The runlevels used by RHS are:
#   0 - halt (Do NOT set initdefault to this)
#   1 - Single user mode
#   2 - Multiuser, without NFS (The same as 3, with no  networking)
#   3 - Full multiuser mode
#   4 - unused
#   5 - X11
#   6 - reboot (Do NOT set initdefault to this)
#
id:3:initdefault:
```

The third section of the /etc/inittab file details the boot sequence. It starts the system initialization with the rc.sysinit script (which we will discuss later in this chapter in the "Understanding System Initialization Scripts" section). It then calls the rc files shown in the following codes.

```
# System initialization.
si::sysinit:/etc/rc.d/rc.sysinit

l0:0:wait:/etc/rc.d/rc 0
l1:1:wait:/etc/rc.d/rc 1
l2:2:wait:/etc/rc.d/rc 2
l3:3:wait:/etc/rc.d/rc 3
l4:4:wait:/etc/rc.d/rc 4
l5:5:wait:/etc/rc.d/rc 5
l6:6:wait:/etc/rc.d/rc 6

# Things to run in every runlevel.
ud::once:/sbin/update
```

The fourth section sets specific commands and options. In particular, it maps the Ctrl+Alt+Delete key sequence, which automatically reboots the system. You can disable or change that option here. This section also has some options regarding SmartUPS settings. If the system is connected to a UPS with serial feedback that instructs the system when the UPS will run out of power, the system can automatically shut itself down with this entry:

```
# Trap CTRL-ALT-DELETE
ca::ctrlaltdel:/sbin/shutdown -t3 -r now

# When our UPS tells us power has failed, assume we have a few
# minutes of power left.  Schedule a shutdown for 2 minutes from
# now. This does, of course, assume you have power installed and
# your UPS connected and working correctly.
pf::powerfail:/sbin/shutdown -f -h +2"Power Failure;System Shutting
Down"

# If power was restored before the shutdown kicked in, cancel it.
pr:12345:powerokwait:/sbin/shutdown -c"Power Restored;Shutdown
Cancelled"
```

The fifth section of the /etc/inittab file sets up your virtual consoles (also discussed in Chapter 6). This specific setup is the default and allows up to six virtual consoles. To add additional virtual consoles, duplicate the lines and then change the first field as well as the **tty** field to represent the appropriate number of your virtual console. Here is a snippet of the /etc/inittab file that sets your virtual consoles:

```
# Run gettys in standard runlevels
1:2345:respawn:/sbin/mingetty tty1
2:2345:respawn:/sbin/mingetty tty2
```

```
3:2345:respawn:/sbin/mingetty tty3
4:2345:respawn:/sbin/mingetty tty4
5:2345:respawn:/sbin/mingetty tty5
6:2345:respawn:/sbin/mingetty tty6

# Run xdm in runlevel 5
# xdm is now a separate service
x:5:respawn:/etc/X11/prefdm -nodaemon
```

As set in the /etc/inittab, root can use **init** and **telinit** to access other runlevels during regular operation. You can also use these two commands to shut down or reboot a system. You don't have to memorize these **init** commands; Red Hat Linux offers the **shutdown** command, which allows you to safely shut down your system. With **shutdown**, you can specify to halt with the "–h" option and reboot with the "–r" option. Passing a "–t" option in addition to either the "–r" or "–h" option allows you to specify the time. For instance, **shutdown –r** specifies a reboot right now, whereas **shutdown –ht 300** specifies a shutdown in 300 seconds.

Understanding System Initialization Scripts

System initialization scripts, all of which are found under the /etc/rc.d/ directory, are used to boot the system. Some of the most popular system initialization scripts are /etc/rc.d/rc.sysinit, /etc/rc.d/rc.serial, etc/rc.d/rc.local, and /etc/rc.d/rc0.d through /etc/rc.d/rc6.d (run-level directories).

rc.sysinit

The /etc/rc.d/rc.sysinit script is the main startup script. Its main purpose is to check all the local filesystems. If there is a problem with performing the filesystem check, the rc.sysinit script is instructed to drop out of the existing shell, send the administrator an error message, and reboot the system. In addition, the rc.sysinit script instructs a filesystem to use quotas. Listing 8.1 includes some excerpts of the rc.sysinit script. This script is quite lengthy, so I have removed some of the extensive sections. For a complete look, take a glance at your /etc/rc.sysinit file. The excerpts include the information related to filesystem checking and quotas.

Listing 8.1   Excerpts of the rc.sysinit script.

```
# Start up swapping.
action "Activating swap partitions" swapon -a
```

```
# This sets up some filesystem check options
if [ -f /fsckoptions ]; then
      fsckoptions='cat /fsckoptions'
   else
      fsckoptions=
fi

if [ -f /forcefsck ]; then
      fsckoptions="-f $fsckoptions"
fi

_RUN_QUOTACHECK=0
if [ ! -f /fastboot ]; then
       STRING="Checking root filesystem"
      echo $STRING
      initlog -c "fsck  -T -a $fsckoptions /"
      rc=$?

      if [ "$rc" = "0" ]; then
            success "$STRING"
           echo
      elif [ "$rc" = "1" ]; then
            passed "$STRING"
            echo
       fi

      # A return of 2 or higher means there were serious problems.
if [ $rc -gt 1 ]; then
            failure "$STRING"
            echo
            echo
            echo "*** An error occurred during the file system
               check."
            echo "*** Dropping you to a shell; the system will
                reboot"
            echo "*** when you leave the shell."

            PS1="(Repair filesystem) \#"; export PS1
            sulogin

            echo "Unmounting file systems"
            umount -a
            mount -n -o remount,ro /
            echo "Automatic reboot in progress."
            reboot
         elif [ "$rc" = "1" ]; then
            _RUN_QUOTACHECK=1
```

```
        fi
fi

# Remount the root filesystem read-write.
action "Remounting root filesystem in read-write mode" mount -n -o
remount,rw /

# Update quotas if fsck was run on /.
if [ X"$_RUN_QUOTACHECK" = X1 -a -x /sbin/quotacheck ]; then
    action "Checking root filesystem quotas"  /sbin/quotacheck -v /
fi
# XXX Disabled to avoid complaints on root later with quotaon -a
#if [ -x /sbin/quotaon ]; then
#   action "Turning on user and group quotas for root filesystem"
    /sbin/quotaon /
#fi

# Check filesystems
if [ ! -f /fastboot ]; then
   STRING="Checking filesystems"
      echo $STRING
      initlog -c "fsck  -T -R -A -a $fsckoptions"
      rc=$?
      if [ "$rc" = "0" ]; then
            success "$STRING"
            echo
      elif [ "$rc" = "1" ]; then
             passed "$STRING"
             echo
      fi

      # A return of 2 or higher means there were serious problems.
      if [ $rc -gt 1 ]; then
            failure "$STRING"
            echo
            echo
            echo "*** An error occurred during the file system
                  check."
            echo "*** Dropping you to a shell; the system will
                  reboot"
            echo "*** when you leave the shell."

            PS1="(Repair filesystem) \#"; export PS1
            sulogin

            echo "Unmounting file systems"
            umount -a
```

```
            mount -n -o remount,ro /
            echo "Automatic reboot in progress."
            reboot
        elif [ "$rc" = "1" -a -x /sbin/quotacheck ]; then
         action "Checking filesystem quotas" /sbin/quotacheck -v -R
            -a
        fi
fi

# Mount all other filesystems (except for NFS and /proc, which is
3already mounted). Contrary to standard usage,
# filesystems are NOT unmounted in single user mode.
action "Mounting local filesystems" mount -a -t nonfs,smbfs,ncpfs,proc

if [ -x /sbin/quotaon ]; then
    action "Turning on user and group quotas for local filesystems"
    /sbin/quotaon -a
fi

# Now we have all of our basic modules loaded and the kernel going,
# let's dump the syslog ring somewhere so we can find it later
dmesg > /var/log/dmesg
```

rc.serial And rc.local

The /etc/rc.d/rc.serial file was used in older versions of Linux. It is rarely used on any current systems, and when it is, it is only for backward compatibility. Most of the functionality of the old rc.serial file can now be found in the rc.local file.

The /etc/rc.d/rc.local file is used to configure local machines. All the commands and scripts that run with this file are executed after the machine boots, but before anyone logs in to the system. The rc.local is also executed after a system runlevel is changed. One of rc.local's jobs is to create the login banner that by default displays your kernel version and machine type. To change this, you can simply edit this file. A sample /etc/rc.d/rc.local file follows:

```
#!/bin/sh

# This script will be executed *after* all the other init scripts.
# You can put your own initialization stuff in here if you don't
# want to do the full Sys V style init stuff.

if [ -f /etc/redhat-release ]; then
    R=$(cat /etc/redhat-release)
```

```
arch=$(uname -m)
a="a"
case "_$arch" in
        _a*) a="an";;
        _i*) a="an";;
esac

# This will overwrite /etc/issue at every boot.  So, make any
# changes you want to make to /etc/issue here or you will lose them
# when you  reboot.
    echo "" > /etc/issue
    echo "$R" >> /etc/issue
    echo "Kernel $(uname -r) on $a $(uname -m)" >> /etc/issue

    cp -f /etc/issue /etc/issue.net
    echo >> /etc/issue
fi
```

The actual prompt is displayed by /etc/issue and /etc/issue.net. The file, however, is overwritten by /etc/rc.d/rc.local. Therefore, any manual changes you make to the /etc/issue and /etc/issue.net files must also be reproduced in the rc.local file.

Run-Level Directories

The system run-level directories are /etc/rc.d/rc0.d through /etc/rc.d/rc6.d. These directories don't actually contain real files or scripts. Instead, they contain links to scripts that are located in the /etc/rc.d/init.d directory.

The links in the rcX.d directories are run through when the system accesses the rc.sysinit system initialization script. Each directory contains symlinks to real scripts. Here is an excerpt of the files in /etc/rc.d/rc0.d:

```
lrwxrwxrwx 1 root root 13 Jun 15 23:55 K10xfs -> ../init.d/xfs
lrwxrwxrwx 1 root root 13 Jun 15 23:57 K15gpm -> ../init.d/gpm
lrwxrwxrwx 1 root root 15 Jun 16 00:02 K15sound -> ../init.d/sound
lrwxrwxrwx 1 root root 13 Jun 15 23:59 K20nfs -> ../init.d/nfs
```

Each symlink in each of the rcX.d files is noted with an S or K at the beginning of the symlink file name. S indicates that the script is to be started; K indicates that it should be stopped. Following the S or K is a two-digit number that indicates the order in which the scripts are to be run. For example, 10 gets run before 15.

The following lists the scripts that are started or stopped between the seven runlevels. Each time another runlevel is accessed, such as with **init 1**, all the services in the associated rcX.d directory are performed.

➤ **rc0.d**   K00linuxconf, K05keytable, K10xfs, K15gpm, K15httpd, K15sound, K20nfs, K20rstatd, K20rusersd, K20rwhod, K30sendmail, K45sshd, K50inet, K55routed, K60atd, K60crond, K60lpd, K80random, K85netfs, K89portmap, K90killall, K90network, K92apmd, K96pcmcia, K99syslog, S00halt

➤ **rc1.d**   K00linuxconf, K05keytable, K10xfs, K15gpm, K15httpd, K15sound, K20nfs, K20rstatd, K20rusersd, K20rwhod, K30sendmail, K45sshd, K50inet, K55routed, K60atd, K60crond, K60lpd, K85netfs, K89portmap, K90network, K92apmd, K96pcmcia, K99syslog, S00single, S20random

➤ **rc2.d**   K15httpd, K15sound, K20nfs, K20rstatd, K20rusersd, K20rwhod, K45sshd, K50inet, K55routed, K60atd, K85netfs, K89portmap, S05apmd, S10network, S20random, S30syslog, S40crond, S45pcmcia, S60lpd, S75keytable, S80sendmail, S85gpm, S90xfs, S99linuxconf, S99local

➤ **rc3.d**   K10xntpd, K15postgresql, K20rstatd, K20rusersd, K20rwhod, K35smb, K45arpwatch, K55routed, K87ypbind, S05apmd, S10network, S11portmap, S15netfs, S20random, S30syslog, S40atd, S40crond, S45pcmcia, S50inet, S55sshd, S60lpd, S60nfs, S75keytable, S80sendmail, S85gpm, S85httpd, S85sound, S90vmware, S90xfs, S99linuxconf, S99local

➤ **rc5.d**   K15postgresql, K20rstatd, K20rusersd, K20rwhod, K35smb, K45arpwatch, K55routed, S05apmd, S10network, S11portmap, S15netfs, S20random, S30syslog, S40atd, S40crond, S45pcmcia, S50inet, S55sshd, S60lpd, S60nfs, S75keytable, S80sendmail, S85gpm, S85httpd, S85sound, S90xfs, S99linuxconf, S99local

➤ **rc6.d**   K00linuxconf, K05keytable, K08vmware, K10xfs, K15gpm, K15httpd, K15sound, K20nfs, K20rstatd, K20rusersd, K20rwhod, K30sendmail, K45sshd, K50inet, K55routed, K60atd, K60crond, K60lpd, K80random, K85netfs, K89portmap, K90killall, K90network, K92apmd, K96pcmcia, K99syslog, S00reboot

Understanding The Linux Kernel

The Linux kernel is the very fundamental foundation on which Linux is based. The Linux kernel, in fact, is where Linux gets its name. As discussed in Chapter 3, the Linux kernel was developed as a hobby by a student named Linus Toorvalds in Helsinki, Finland. The Linux kernel, combined with many applications and GNU tools, is what makes up Red Hat Linux today. In this section, we will discuss technicalities of the kernel, good housekeeping practices, kernel modules, kernel configuration, kernel compiling, and more.

Kernel Basics

There are two types of Linux kernels: *monolithic* and *modular*. Monolithic kernels are much like old-style Unix kernels. All the system support is compiled directly in the kernel. Therefore, if SCSI support is required, all the SCSI drivers and so on are compiled directly in the kernel. This creates a much larger kernel, but runs a little faster at boot-time. In addition, monolithic kernels use a constant amount of RAM.

On the other hand, the only drivers that modular kernels need compiled are those required at boot-time. Remaining drivers and support are installed as modules and are loaded only when needed. The modular kernel method is less secure than the monolithic kernel method; however, it is more memory efficient and allows the kernel to be much smaller.

Some systems require the use of ramdisks. Ramdisks are required when support such as SCSI support during boot is needed. The ramdisk is noted in your /etc/lilo.conf file as an **initrd=** comment. We will discuss creating this file later in this chapter.

Kernel Housekeeping

Good kernel housekeepers know how to keep their kernels clean and their systems functioning. It is a good habit to never delete an existing kernel when you compile a new one. Rather than overwriting your existing kernel, rename it. You can then set up LILO, the Linux boot loader, to boot your existing kernel as a choice, just in case your new kernel is unbootable.

If your new kernel is unbootable, do not fret. You kept your existing kernel to boot from, didn't you? Chances are you may have misconfigured your system, maybe even set the wrong options during your configuration, or possibly have missing or corrupt kernel source. If any of these situations happens, try debugging your kernel problems by the errors you receive when compiling or booting. If the problem turns out to be something unsolvable, try and try again. Just remember that wherever you visit, clean up after yourself. Leaving behind old configurations from previous trials may make future attempts less successful.

Kernel Modules

Kernel modules are used in modular kernels. They are loaded as needed when support for a specific device, protocol, and so on is required. Modules that the kernel uses are located in the /lib/modules/ directory. The files located under

/lib/modules/ are separated by kernel versions. For instance, on my system, I have installed kernel 2.2.5 and 2.2.10. Therefore, I have a directory under /lib/modules/ for each kernel.

When a request is made for a service from a module that has either not been loaded or isn't compiled directly into the kernel, the kernel (using kmod) looks to load the needed module. To find the needed module, kmod looks into /lib/modules/, then into the appropriate kernel directory, and then into the appropriate device directory, if needed.

Red Hat Linux packages a number of tools that make controlling modules simpler. They include **lsmod, insmod, rmmod,** and **modprobe.** The **lsmod** tool tells you what modules are running. A sample output of **lsmod** follows.

```
Module                 Size  Used by
nls_iso8859-1          2020     1  (autoclean)
isofs                 17400     1  (autoclean)
ide-cd                22516     2  (autoclean)
cdrom                 13272     0  (autoclean) [ide-cd]
floppy                45964     1  (autoclean)
vmnet                  9200     4
vmmon                 10496     1
nfsd                 150008     8  (autoclean)
lockd                 30856     1  (autoclean) [nfsd]
sunrpc                52548     1  (autoclean) [nfsd lockd]
pcnet_cs               7572     1
8390                   5920     0  [pcnet_cs]
ds                     5740     2  [pcnet_cs]
i82365                22576     2
pcmcia_core           39912     0  [pcnet_cs ds i82365]
uart401                5968     0
sound                 57176     0  [uart401]
soundlow                300     0  [sound]
soundcore              2372     3  [sound]
```

The **insmod** tool loads a specific module manually. The **rmmod** tool removes any idle modules that aren't being used. The **modprobe** tool automatically loads all base modules that are needed for a specific service.

Module Configuration

Module loading and so on used to be handled in Red Hat Linux by **kerneld.** As of Red Hat Linux 6.0, however, **kerneld** is obsolete. The Red Hat Linux kernel now uses kmod to handle the loading of kernel modules.

One configuration file used with modularized kernels is /etc/conf.modules. The /etc/conf.modules file specifies commands, options, paths, and so on for modules. In addition, this file sets up any module aliases and parameters that may be required.

Red Hat Linux also has a kernel configuration tool (**kernelcfg**) that is used in X to help configure kernel modules. To run this tool, simply type "kernelcfg" at the root prompt. The window, shown in Figure 8.1, appears.

The kernel configurator lists the installed modules on your system. You can then add or delete modules with the Add and Remove buttons located at the bottom of the window. In addition you can edit current modules to add any arguments you may require. The fourth button, Restart kerneld, allows you to restart kerneld on older Red Hat Linux systems. With kmod, this button is deprecated.

Kernel Configuration

The files you need to boot a kernel are located in the /boot directory. These files include System.map, boot.b, boot.0300, initrd, and kernel boot images (typically named with the vmlinuz prefix). The System.map file is a file that you use to debug the kernel. The boot.b file is the file that LILO creates; it is used in the second stage of LILO and is pointed from LILO in the master boot record. The boot.0300 file is a backup of your master boot record that is created when you install LILO. The initial ramdisk used to boot a system that uses SCSI during the boot process is called initrd. The vmlinuz files are the kernel boot images that are created during the kernel's **make** process.

Kernel source and documentation are located under the /usr/src/linux directory. Under this directory you will find a number of files and resources that you might find helpful when compiling or even debugging your kernel. Some of these files include the **CREDITS file**, which gives credit to many of the contributors to the Linux kernel, as well as the **Documentation directory**, which contains many text files with details about hardware, kernel files, and more. It also contains files that are required for compiling a kernel, such as Makefile

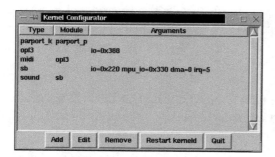

Figure 8.1 The kernel configurator.

and System.map. By default, any work you do with the Linux kernel will take place under this directory.

Kernel Configuration Tools

The first step in compiling (or recompiling) a kernel involves the **make** tool, which allows you to select and deselect exactly what options you want to include and modularize for the new kernel. These configuration settings are stored in a file in /usr/src/linux/.config. There are three methods of using **make** to help you configure your kernel: **make config**, **make menuconfig**, and **make xconfig**. Each of these methods creates a file with the .config extension that is used when making the zImage or bzImage of the kernel.

> *Note:* *To successfully use **make**, be sure you have all the appropriate packages installed. All methods of **make** require the glibc-devel, egcs, make, kernel-headers, kernel-source, bin86, and cpp packages. If you opt to use the **make menuconfig** option, you must also have the ncurses and ncurses-devel packages installed. If you opt for the **make xconfig** option, you must have X Window support.*

The first method, **make config**, is a text-based tool that you use to configure your kernel options. It is revered as the most difficult interface to configure a kernel. However, **make config** is a standard tool and is used amongst all Linux distributions. When you use **make config**, you are prompted line by line to include support for a specific item. Following each question, you are given up to four options: "y" for yes, "n" for no, "m" for modularize, and "?" for help. Pressing the "?" option gives you details for what the particular item is and what the default settings are. The default settings for a particular item are noted with the option being capitalized. For instance, the first question, "Prompt for development and/or incomplete code/drivers (CONFIG_EXPERIMENTAL) [Y/n/?]" has a default answer of "Y" or yes. To simply use the default answer, you can press Enter. The following displays the interface used in **make config**:

```
rm -f include/asm
( cd include ; ln -sf asm-i386 asm)
/bin/sh scripts/Configure arch/i386/config.in
#
# Using defaults found in .config
#
*
* Code maturity level options
*
```

```
Prompt for development and/or incomplete code/drivers
(CONFIG_EXPERIMENTAL) [Y/n/?]
*
* Processor type and features
*
Processor family (386, 486/Cx486, 586/K5/5x86/6x86, Pentium/K6/TSC,
PPro/6x86MX) [PPro/6x86MX]
  defined CONFIG_M686
Math emulation (CONFIG_MATH_EMULATION) [N/y/?]
MTRR (Memory Type Range Register) support (CONFIG_MTRR) [Y/n/?]
Symmetric multi-processing support (CONFIG_SMP) [N/y/?]
```

The second type of **make** method is **make menuconfig**. This method is one of the most popular used amongst Red Hat Linux users. It gives you a graphical window-based display without requiring you to use the X Window system. When you use **make menuconfig**, you are presented with a directory tree menu system. Following each selection, you are presented with the available options. To include an option, use the "Y" key; to exclude it, use the "N" key; and to modularize it, use the "M" key. Letters that are highlighted are considered hotkeys and allow you to quickly maneuver through the menu options. To exit a window, select the Exit option, or press Esc twice. Figure 8.2 shows you the **make menuconfig** interface.

The third type of **make** method is **make xconfig**. This method is very popular amongst new Linux users and users who are accustomed to graphical interface tools. The **make xconfig** tool requires that full X window system support be used. When starting **make xconfig**, you are presented with a window with buttons for each class of configuration. Pressing a configuration button, you are prompted, in a tree style, the options available. You can then select, deselect, or modularize each option by pressing the corresponding button next to the item.

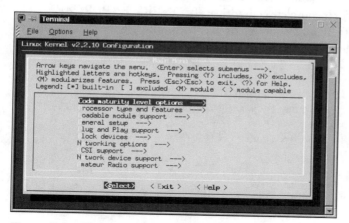

Figure 8.2   The **make menuconfig** interface.

One of the benefits of using this **make** method over the standard **make config** method is the backward mobility of the configuration. This means that if you change your mind, or make a mistake, you can move back and change the option with **make xconfig**; you can't do this with **make config**. With the **make config** method, you must restart your configuration process. Figure 8.3 shows the graphical user interface used with the **make xconfig** method.

Kernel Configuration Options

When configuring a kernel using any of the **make** tools described earlier in this chapter, you are presented with at least 24 divisions of configuration options. These options range everywhere from configuration tool preferences to hardware support and even development tools. This section discusses the different categories of options available, what settings are available, and what the standard preferences and practices are for each category.

> *Note: The options described in the following sections are not necessarily listed in the order in which your **make** option presents them. The order in which you configure your kernel does not affect the kernel in any way. These options and descriptions are based on the compilation of kernel 2.2. Options for other kernels, older or newer, may have fewer or additional options and categories because more hardware and other technologies are supported.*

Code Maturity Level

One of the first categories concerns code maturity level options. The code maturity level question sets whether the kernel configuration tool prompts you for development or incomplete support options within the kernel. If you specify

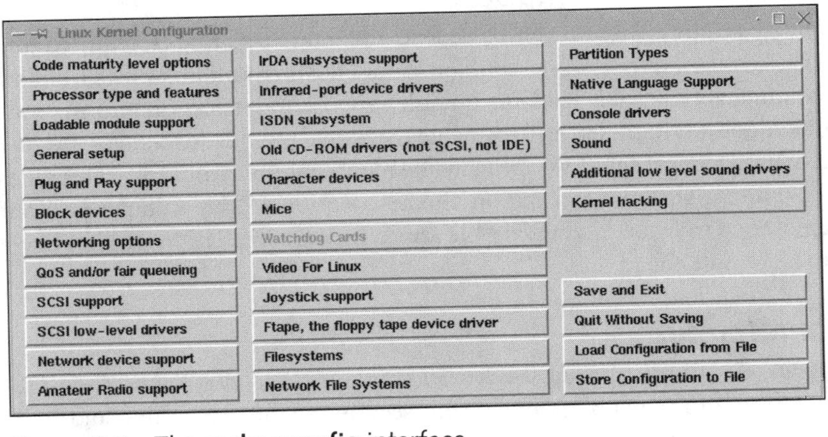

Figure 8.3   The **make xconfig** interface.

no for this option, all development or incomplete support options are automatically disabled. It is recommended that you answer yes to this option. Many tools require development packages in order to work properly.

Processor Family

The first question, regarding Processor family, sets certain assumptions for the kernel. When set to 386, the kernel you compile should run on *any* x86-compatible processor. Using any higher CPU family makes the kernel assume certain capabilities in the processor (which may have a large impact on performance on that type of CPU). Therefore, the resulting kernel probably won't run on anything lower than the family you specify.

The Math Emulation option turns on the kernel software floating point emulation. This is safe to turn on even for CPUs with hardware floating point units because the kernel detects the FPU at boot and disables emulation. Turning this option on increases the size of the kernel, however, so it is really necessary only for 386, 486SX, and other CPUs without hardware floating point.

The MTRR Support option can have a huge impact on performance. It allows you to turn on write-combining for certain cards, such as video cards on the PCI or AGP bus. This option is available only on Pentium II (and higher) and K6-2 (and higher) CPUs. It is safe to turn this option on for CPUs that do not support it because it adds just a small amount of additional code to the kernel.

The Symmetric Multi-Processing Support option turns on SMP support in the kernel. This is also safe for uni-processor systems. However, turning on this option may slow such systems down slightly and adds a small amount of code to the kernel.

Loadable Module Support

You are given the option to configure loadable module support—required for modular kernels—during kernel configuration. The three options available under this heading are to enable loadable module support, to set version information on all symbols for modules, and to enable the kernel module loader. For modular kernels, you must select yes for loadable module support and kernel module loader. The set version information choice is optional. The modular version setting is used to make modules usable after a kernel compilation without having to recompile the module.

General Setup

The general setup section of the kernel configuration options has about 28 options. Two of the main options in this section are for networking and PCI support. If you answer no to the networking support option, the configuration tool automatically disables all networking-related configuration options. If you want any networking connectivity, you should answer yes to this option.

As with the networking option, choosing no for the PCI support automatically disables all PCI support-related configuration options. If your motherboard has any PCI slots or PCI support, choose yes for this option. Most 586 (and above) processors and motherboards have PCI onboard. If not, choose no.

The remaining options in this section set system preferences. Options for other hardware support and other system options are available here. Kernel support for specific types of binaries (such as a.out, java, and ELF binaries) is located here. In addition, specific hardware support, such as whether to support PC style or foreign hardware, is set here.

Your power management support is also located in this set of options. If your BIOS can support Advanced Power Management (APM), you should select yes here. The remaining APM options allow you to specify how APM manages CPU calls, shutdown options, suspend options, and more.

Plug And Play

Most Intel machines use some sort of plug-and-play hardware. Therefore, under the Plug And Play Support category, you can decide whether to supply support for plug-and-play hardware in your kernel. Most administrators answer yes to this option. Also found in this category is support to auto-probe for parallel devices on your system. If any parallel devices will be used on your system, enable this option. It is advised to modularize this option so that the support is loaded only when needed.

 With 2.2.x (and newer) kernels, Plug and Play support is only used for parallel devices.

Block Devices

The block devices section of kernel configuration is quite extensive and very specific. Within this section, you can specify floppy disk support, CD-ROM, Tape, IDE, and Atapi device support. With the exception of IDE disk support, most of these options are simply modularized to be loaded as needed.

In addition to these media devices, PCI and IDE chipset support options are available. Here, you enable whichever chipset you have on your system and disable the rest. Besides the chipset information, you can select device support, such as loopback, network block, multiple device driver, and ramdisk support. Loopback device support is typically modularized, whereas network block and multiple device driver support is enabled only if needed. RAM disk support is required by SCSI-booted systems that need to use initial ramdisks (initrd) to boot. If you use SCSI hard drives, you should enable this option.

The final options in this section include XT hard disk support and parallel port IDE device support. If your system will access an XT hard disk, you should enable the support. If you think you may ever connect a parallel port IDE device, such as CD-ROM, tape drive, or other IDE device, it is recommended to modularize this support.

Networking Options

The Networking Options section contains all the configuration options for everything related to networking, including hardware, software, and protocols. The packet socket option turns on an interface that allows programs to communicate directly with network devices. Programs like **tcpdump**, packet sniffers, and **dhcpcd** (a DHCP client), use the interface to send and receive packets without going through the kernel TCP stack.

The Kernel/User Netlink Socket option turns on support for communication between certain network-related parts of the kernel and user processes. It is currently used by the kernel to publish routing messages (when CONFIG_RTNETLINK is on) and by **arpd** and the ethertap device.

The next two prompts are related to kernel firewalling options. The first prompts for support for network firewalls. Answering yes turns on support for IP firewalling, masquerading, and so on. The second prompts for support for socket filtering. Answering yes enables support for user-space socket filters.

The Unix domain socket option turns on support for Unix domain sockets, which are heavily used by many programs, such as **syslogd** and X, even when a system is not connected to a network. You should enable this option except in embedded applications where you know no communication over Unix domain sockets will occur.

Enabling support for the TCP/IP networking option includes support for TCP/IP networking, which many normal programs use heavily. Again, turn this option on except in embedded applications where you know you won't use TCP/IP.

Several other TCP/IP-related configuration options appear in this section. The first includes experimental support for the new IPv6 networking protocol, which will sometime soon replace the current TCP/IP protocol (IPv4) used on the Internet. If you want to test IPv6 on your network, turn on this driver.

Within this section, you are also prompted for support of other networking protocols such as IPX and AppleTalk DDP. Enabling the IPX option turns on support for the IPX protocol, which older versions of Novell's NetWare NOS use. Enabling the AppleTalk DDP option turns on support for the AppleTalk protocol, which Apple Macintosh networks use to share files and printers.

Three experimental options are available to enable support for networking over amateur radio links: CCITT X.25 Packet Layer, LAPB Data Link Driver, and 802.2 LLC. You can use X.25 over amateur radio, as well as over serial links and Ethernet. LAPB is a link-level protocol that is used with the X.25 protocol. The 802.2 LLC choice is another option for a link-level protocol (over Ethernet) for X.25.

The next options allow you to enable support for various network operations. The first option allows experimental support for bridging. Enabling this option allows the Linux kernel to act as an Ethernet bridge. The second option can enable support for Wide Area Network (WAN) routing. This new option allows you to configure support for WAN adapter cards such as Sangoma frame relay cards. A third, new network operation option is for fast switching. This new option allows support for direct NIC-to-NIC transfers. Be leery of this option, however, because it is not compatible with several other network options (such as kernel firewalling). Enable this option only if the system will act as a dedicated router.

A few options that manage network connectivity and flow are also available. One of the first enables forwarding between high-speed interfaces. This option turns on support for hardware throttling when the network is congested. See the help for this option if this sounds like something you need. Another option is new: support for CPUs that you suspect are too slow to handle the full bandwidth of the network they are attached to. Most often, you do not need to enable this option.

SCSI Support

The first option for SCSI support is simply to enable SCSI support, which turns on support for SCSI devices. If you turn this option on, you are given the opportunity to configure various driver options, as well as support for various types of devices and interface cards. Unless you are booting off an SCSI device, it is safe to simply modularize this option in the event you install an SCSI card or other SCSI device.

Network Device Support

There are several options available under the network device support section. The first option is to enable support for network devices, which allows you to configure support for various network devices. If you enable this option, you are prompted for specific network device support. If you answer no to this option, the following network devices are automatically disabled.

One of the first network device options is to enable ARCnet support. This option allows you to turn on support for old ARCnet cards. ARCnet is an old networking system that somewhat resembles Ethernet used primarily on PCs.

Another network device option is for dummy net driver support. Enabling this option allows you to include support for a "dummy" network interface. Traffic sent to this interface is simply discarded. This option is useful for keeping a permanent IP address associated with a system, even though its only "real" network interface is PPP or SLIP.

A handy option located here is support for EQL (serial line load balancing). Enabling this option turns on support for load balancing over PPP or SLIP interfaces. You can use this to combine multiple lower-speed serial links into a single higher-speed network interface. Note that the other end of the link must also support this protocol.

The most needed option in this category is to enable Ethernet support. This option allows you to configure support for various Ethernet controllers. This includes support for both 10MB and 100MB controllers.

Another device that you can enable is support for FDDI drivers. Turning this option on allows you to configure support for FDDI adapter cards. In addition to FDDI, there is an option to enable frame relay DLCI support. Turning on this option allows you to configure support for frame relay adapter cards.

The next three options, PLIP, PPP, and SLIP support, allow you to enable these types of network connections. Enabling PLIP support enables parallel port connections. This option turns on support for the Parallel Line Internet Protocol, which works over specially modified parallel cables. Enabling PPP support enables point-to-point connections. This option turns on support for the PPP protocol, which is most commonly used to do networking over serial links such as modems. Enabling the SLIP support enables serial line connections. This option turns on support for SLIP, a protocol that pre-dates PPP and that is used to network over serial links. PPP is a more robust protocol, so you generally won't need SLIP support. Turning the SLIP option on also allows you to configure various SLIP driver options.

One of the final options in this category is to enable token ring driver support. Turning this option on allows you to include support for a few token ring adapter cards in the kernel. Token ring is an old, slow, and expensive local area network system that IBM developed and heavily pushed several years ago. It is still commonly found in large IBM-centric organizations.

Amateur Radio Support

One of the shorter categories, there are options in your kernel configuration for amateur radio support. Turning on this option allows you to configure support for networking over amateur radio. You should enable this only if you plan to work with radio networking.

Infrared Support

Another short category enables the new option of support for infrared devices. The main question in this category is to enable IrDA subsystems support. Enabling this option allows you to configure support for communication over certain infrared interfaces. This category includes an option to do networking between infrared interfaces.

ISDN Support

You can select support for ISDN with the ISDN Support option. Enabling ISDN support allows you to configure kernel support for ISDN adapter cards as well as networking over ISDN.

Old CD-ROM Driver Support

Some systems use CD-ROM drives other than SCSI or current IDE CD-ROM drives. Enabling this option allows you to configure support for CD-ROM drives that use old proprietary interfaces, such as those commonly found on older sound cards. Typically, you do not need to enable this support.

Character Devices

Within the character devices category, there are approximately 12 configuration options available. One of the first options is to enable support for virtual terminal devices. This is the standard way of supporting the system keyboard/mouse/monitor combination of a system in Linux. You should consider this a required option on all systems other than embedded devices. Another option allows the system console to be set to a virtual terminal. The system console is where kernel messages go and where logins are allowed in single-user mode. You should turn this option on except if you are sure you will always use another device, such as a serial port, for the system console.

Another character device option in this category is to enable support for standard generic dumb serials. Turning this option on allows you to set a serial port as the system console. To enable console support on the dumb terminal, you must enable support for the console on the serial port. Some additional serial support options include extended dumb serial driver and non-standard serial port support. Enabling the extended dumb serial driver options allows you to turn on certain options for the standard serial driver, such as support for IRQ sharing. Enabling the non-standard serial port support option allows you to configure support for various intelligent serial boards.

The next option in this category is to enable support for Unix98 PTY. Turning this option on includes kernel support for the /dev/pts/*number* naming scheme for pseudo terminal devices mandated by the UNIX98 specification. This system is supported in the GNU C library version 2.1 and higher. It is used by default in Red Hat 6.0 and higher.

If you plan to connect a parallel printer to the system, you must enable parallel printer support. In addition, there is an option to enable printer read-back. It turns on support for status read-back from printers. When this option is turned on, you get status information about the printer when you execute **cat** /**dev**/*lp0* (or whatever the printer device is).

If you plan to connect a mouse with an interface other than serial, such as PS/2, you must enable the mouse support option in this category. Turning this option on allows you to configure support for various non-serial mouse interfaces, such as the PS/2 interface found on most recent systems.

Some older systems use an old style QIC-02 tape drive. To enable support for this type of tape drive, you must turn on the QIC-02 tape support option.

Another option in this category is to enable watchdog timer support. Doing so allows you to configure support for the watchdog device, which is used to monitor system health by triggering a reboot if the device isn't written to in a certain period of time. The idea is that if a process's only job is to occasionally write to this device, and that process fails, something bad must have happened to the system. The watchdog device can be driven entirely by software that may not be reliable if the system has crashed. It can also be tied to special hardware-monitoring cards. Most administrators don't use this option.

To be able to read and write to a PC's CMOS, you must enable /dev/nvram support. This option turns on support for reading and writing a system's non-volatile RAM (NVRAM) area. On PCs, this is usually called the CMOS. This can be used, for example, to store a small amount of information that will persist over reboots. Doing so can be very dangerous, though, because over-writing the NVRAM on a system will probably make it unbootable. Most administrators don't enable this option.

The last option in this category is for enhanced real-time clock support. This option turns on extended support for the real-time clock chip on most systems. This is generally handy to have available, and it is required for synchronization on SMP systems.

Video For Linux

The category for video for Linux is a bit misleading. This category is not for video display support, such as X support, but for additional video option support. Enabling support for video for Linux allows you to configure support for various video capture cards, TV tuner cards, and FM radio cards.

Joystick Support

Joysticks are typically connected to the standard PC game port. Enabling the joystick support option allows you to configure support for joysticks on the standard PC game port as well as support for many newer digital joysticks.

Ftape Support

Ftape is the floppy tape device. Enabling the Ftape (QIC-80/Travan) support option allows you to configure kernel support for various tape drives that use the standard PC floppy disk interface.

Filesystem Support

The filesystem support category for kernel configuration currently contains options for about 14 filesystem types and options. One of the first is quota support. Enabling this option turns on support for user and group quotas (usage limits) on filesystems.

Another option is for kernel automounter support. This option turns on kernel support for a daemon that can be used to automatically mount both local and remote filesystems. This option can be extremely convenient, especially on desktop systems.

One of the first options for types of filesystems is the experimental support option for the read-only ADFS filesystem support. There are also options for the Amiga FFS filesystem support and the experimental Apple Macintosh filesystem support. These options allow you to configure support for the native filesystems used by Acorn's RiscOS, AmigaOS, and MacOS, respectively.

To read DOS- and Windows-style FAT filesystems from Linux, you must have support for these filesystems. Enabling the DOS FAT fs support option allows you to configure support for DOS- and Windows-style FAT filesystems.

The standard filesystem used on CD-ROMs is the ISO9660 filesystem. To enable support for this system, you must answer yes to the ISO 9660 CD-ROM filesystem support option.

Some additional options for foreign filesystem support include the Minix fs support option, read-only NTFS filesystem support, and read-only OS/2 HPFS filesystem support. These options turn on support for the native filesystems of Minix (which was also once the native Linux filesystem), Windows NT, and OS/2, respectively.

The /proc filesystem support options turn on support for the /proc filesystem. An option that comes after this, /dev/pts filesystem for Unix98 PTYs, turns on support for the devpts virtual filesystem. This filesystem is used to create and remove pseudo terminal device entries in /dev/pts as needed. If you have turned on support for Unix98 PTYs, turn this on.

The next option is QNX filesystem support. This support is experimental, and when enabled, provides support for the filesystem used by the QNX real-time OS. For read-only media, the ROM filesystem support option is used. This option turns on support for a lightweight filesystem designed for read-only media. It is generally useful only for install media and embedded systems.

A very important option is for the second extended filesystem, which is the standard filesystem on Linux. The second extended fs support option turns on support for this.

Two options that support other Unix filesystems include the System V and Coherent filesystem support and the UFS filesystem support. These two options allow you to turn on support for the filesystems used in many other Unix (or Unix-like) systems, especially some of the "genuine" Unix systems derived from AT&T or BSD code. The System V filesystem is used by some SysV-based systems like SCO. UFS is used by many BSD-based systems.

Network File Systems

There are six options available under the Network File Systems category. The first enables support for the Coda filesystem, an experimental filesystem that supports advanced features like client caching of files.

The next two options deal with network filesystem (NFS) support. The first enables direct support for the NFS filesystem and turns on support for the kernel client. This is the standard method of file sharing between Unix (and Unix-like) systems. Such support is generally good to have available. The second option enables support for the NFS server. This is new in the 2.2.x kernels. Using the new **knfsd** tools, the kernel does the work that was previously done with a user-space **nfsd** on earlier Linux systems. The knfsd tools are much more robust, and much cleaner, because the user-space nfsd could not easily access information like inode numbers, which are passed between the NFS server and client.

The next two options set up support for Samba filesystems. The first enables SMB filesystem support. This option turns on support for the kernel SMB (LanManager/Samba/Windows NT) client. Mounted SMB shares appear as standard Unix-like filesystems. The second option enables the Samba Windows 95 bug workaround. The one case where you should turn this option on is for systems where the only SMB shares that will be mounted are on Windows 95 systems.

The final option in this category is for NCP filesystem support. This is used to mount NetWare volumes. Enabling this option turns on support for NetWare client support in the kernel. Mounted NetWare volumes appear as standard Unix-like filesystems.

Partition Types

You can enable five major partition types in the kernel. These options turn on support for various partition table formats that various operating systems use. The first option is for BSD disklabel support, which enables support for BSD-style partition tables. The second option is for Macintosh partition map support. This is used on the Macintosh platform. The third option is for SMD disklabel support, which enables support for Sun partition tables. The fourth option is for support of the x86 Solaris partition table. The last option is the experimental support for Unixware slices. By default, Linux uses the DOS-style partition table format.

Native Language Support

If you turn on FAT support, or support for the Microsoft Joliet extension to ISO9660, you are prompted for support for NLS, which is used to support the various character sets used around the world. These character sets are labeled by codepage and their appropriate number, such as codepage 437, which is the United States, Canada character set. Approximately 27 character sets, ranging from United States to Turkish to Russian, are available.

Console Drivers

The four options under the Console Drivers category allow you to enable options for your Linux console. The first is the VGA text console support option. This option turns on support for the standard PC-style VGA text console. You should almost always turn this on for x86 systems.

The second is the video mode selection support option. It includes support in the kernel for switching VGA text modes using the BIOS before the kernel boots into protected mode (and can no longer use the BIOS). To use this option, you must boot the kernel with the "vga=" option.

The third option is support for the dual-headed MDA text console. Enabling this new experimental option allows you to run with an old Hercules monochrome adapter and monitor on your system. This can be very handy for keeping something such as the system log displayed on a second display at all times.

The final option in this category is new: support for frame buffer devices. This option turns on support for frame buffer console devices, which are used primarily on non-x86 systems for graphical console support. On x86, this can still be useful because there is an option for VESA frame buffer support, which lets you run with a graphical console at high resolution on any VESA 2.0-compatible video card.

Sound Support

For systems with sound cards, you should enable sound support. The prompt to enable sound support is simply sound card support. Turning this option on allows you to configure support for sound cards as well as configure various options for the Linux kernel sound driver.

Kernel Hacking

A final category for configuring your kernel is Kernel Hacking. This category has only one option, which you use to configure support for the SysRq key. This option turns on support for various "magic" key sequences using Alt+SysRq (also Print Screen) on the standard PC keyboard. These sequences can sync all mounted filesystems, kill all processes on the virtual console, reboot the system, and so on. This option can be very convenient, but you should not turn it on for systems where access to the system's console could be a security risk.

Compiling And Installing A Custom Kernel

When compiling and installing a kernel, you use various **make** options. There are as many as 11 options that you can use when compiling and installing your kernel from start to finish; we will describe them in this section. Follow these steps to compile and install a new kernel:

1. You must first configure your kernel as discussed in the "Kernel Configuration Options" section earlier in this chapter. There are several options available to configure your kernel. First, to compile your kernel, you must be in the /usr/src/linux directory. Next, if you plan to configure your kernel completely by scratch, first use **make mrproper**. Doing so removes your current .config file and allows you to set up all new options for your kernel without knowing your current default configuration. If you wish to see your current default options, skip the **make mrproper** step. To finish configuring your kernel, use your choice of **make config**, **make menuconfig**, or **make xconfig**, as discussed earlier in this chapter.

2. Next, you must do some general kernel housekeeping. This means that you need to clean up any unneeded or temporary files from the kernel source tree. To clean the source tree, run **make clean**.

3. Next, you must ensure that all dependencies are available and correctly placed. The two dependencies in particular are the kernel header files /

usr/src/linux/config.h and /usr/src/linux/proc_fs.h. To check for these dependencies, run **make dep**.

4. You must next create the kernel image. Your two options are **make zImage** and **make bzImage**. Both methods compile a kernel image and place it in the /arch/i386/boot directory and then call the image either zImage or bzImage (depending on what method you use). The method you use depends on the size of your kernel. If your kernel image plus the compressed kernel image is smaller than 640K, you can use zImage. However, if your kernel is monolithic, or otherwise larger than 640K, you should use bzImage. Unless you're attempting to make the smallest possible kernel, it's always safe to use bzImage. After the image is created, copy the zImage or bzImage from the /usr/src/linux/arch/i386/ boot directory to the /boot directory. In the /boot directory, you may wish to rename the image to something like vmlinuz-*the.kernel.version*, such as 2.2.10.

5. Next, you compile your modules. If you made a completely monolithic kernel, skip ahead to Step 7. Otherwise, run **make modules** to compile all of your selected modules.

6. You must next install your compiled modules by running **make modules_install**. When you install the modules with this **make** option, **make** installs them to /lib/modules.

> With the post-configuration **make** options—such as **make clean, make dep, make bzImage, make modules**, and **make modules_install**—you don't have to invoke each **make** command one at a time. You can string them together to run automatically without user intervention by simply running **make clean dep bzImage modules modules_install**. While letting this run, you can do whatever you want; you do not need to wait for any specific task until all **make** options are finished.

7. Next, create the ramdisk image (if required). The ramdisk image is used to preload block device modules (such as SCSI drivers to access SCSI hard drives) that are required during boot-time to access the root filesystem. To create this ramdisk image, use the **mkinitrd** command in the format **mkinitrd /boot/***newimage the.kernel.version*, where *newimage* is the name of the new ramdisk image and *the.kernel.version* is the kernel version.

8. Lastly, you set up LILO for your new kernel by editing the /etc/lilo.conf file. If you are installing your new kernel the recommended way (by

adding it as an additional boot option to your existing kernel), you simply add an additional boot image section to /etc/lilo.conf. Otherwise, you change the current boot image section to reflect your new kernel image name and initrd image (if necessary). For instance, if you just compiled kernel 2.2.10, named the image /boot/vmlinuz-2.2.10, and created an initrd image to /boot/initrd-2.2.10, your new boot image section of /etc/lilo.conf should look like this:

```
boot=/dev/hda
map=/boot/map
install=/boot/boot.b
#prompt
delay=20
timeout=2400
root=/dev/hda3
read-only
image=/boot/vmlinuz-2.2.10
        label=2.2.10
        initrd=/boot/initrd-2.2.10
```

Note: After you have edited your /etc/lilo.conf file, make sure to install the new /etc/lilo.conf configuration by running /sbin/lilo.

The Vixie cron System

The Vixie cron system allows your machine to run specific commands at regularly specified intervals. You can set these commands to run hourly, daily, weekly, monthly, or even yearly. Both root and individual users can use the cron system.

The cron system uses configuration files named crontab. The system's (root's) crontab is located in /etc/crontab. User-specific crontabs are in /var/spool/cron/ *username*. If a cron job specifies a standard out request, the output is emailed to the user who owns the group.

Looking At The /etc/crontab File

Root's crontab file is located at /etc/crontab. Taking a look at this file can be quite deceiving because it looks very simple. In fact, the /etc/crontab file, by default, is comprised of only nine lines. Four of them are script settings, and one is a comment. A default /etc/crontab file follows:

```
SHELL=/bin/bash
PATH=/sbin:/bin:/usr/sbin:/usr/bin
MAILTO=root
HOME=/
```

```
# run-parts
01 * * * * root run-parts /etc/cron.hourly
02 4 * * * root run-parts /etc/cron.daily
22 4 * * 0 root run-parts /etc/cron.weekly
42 4 1 * * root run-parts /etc/cron.monthly
```

The layout of root's /etc/crontab file was developed so that you can simply administer cron jobs and the crontab file itself. You don't have to specify line after line of cron jobs to be run; rather, when you set individual cron settings for each script or job, root's /etc/crontab file sets times for a script to execute all scripts within a specific directory. The script used to run the files within the specific directory is **run-parts**, located at /usr/bin/run-parts. Taking a glance at the run-parts script, you can see that it opens the indicated directory, checks to see that is in fact a directory, and runs all the scripts located within that directory. See the following script to understand how run-parts works:

```bash
#!/bin/bash

# run-parts - concept taken from Debian

# keep going when something fails
set +e

if [ $# -lt 1 ]; then
        echo "Usage: run-parts <dir>"
        exit 1
fi

if [ ! -d $1 ]; then
        echo "Not a directory: $1"
        exit 1
fi

for i in $1/* ; do
        [ -d $i ] && continue
        # Don't run [KS]??foo.{rpmsave,rpmorig,rpmnew} scripts
        [ "${i%.rpmsave}" != "${i}" ] && continue
         [ "${i%.rpmorig}" != "${i}" ] && continue
         [ "${i%.rpmnew}" != "${i}" ] && continue

        if [ -x $i ]; then
                $i
        fi
done

exit 0
```

The directories that run-parts is asked to run by default are divided and named by how often the job scripts within the directories are run. For instance, cron.weekly are jobs that are run every week, and cron.daily jobs run daily. Some default jobs in cron.daily might be **logrotate** and **tmpwatch**. If specified, the **logrotate** script rotates all system logs, such as /var/log/messages and /var/log/maillog. The **tmpwatch** script searches the system and removes temporary files that haven't been accessed for a specified length of time.

Setting Up A User's crontab File

Setting up a crontab file for a user is a little more complex than setting up root's crontab. A user can create her own crontab file with the **crontab −e** command, which drops the user into edit mode. The user's crontab file is created in /tmp but is saved in /var/spool/cron/*username*. The user's crontab is created with a similar layout as root's /etc/crontab, but rather than the scripts being split off into directories, they are listed directly in the file, configuring individual time settings, and so on. In the crontab file, you can enter lines that look much like this:

```
#Description of Job to be run and when
* * * * * /path/to/script
```

Typically, it is good practice to add comments to each line for each job you run so that you can remember what job is running and when. You don't want to be manually looking up the script each time. The five asterisks (*) at the beginning of each script line are the five fields for setting when the script is to be run. If the field isn't set, the field has an asterisk. The first field indicates what minute of the hour the script should run. Valid settings for this field are 0 (or 00) through 59. If the five fields read 22 * * * *, the script runs on the 22nd minute of every hour.

The second field specifies the hour of the day. Valid settings for this field are 0 through 23. If the five fields read 00 12 * * *, the script runs every 12th hour at the zero minute of every day.

The third field indicates the day of month. Valid settings for this field are 0 through 31. If the five fields read 0 0 1 * *, the script runs the first day of every month at the zero hour and zero minute.

The fourth field specifies the month of the year. Valid settings for this field are 1 through 12. In addition, you can use names of the month (such as jan, feb, mar, and so on) here. If the five fields read 0 0 1 3 *, the job runs the first day of the third month of every year at the zero hour and zero minute.

The final script specifies the day of the week. Valid settings for this field are 0 through 7, where both 0 and 7 are Sunday. In addition, you can specify the day's name (such as sun, mon, tue, and so on). If the five fields read 0 12 * * 5, the job runs every Friday of every week of every month at the zero minute of the twelfth hour.

Each of the time fields also allows you to specify ranges and multiple run times. Using a dash (-) between two options in a field specifies that the script should run within the valid range. Using a comma to separate two options in a field specifies that it should run at both times. For instance,

```
30 12 1,15 2,4,6,8,10,12 * /usr/sbin/rm -rf /home/user/tmp/*
```

removes all files under the /tmp directory in the user home directory at 12:30 P.M. on the first and fifteenth days of every other month starting in February and including April, June, August, October, and December. On the other hand,

```
30 12 1-15 3-9 * /usr/sbin/rm -rf /home/user/tmp/*
```

removes all the directories in the user's tmp directory at 12:30 P.M. every day between the first and the fifteenth of every month between March and September. If you tossed in a 5 in the fifth directory, the job would run every Friday as well, even outside the March through September range or the first through the fifteenth range.

 When the time on a system is changed for any reason, such as correction, daylight savings time, and so on, the crontab files may be affected. If the time is moved forward by less than one hour, any scripts or jobs scheduled to run during that time are still executed. However, if the time is moved ahead by more than an hour, the scheduled jobs are missed.

On the other hand, similar jobs apply to moving time back. If the time is moved backward by less than one hour, the scheduled jobs are not run again. However, if time is moved back by more than an hour, commands are re-executed.

Bash Configuration

In Chapter 6, we discussed how to configure the bash options for individual users. As a reminder, you should recognize the files .bash_logout, .bash_profile, and .bashrc. These files are modeled after the system-wide bash shell configuration files, and work interactively with these user files to set up the bash shells for each user. By working interactively, I mean that these files call upon one another for system settings, and preferences. Each time a bash shell is executed, three system-wide configuration files are executed and used: /etc/bashrc, /etc/profile, and /etc/profile.d/.

Each time a bash shell is executed, it calls the /etc/profile script, which calls script files that are located under /etc/profile.d. The /etc/profile script calls for a user's .bash_profile (or .profile) for local settings. The user's .bash_profile calls for the user's .bashrc. The user's .bashrc then calls the system's /etc/bashrc.

/etc/bashrc

The /etc/bashrc is the global setup file for the bash shell. Red Hat Linux ships with several shells, including bash, korn, and c, but the standard Red Hat Linux shell is bash. The /etc/bashrc, by default, simply specifies options for the shell prompt. Here is a sample /etc/bashrc:

```
# /etc/bashrc
# System wide functions and aliases
# Environment stuff goes in /etc/profile
# For some unknown reason bash refuses to inherit
# PS1 in some circumstances that I can't figure out.
# Putting PS1 here ensures that it gets loaded every time.
PS1="[\u@\h \W]\\$ "
```

This /etc/bashrc file prints a prompt (notated by the **PS1=** line). It says to print the default prompt (PS1) with the format within the double quotation marks. The **\u@** indicates to print the username@, and the **\h** indicates to print the hostname. The **\W** indicates to print the last directory name within the entered path. The open and close square brackets [] around the statement say to print brackets around the prompt. With the above setting on a system, your default prompt would look something like this:

```
[root@celery root]#
```

You could change the **PS1=** line to become a little simpler. For instance, if you wanted your prompt to simply read the hostname, but print the full path, your /etc/bashrc file would look like this:

```
# /etc/bashrc
# System wide functions and aliases
# Environment stuff goes in /etc/profile
# For some unknown reason bash refuses to inherit
# PS1 in some circumstances that I can't figure out.
# Putting PS1 here ensures that it gets loaded every time.
PS1='\h:\w\$'
```

This /etc/bashrc file would give you this prompt:

```
celery:~$
```

If you are in a directory other than the home directory, you would get

```
celery:/etc$
```

> *Note:* *You may have noticed the difference between the two /etc/bashrc files: One uses double quotation marks ("") around the options, and the other uses single quotation marks ("). The difference is in the way the output is handled. For example, typing echo "$HOME" prints your home directory, whereas typing echo '$HOME' at the prompt prints $HOME exactly.*

/etc/profile

The system administrator uses the /etc/profile script to set the global defaults for all users. The /etc/profile script is run by all bash users at login and calls scripts that are saved in /etc/profile.d/ upon system startup. The following is a sample /etc/profile script:

```
# /etc/profile

# System wide environment and startup programs
# Functions and aliases go in /etc/bashrc

PATH="$PATH:/usr/X11R6/bin"
PS1="[\u@\h \W]\\$ "

ulimit -c 1000000
if [ 'id -gn' = 'id -un' -a 'id -u' -gt 14 ]; then
        umask 002
else
        umask 022
fi

USER='id -un'
LOGNAME=$USER
MAIL="/var/spool/mail/$USER"

HOSTNAME='/bin/hostname'
HISTSIZE=1000
HISTFILESIZE=1000
```

```
INPUTRC=/etc/inputrc
export PATH PS1 HOSTNAME HISTSIZE HISTFILESIZE USER LOGNAME MAIL
INPUTRC

for i in /etc/profile.d/*.sh ; do
      if [ -x $i ]; then
                  . $i
      fi
done

unset i
```

The script starts with the default **PATH** and prompt settings. Next, it specifies the size limit of core files. It then determines the umask of the user shell by determining the user by the user id and whether the user is root. Next, the username, logname, and mail spools are set by determining the login user. Then, the hostname and history options are set. The **histsize** is the number of commands the history file will remember, and the **histfilesize** is the number of lines the history file can host. The next line specifies where the readline startup file is located. The rest of the script sets the options that use the **export** command, then runs any scripts located in the /etc/profile.d/ directory.

/etc/profile.d/

The /etc/profile.d/ directory contains any special scripts that the /etc/profile directory should use. This is important because it allows RPM (or you) to add scripts to the directory rather than having you edit the /etc/profile file. Some scripts that you may see in the /etc/profile.d/ directory set up kde, language, and other shell options. Here is a list of some sample scripts you might find in your /etc/profile.d/ directory:

➤ kde.csh

➤ kde.sh

➤ lang.sh

➤ mc.csh

➤ mc.sh

➤ profile

Practice Questions

Question 1

What script is run for setting bash global defaults for all users?

○ a. /etc/profile

○ b. /etc/bashrc

○ c. /etc/.bashrc

○ d. /etc/.profile

Answer a is correct.

Question 2

How can a user set up his own crontab file?

○ a. **vi /etc/crontab**

○ b. **crontab –e**

○ c. **vi /user/crontab**

○ d. **make cron**

Answer b is correct. Answer a is incorrect because it sets up root's crontab. Answers c and d are incorrect because they are invalid commands.

Question 3

What does the 0 0 1 1 * /home/kara/.happynewyear crontab entry do?

This entry in an /etc/crontab file runs the script .happynewyear from the /home/ kara directory on the first day of the first month of the year at the zero minute and zero hour.

Question 4

Which set of commands successfully compiles a new kernel?

○ a. **make mrproper, make config, make clean, make zImage, make modules_install, make lilo**

○ b. **make mrproper, make menuconfig, make bzImage, make modules, make modules_install**

○ c. **make xconfig, make clean, make dep, make bzImage, make modules, make modules_install**

○ d. **make mrproper dep clean bzImage modules modules_install**

Answer c is correct. Answer a is incorrect because it does not include the **make dep** and **make modules_install** options. In addition, **make lilo** is not valid. Answer b is incorrect because it does not include the **make clean** and **make dep** options. Answer d is incorrect because it has no .configure file to compile from because make **mrproper** deletes the current .config file.

Question 5

What format of partition tables does Linux use?

○ a. Linux

○ b. BSD

○ c. Unixware

○ d. DOS

Answer d is correct. Answer a is incorrect because it isn't a valid partition table format. Answer b is incorrect because BSD disklabels aren't used by Linux by default. Answer c is incorrect because Unixware slices aren't Linux defaults either.

Question 6

The **make menuconfig** option is a menu-driven tool that requires X video support.

○ a. True

○ b. False

Answer b is correct. The **make menuconfig** tool is menu driven, but doesn't require X support. The **make xconfig** command, however, does require such X support.

Question 7

> Who created the Linux kernel?
>
> ○ a. Linus Torvalds
>
> ○ b. Richard Stallman
>
> ○ c. Jon "maddog" Hall
>
> ○ d. Bill Gates

Answer a is correct. Answer b is incorrect because Richard Stallman created most of the GNU tools. Answer c is incorrect because Jon "maddog" Hall is the director of Linux International. Answer d is incorrect because Bill Gates was affiliated with Xenix back in the early '80s.

Question 8

> To halt a Linux system, what can you do?
>
> ○ a. Ctrl+Alt+Delete
>
> ○ b. **shutdown –h**
>
> ○ c. **shutdown –r now**
>
> ○ d. **init 0**

Answer d is correct. Answers a and c are incorrect because both reboot the system, not halt it. Answer b is incorrect because it isn't complete.

Question 9

> What is the main difference between runlevel 2 and runlevel 3?

Both runlevels 2 and 3 are multi-user runlevels. The biggest difference between the two is simply networking support. Runlevel 2 is full multi-user mode without networking, and runlevel 3 is full multi-user mode with networking support.

Question 10

What command is used to set user and group quotas?

○ a. **/usr/sbin/quota**

○ b. **/sbin/quotaon**

○ c. **/sbin/edquota**

○ d. **/sbin/usrquota**

Answer c is correct. Answers a and d are incorrect because they are not valid commands. Answer b is incorrect because it turns quotas on but doesn't set them up.

Task 1

Recompile your kernel. Use the different **make** configuration tools, such as **make config**, **make menuconfig**, and **make xconfig**, to discover how these **make** options differ and to decide which method you prefer.

Task 2

Set up two new kernels, one monolithic and one modular. Do you notice any differences?

Need To Know More?

Æleen Frisch. *Essential System Administration*, O'Reilly & Associates, Sebastopol, CA, 1995. ISBN:1-56592-127-5. Chapter 14 discusses Unix style boot processes and Chapter 15 discusses compiling a Linux kernel.

http://metalab.unc.edu/LDP/HOWTO/HOWTO-INDEX

The Linux Documentation Project provides an excellent resource on all aspects of Linux, including an entry regarding compiling Linux kernels.

9

X Window System

Terms you'll need to understand:

√ Graphical user interface (GUI)

√ Client/server relationship

√ Root window

√ Window manager

√ Terminal emulator

√ Desktop environment

√ Remote host

Techniques you'll need to master:

√ Understanding X client/server relationships

√ Selecting the proper XFree86 (XF86) server for specific hardware

√ Configuring an X server

√ Understanding desktop environments

√ Setting up remote X access

The X Window system is the GUI used when Linux is running. Most administration tools used on Linux have a GUI interface that can be used with the X Window system. Most administrators use the X Window system on their Red Hat Linux machines. Therefore, it is imperative that when you are studying for the RHCE 300 exam, you understand the X Window system, X servers, X clients, and remote X applications.

X Concepts

The X Window system is not a new concept. In fact, it has been implemented on several Unix systems before Linux was even created! One of the best explanations for where the X Window system came from can be found in the X Window system HOWTO, maintained by Ray Brigleb, found in the LDP (Linux Documentation Project, **http://metalab.unc.edu/LDP**). The HOWTO explains that the X Window system was developed in the Laboratory for Computer Science at the Massachusetts Institute of Technology and first released in 1984. The origins of X are based on the W Windowing package, developed by Paul Asente at Stanford.

The HOWTO continues to explain that in September 1987, MIT issued the first release of the X11 that we know and use today. As of X11R2, however, development and control passed from MIT to the X Consortium, formed in January 1988.

The X Window system is currently developed and distributed by the X.org. A liberal license permits the existence of free and low-cost implementations. Linux uses the XFree86 version of the X Window system. The XF86 version, which is freely distributable, is a collection of X servers for Unix-based operating systems on Intel x86 platforms. The work is derived from X386, and much of the new work is contributed back into the X11R6 project thereafter.

X Window System Components

The X Window system is made up of four main components that interact with one another to function: an X server, an X client, the X protocol, and an X window manager. We will discuss the server, client, and window managers later in this chapter.

You can establish the X Window system client/server relationship in two ways. Typically, on a Red Hat Linux system, the X client and X server are located on the same machine. In this scenario, the X application acts as the X client and the hardware display adapter acts as the X server. In other instances, especially within large Red Hat Linux networks, the client/server relationship is established between two separate machines—a physically separate X client and a separate X server.

With both client/server relationships, however, the X client makes requests to the X server. The X server responds by telling the X client how to draw the windows on the X client display. The X server's response translates the X client's request into hardware instructions, such as put a pixel here, change this pixel color there, do a screen refresh, and so on.

All the request and response exchanges between the X client and X server are carried over the X protocol, the X Window system's underlying network transparent protocol. The X protocol is used to enable programs to display graphic images on your monitor.

The traffic that is set up between the X client and X server does not simply work by itself between the client and server. In fact, an X window manager is required. The X window manager, of which there are several types, acts like "middle management" between the X client and X server.

X Server

The X server is responsible for listening for X client requests for hardware instructions about how to draw windows in a specific way on the X client. If the X server is running without a client that makes requests, your monitor has a gray pixel screen without any features or windows displayed. To understand the X Window system, and to pass the RHCE 300 exam, you must know about the various XF86 servers available and X configuration.

XFree86 Servers

Most Linux distributions use the XFree86 servers supplied by the XFree86 Project. The XFree86 Project, Inc. is a non-profit organization that produces XFree86, a freely distributable implementation of the X Window system that runs on Linux and other x86-based Unix based operating systems. The XFree86 Project currently has over 15 available XF86 servers. However, all of these servers will be combined into one with the release of XF86 version 4.0, scheduled for release later in 1999. Each server supports a specific type or family of video chipsets. Some of the most common servers are the FBDev, I128, Mach8, Mach32, Mach64, S3 Virge, SVGA, and VGA16. The majority of video cards used today use the SVGA, Mach64, and S3 XF86 servers.

> *Note:* *When all servers are compiled into one server with the release of XF86 version 4, individual chipset support will be modularized for use with the single XF86 server.*

To see if an XF86 server included in your Red Hat Linux distribution supports your video hardware, check Red Hat Software's hardware compatibility lists (http://www.redhat.com). For hardware support of other versions of XF86, visit **http://www.xfree86.org**, the Web site of the XFree86 Project, Inc. At this Web site, you can also download new versions of the XF86 server.

X Server Configuration

Setting up the X Window system involves many files, options, and settings. All the configuration files used for the X Window system, as well as several programs and configuration tools, are found in the /etc/X11/ directory. The most important programs and tools include **X** and **xinit**, as well as **Xconfigurator**, **XF86Setup**, and **xf86config** (discussed shortly).

The **X** file is actually a symlink to the X server you are using. The X server you are using is in the /usr/X11R6/bin/ directory. Therefore, if you were using the XF86_S3 X server, your **X** file could be symlinked to /usr/X11R6/bin/ XF86_S3.

The **xinit** program is used to start the X Window system. When executed without a specific client program indicated, **xinit** looks for a file named .xinitrc in the user's home directory. The .xinitrc file is a script used to start up client programs as the user has specified. If no .xinitrc is found in the user's home directory, **xinit** uses the following by default:

```
xterm -geometry +1+1 -n login -display :0
```

Xconfigurator

Xconfigurator is Red Hat's X Window system configuration program. To invoke this program, type "Xconfigurator" at the shell prompt. The **Xconfigurator** program creates a basic XF86Config file that is based on the selections you make within the menu interface. This XF86Config file (on Red Hat systems) is under /etc/X11 (which happens to be symlinked to from /usr/X11R6/lib/ X11).

When running Red Hat's **Xconfigurator**, you are presented with a menu-based screen with a blue, red, yellow, and gray color scheme (as was used during the Red Hat Linux installation). Figure 9.1 shows the interface used with **Xconfigurator**.

Xconfigurator has two modes of operation: interactive and kickstart. In interactive mode, **Xconfigurator** prompts you for the type of video card and monitor attached to the system. Some of this information may be automatically probed and filled in for you. However, if you apply an "--expert" option to **Xconfigurator**, you can override any probed values.

Figure 9.1 Red Hat's **Xconfigurator** program.

In kickstart mode, **Xconfigurator** tries to autoprobe all required information automatically. This is most useful when you are using PCI video cards because **Xconfigurator** typically autoprobes them properly. If no card is detected, you are prompted to select your video card manually.

XF86Setup

The **XF86Setup** program is the XFree86 Project's graphical user interface configuration tool. You usually use **XF86Setup** to initially set up the XF86 servers, or to adjust current configurations. To invoke the **XF86Setup** program, type "XF86Setup" at the shell prompt. When running, **XF86Setup** presents you with a gray, blue, and teal button-style interface that runs on a generic VGA16 server. Figure 9.2 shows **XF86Setup**'s interface.

As you can see in Figure 9.2, **XF86Setup** presents you with six buttons used for X Window system configuration. The first button, Mouse, allows you to configure your mouse settings. Within this menu, you can choose what type of mouse protocol to use (such as PS/2, Microsoft, Logitech, and so on) and other mouse options such as the mouse device (/dev/ttyX or /dev/psanx) and button settings.

Figure 9.2 **XF86Setup** interface.

The second button option in the **XF86Setup** window is Keyboard. This menu presents you with options to select your keyboard model and language. In addition, you can select options such as Shift/Lock behavior and the position of your Control key.

The third button option in the **XF86Setup** window is Card. This menu allows you to choose which type of XF86 server to use In addition, you are presented with options to select specific chipsets, RamDac options, ClockChip, and any other options you would like to have automatically added to the XF86Config file.

The fourth option in the **XF86Setup** window is Monitor. This menu allows you to select your monitor type as well as horizontal and vertical sync rates. It lists many common monitor settings that automatically set the horizontal and vertical sync rates. If you know your monitor's capabilities, or if your monitor is not listed, you must specify the horizontal and vertical sync rates manually at the top of the screen. Figure 9.3 shows the monitor configuration interface for **XF86Setup**.

The fifth button in the **XF86Setup** window is Modeselection. This menu allows you to configure your display resolution and color depth. You can select one of several resolutions (the options differ depending on what server and monitor you choose) that range from (and beyond) 320×200 to 1600×1200. You can also choose at what color depth you want to run the X Window system. Some options include 8bpp (bits per pixel), 16bpp, 24bpp, and 32bpp. If you attempt to select any option that your card or monitor does not support, you receive an error and are then automatically returned to the configuration menu.

The final button on the **XF86Setup** window is Other. This menu allows you to select optional server settings. Some of the options available include enabling

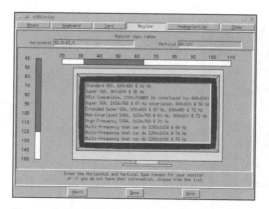

Figure 9.3   **XF86Setup**'s monitor configuration.

the hotkey sequence (Ctrl+Alt+Back Space) to kill the XF86 server, enabling video mode switching, and allowing changes from other hosts.

xf86config

The **xf86config** program is a text-based configuration tool that is used to configure the XF86Config file. To invoke **xf86config**, type "xf86config" at a root prompt.

With the **xf86config** tool, you are prompted to configure your mouse, keyboard, card, and monitor settings with a text-based prompt method. Each of the options prompts you with a list of available numbered options for selection, or for a yes or no answer. The **xf86config** tool is the least used tool for configuring the X Window system. Figure 9.4 shows an example of the **xf86config** tool interface.

X Client

An X client is the software that sends requests to the X server. The response from the X server is then displayed on the X client. An X client can be either the software on the same machine as the X server, or on a remote host. We will discuss the remote X applications later in this chapter.

A special type of X client is the desktop client. The desktop client is actually a window manager that controls how the title bar, task bar, and other features of a window are handled.

The standard X desktop is made up of many services and programs, which vary depending on what window manager or environment you use. However, several standard terms and applications apply. When using an X client, you should be aware of the following terms and their differences:

Figure 9.4 The **xf86config** interface.

➤ **screen**   Your whole desktop. The terms "screen" and "desktop" are often interchanged. Technically, the screen is the primary video display with which you view your X Window system.

➤ **root window**   The background of your screen. The root window doesn't have any of the standard characteristics of any other window, but it does have some unique applications. The root window is where you can customize your background images and so on.

➤ **window manager**   The main interface between the X Window system and the user. The window manager provides functionality such as window borders, menus, icons, desktops, button, and toolbars, and it allows the user to customize them all. We will discuss the various window managers later in this chapter.

➤ **pointer**   The arrow or other indicator that represents the location of your mouse, trackball, glide point, or other pointing device that corresponds to the location on the screen. Quite often, the shape, color, or size of the pointer changes to indicate that the mouse has a particular function on that specific area of the screen.

➤ **window**   A frame where any given application resides and is managed by the window manager. The active window, the window you are currently using on your desktop, is usually indicated by being on top, in focus, or highlighted compared to the inactive windows on the screen.

➤ **terminal emulator**   A window with just text that basically emulates a console. One example of a terminal emulator is an xterm.

Window Managers

Many window managers—such as AfterStep, Enlightenment, fvwm, and Window Maker—are available for use with your X client. You should not confuse window managers with desktop environments, such as GNU Network Object Model (GNOME) and K Desktop Environment (KDE). We will discuss these desktop environments later in this chapter.

AfterStep

AfterStep, shown in Figure 9.5, was originally designed to look and feel like the NeXTStep interface used on NeXT machines before Apple bought the company.

Figure 9.5   AfterStep's desktop.

Enlightenment

Unlike AfterStep or a few of the other window managers, Enlightenment, shown in Figure 9.6, is not modeled to look or feel like any existing window manager or other operating system environment. It is a highly graphical window manager that is developed and changed often.

> *Note: This window manager is not recommended for users of machines with low memory resources or disk space.*

fvwm

The fvwm window manager, shown in Figure 9.7, is one of the oldest window managers available for Linux. It is very small compared to some of the newer ones, such as Enlightenment, and requires less memory and fewer CPU resources. You can configure the fvwm window manager to look like Motif or even Windows 95.

Window Maker

Window Maker, shown in Figure 9.8, is another window manager modeled to look like NeXTStep. Window Maker is designed to give additional integration support for GNUstep applications. Window Maker is relatively fast, easy to use, and popular amongst many Linux users.

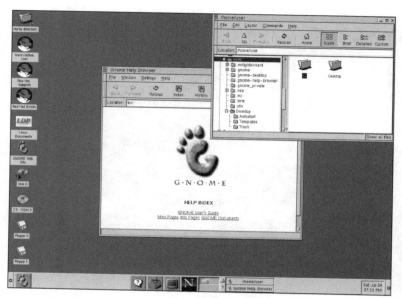

Figure 9.6 Enlightenment and GNOME.

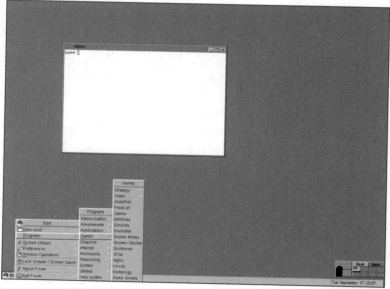

Figure 9.7 fvwm.

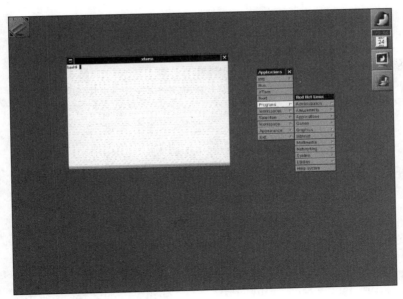

Figure 9.8   Window Maker.

X Server Tools, Tips, And Tricks

Various tools, tips, and tricks are available to assist you in managing and configuring your window manager options. For example, you can set up your Red Hat Linux 6.0 installation to automatically boot into your favorite window manager by default. To do this (assuming you didn't select the window manager during installation), edit your /etc/inittab file. To automatically start into your window manager, you must set your /etc/inittab file to boot into runlevel 5. You set this in one of the first options in the file, in the string

```
id:X:initdefault:
```

where *X* is the default runlevel at boot. To automatically boot into runlevel 5, this configuration string should read

```
id:5:initdefault:
```

If you are running in runlevel 3 (console mode), you have two options to run the X Window system. You can either boot into runlevel 5 with the **init 5** command, or simply start the X Window system using **startx**. Typically, **startx** is the preferred method for starting the X Window system from the console.

The shell script used to specify a user's display manager (gdm, kdm, or xdm) is **Xsession**. The default **Xsession** script, located in the /etc/X11/xdm/ directory, is used if the user does not have an .xsession file or .Xclients file in his home directory. The .xsession and .Xclients files are used to specify certain display environments or window managers for the user, typically if the user wishes his setup to be different from the default system setup. The script used to execute the window manager is **xinitrc**. If a user has an .xinitrc in his home directory, his personal startup script is used. Otherwise, the default, **/etc/X11/xinit/xinitrc**, is used.

If present in a user's home directory, the .xsession, .xinitrc, and .Xclients files must all have the appropriate permissions set before they can be used. Therefore, all three of these files should have the executable permission set (**chmod +x**).

A final trick for helping to manage window managers is a tool called **switchdesk**. If you want to change your window manager the next time you start your X Window session, the **switchdesk** program prompts you for the new window manager. To invoke this program, type "switchdesk" at a shell prompt. The **switchdesk** program automatically creates an .Xclients-default that specifies what window manager or environment to run.

Desktop Environments

Over the past couple of years, window managers have escalated to becoming integrated with entire desktop environments. Desktop environments control not only the look and feel of your desktop, but also the tools and applications that are available for your desktop. The two main desktop environments shipped with Red Hat Linux are GNOME and KDE.

GNOME

GNOME is based on CORBA and allows programmers to import and export component type resources of their choice. This means that a program can use any editor it needed as long as the editor supports a standard interface via CORBA. Currently, the GNOME development project is partially funded by RHAD Labs, a division of Red Hat Software, Inc.

GNOME is used primarily as a base desktop environment for other window managers. By default, window managers such as Enlightenment and Window Maker use GNOME as the base environment. In addition to the styles and tools that the window managers add, GNOME offers several GNOME utilities to make the desktop more user-friendly. GNOME is based on the GTK+ (GIMP tool kit).

One of GNOME's tools is the GNOME Midnight Commander (GMC). GMC is a file manager. This manager allows capabilities such as drag and drop to the desktop features and file browsing similar to the Windows Explorer. Another tool GNOME uses is GDM, the GNOME Display Manager. GDM is more robust than the default X Display Manager (XDM). GDM allows the user to login to GNOME, KDE, or AnotherLevel. GDM allows the user to change the environment choice at login. GDM also provides a failsafe mode in case a problem occurs in the user environment, by bringing up an xterm to bypass the window manager.

KDE

Unlike GNOME, KDE has a built-in window manager. You can, however, use KDE with other window managers including AfterStep, Enlightenment, and Window Maker. KDE is based on the Qt toolkit, developed by the Norwegian-based company Troll Tech. Figure 9.9 shows a KDE desktop using the default KDE window manager.

KDE incorporates many KDE tools, applications, and functionality to the window manager. KDE incorporates KDE File Manager (KFM). Like GMC, KFM provides drag and drop functionality to the desktop, provides an Explorer-style file manager, and has incorporated Web-browsing functionality. Like GNOME, KDE has its own display manager, called KDE Display Manager (KDM).

Other programs that are available for KDE include applications such as killustrator and klyx. The killustrator program is a vector-based graphics program similar

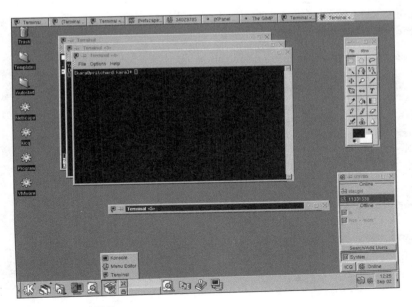

Figure 9.9 KDE.

to Adobe Illustrator or Corel Draw. The klyx program is a modern approach to writing documents with a computer based on LyX formatting. Some popular information management tools available for KDE include kalendar and korganizer. The kalendar program is a simple KDE-based calendar and to-do-list manager. The korganizer is a bit more complex program that involves a calendar and appointment manager similar to those of Microsoft Outlook and Netscape's NSCAL. You can find many additional applications for KDE at www.kde.org.

Remote X Applications

A very popular feature of the X Window system is that it can display an X application on a remote host, as mentioned earlier in this chapter. X is an entirely network-transparent system that can provide seamless access from one workstation to another that is running applications. This is even possible to display to other machines, even if the other machine is not running the same operating system! To set up such access, you must use a host authentication program, such as **xhost** or **xauth**, and use the command to export the DISPLAY environment variable, such as **export DISPLAY= remotehost:0**.

Setting Up Remote Access

You use the **xhost** program to grant permission to host applications to other machines. Using **xhost** is simple. To enable permission to display remote applications, use **xhost +***remotehost*. To disable permission to display remote applications, use **xhost −***remotehost*.

To display a shell to another host, use this string:

```
export DISPLAY=remotemachine:0.0
```

After this string is executed, that shell's display is set to the remote machine specified. Any commands executed in that shell are then displayed to the remote machine.

To display a single command to another host, use the

```
command DISPLAY=remotemachine:0 command
```

command, where *remotemachine* is the machine that the application is to be displayed to, and *command* is the command to be exported to the remote machine.

Practice Questions

Question 1

How do you display a single X application to a remote X host?

- ○ a. **DISPLAY=remoteXhost:0 application**
- ○ b. **export DISPLAY=remoteXhost:0.0**
- ○ c. **export xeyes:remoteXhost :0**
- ○ d. None of the above

Answer a is correct. Answer a instructs the machine to display *application* to the *remoteXhost*. Answer b is incorrect because it simply changes the **DISPLAY** variable to the remoteXhost and doesn't send any applications. Answer c is incorrect because it is not a valid option.

Question 2

What is one of the biggest differences between GNOME and KDE?

- ○ a. One is a window manager and the other is a desktop environment.
- ○ b. GNOME is an operating system, and KDE is a desktop environment.
- ○ c. GNOME is an application, and KDE is a desktop environment.
- ○ d. GNOME is based on GTK+, and KDE is based on Qt.

Answer d is correct. GNOME and KDE are based on different tool kits; GNOME is based on GTK+, and KDE is based on Qt. Answer a is incorrect because both GNOME and KDE are desktop environments, although KDE has a built-in window manager as well. Answer b is incorrect because GNOME is not an operating system. Answer c is incorrect because GNOME is not an application.

Question 3

> What tool allows you to change your default X Window desktop manager?
>
> ○ a. **xinitrc**
>
> ○ b. **switchdesk**
>
> ○ c. **Xchange**
>
> ○ d. All of the above

Answer b is correct. The **switchdesk** tool allows you to specify which installed window manager or desktop environment to use by default the next time you run X. Answer a is incorrect because **xinitrc** is the script that executes the X Window system. Answer c is incorrect because **Xchange** is not a valid option.

Question 4

> In what file can you specify to boot into the X Window system by default?
>
> ○ a. Xdefaults
>
> ○ b. xinitrc
>
> ○ c. /etc/inittab
>
> ○ d. .xdefaults

Answer c is correct. In the /etc/inittab file, you can specify the default runlevel in the string **id:5:initdefault:**. Answers a and b are incorrect because they are used when starting the X Window system, not to specify boot-time options. Answer d is incorrect because it is not a valid option.

Question 5

> What is the difference between a window and a terminal emulator?
>
> _____

A terminal emulator is a type of window. The difference simply is that a window can display either an X application or a terminal emulator, but a terminal emulator displays only text-based tools and command lines.

Question 6

What X interfaced tool is available for configuring the X Window system?

- ○ a. **XF86Setup**
- ○ b. **Xconfigurator**
- ○ c. **xf86config**
- ○ d. All of the above

Answer a is correct. **XF86Setup** is an X-based tool that invokes a minimum X server, allowing you to use X-based button-style tools to configure the XF86 configuration. Although answers b and c configure the X Window system, they are not X-based tools. Therefore, they are incorrect.

Question 7

What project is currently developing X server support?

- ○ a. RHAD Labs
- ○ b. XFree86 Project, Inc.
- ○ c. GNOME Project
- ○ d. None of the above

Answer b is correct. XFree86 Project, Inc. is primarily responsible for the development of the XF86 X server and support. Answer a is incorrect because RHAD Labs is a division of Red Hat Software. Answer c is incorrect because the GNOME Project is responsible for the development of the GNOME desktop environment, not X server support.

Question 8

What is the difference between an X client and an X server?

The X client is the software located either on a remote machine or the same machine that sends X display requests to the X server. The X server is the hardware server responsible for responding to drawing requests from the X client.

Question 9

> The XFree86 Project develops only the X Window system for Linux.
>
> ○ a. True
>
> ○ b. False

Answer b is correct. The XFree86 Project is developing X Window system support for all Unix-based operating systems.

Task 1

Set up your X Window system by using each of the available X tools mentioned in this chapter. After setting up a specific window manager, use **switchdesk** to set your window manager default to another available window manager. View the .Xclients-default file and see what changes were made. Manually edit this file to reflect your original window manager setting. Restart your X session. Did your preferred window manager return?

Task 2

Set up another machine on your network. Set the remote machine to accept remote applications from your machine. Display **xeyes** to the other host. What happened? Login to the other host and display an **xterm** back to your machine. Type "xcalc" in the new xterm displayed on your machine. What happened?

Need To Know More?

 Mui, Linda and Eric Pearce. *X Window System Administrators Guide*, O'Reilly & Associates, 1992. ISBN 0-93717-5838. This book discusses the issues of system administration for X and X-based networks.

 Pennington, Havoc. *GTK+/GNOME Development*, New Riders Publishing, 1999. ISBN 0-73570-0788. This book (scheduled for release in Fall 1999) discusses details involving GTK_ and GNOME development.

 Wells, Nicholas. *Using KDE*, Que, 1999. ISBN 0-78972-2143. This book (scheduled for release in Fall 1999) discusses skills required for programming with KDE and related skills to achieve advanced-level knowledge required for administering KDE.

 http://metalab.unc.edu/LDP/HOWTO/HOWTO-INDEX-3.html

This is the Linux Documentation Project Web site, whose links to X, X Window system, and XFree86 supply the latest information regarding the X Window system.

 http://www.afterstep.org/

This is the AfterStep Web site, which shows the latest developments for the AfterStep window manager.

 http://www.enlightenment.org/

This is the Enlightenment Web site, which shows current development and documentation for the popular Enlightenment window manager.

 http://www.gnome.org/

This is the GNOME Web site, which shows the latest development, documentation, and applications for the GNOME environment.

 http://www.kde.org/

This is the KDE Web site, which shows current development of the KDE environment, and contains links to many applications developed for KDE.

http://www.windowmaker.org/

This is the Window Maker Web site, which shows the latest development and documentation for the window manager Window Maker.

 http://www.xfree86.org/

This is the XFree86 Project, Inc. Web site, which gives the latest information, documentation, and drivers for the X Window system.

Standard Networking Services

Terms you'll need to understand:

√ Web server

√ Hyper Text Transfer Protocol

√ Virtual hosts

√ Mail agents

√ Domain Name Service

√ Forward and reverse DNS

√ File Transfer Protocol

√ Dynamic Host Configuration Protocol

√ Proxy Server

Techniques you'll need to master:

√ Configuring an Apache Web server

√ Configuring virtual hosts

√ Using Sendmail

√ Configuring and using DNS (BIND)

√ Configuring DNS entries

√ Setting up anonymous FTP servers

√ Setting up and using NFS

√ Setting up Windows client file sharing

√ Setting up and using DHCP

The largest portion of the RHCE 300 exams centers on setting up Red Hat Linux networking services. The reason for such focus is that the greatest percentage of Red Hat Linux machines are installed to be used as either a client or a server on a network. Networking support is the strongest feature and most common use of Linux. To be not only successful on the RHCE 300 exam, but also successful as an RHCE, you must be comfortable with installing, configuring, and using many Linux networking services. In this chapter, we will discuss Apache, email, Domain Name Services (DNS), File Transfer Protocol (FTP), Network File Systems (NFS), Samba (SMB), the Dynamic Host Configuration Protocol (DHCP), time services, and the Squid proxy server.

Apache

Apache is the world's most popular Hypertext Transport Protocol (HTTP) server in the world, running on more than 55 percent of the world's Web servers. Apache was based originally on the most popular Web server in 1995, NCSA's httpd 1.3. As the first version of Apache was simply different patches applied to NCSA's httpd, Apache was often referred to as "a patchy server," which is how Apache got its name (A+PAtCHy). In this section, we will discuss how to set up Apache, and how to set up virtual Apache hosts.

Setting Up Apache

Red Hat Linux 6.0 is shipped with Apache 1.3. You can install it either during the installation of Red Hat Linux, or by installing the RPM file apache-1.3.6-7.i386.rpm which is located on your Red Hat Linux 6.0 CD in the /RedHat/RPMS directory.

The installation of Apache places all the appropriate configuration files in the /etc/httpd/conf/ directory. There are three main configuration files found in the /etc/httpd/conf/ directory. They include access.conf, httpd.conf, and srm.conf.

access.conf

The access.conf file is the global access configuration file, which defines what and when services are allowed to be executed. Listing 10.1 is a sample access.conf file, with a majority of the comments removed from the code.

Listing 10.1   The access.conf file.

```
##
## access.conf -- Apache HTTP server configuration file
##
<Directory />
```

```
Options None
AllowOverride None
</Directory>
# Note that from this point forward you must specifically allow
# particular features to be enabled - so if something's not working
# as you might expect, make sure that you have specifically enabled
# it below.

<Directory /home/httpd/html>

# This may also be "None", "All", or any combination of "Indexes",
# "Includes", "FollowSymLinks", "ExecCGI", or "MultiViews".

Options Indexes Includes FollowSymLinks

# This controls which options the .htaccess files in directories
# can override. Can also be "All", or any combination of "Options",
# "FileInfo", "AuthConfig", and "Limit"

AllowOverride None

# Controls who can get stuff from this server.

order allow,deny
allow from all

</Directory>

# /home/httpd/cgi-bin should be changed to whatever your
# ScriptAliased CGI directory exists, if you have that configured.

<Directory /home/httpd/cgi-bin>
AllowOverride None
Options ExecCGI
</Directory>

#<Location /server-status>
#SetHandler server-status

#order deny,allow
#deny from all
#allow from .your_domain.com
#</Location>

# Allow access to local system documentation from localhost
Alias /doc /usr/doc
<Directory /usr/doc>
```

```
order deny,allow
deny from all
allow from localhost
Options Indexes FollowSymLinks
</Directory>

#<Location /cgi-bin/phf*>
#deny from all
#ErrorDocument 403 http://phf.apache.org/phf_abuse_log.cgi
#</Location>
```

A few of the most important lines in the access.conf file are highlighted in Listing 10.1. The first highlighted line of code specifies the **document root** location. The **document root** is the directory on the Web server where the HTML files for hosted Web sites are located.

The second set of highlighted lines specifies who can access your Web files. This is achieved by using **deny** and **allow** entries. With **deny** and **allow** entries, you can use either specific domains or IP addresses to specify whether they can (using **allow**) or cannot (using **deny**) access the documents. For instance, specifying **deny redhat.com** would not allow any users from redhat.com to access your Web files. You can also use generic terms such as **from all**. Specifying **allow from all** would allow all users to access your Web files.

 You must specify to "allow from all" if you want to grant to all users access to your Web files. If no entry to allow is here, all users will get "access denied" errors when trying to access your Web files.

httpd.conf

The /etc/httpd/conf/httpd.conf file is the main httpd server configuration file. The entries in the httpd.conf file often refer to the entries in both the srm.conf and access.conf files to properly configure Apache. The following section will display snippets of code from the httpd.conf file and what they are used for.

Note: The httpd.conf file is extensive. Only sections that are imperative to successfully configuring Apache for the RHCE 300 exam are shown here.

```
# ServerType is either inetd, or standalone.
ServerType standalone

# Port: The port the standalone listens to. For ports < 1023, you
# will need httpd to be run as root initially.

Port 80
```

This snippet of code specifies whether to run **httpd** standalone or through **inetd**, and what port on the server **httpd** should listen from if the server runs standalone. The default setting for Apache is to run the server standalone. Running the server through **inetd** is not advised as it causes **inetd** to **fork()** repeatedly, with each **fork()** running its own instance of **httpd**. This causes the Web server to be very slow. With standalone servers, you must also specify what server **httpd** should listen on. The default setting is port 80.

```
ServerAdmin root@localhost
```

This line of code assigns the email address that **httpd** emails if there are any errors or other problem information. The default setting is root@localhost. The following code snippet of the httpd.conf file is the location of the error log file where **httpd** can log any errors it receives. The default setting for this option is logs/error_log:

```
# ErrorLog: The location of the error log file. If this does not
# start with /, ServerRoot is prepended to it.
```

```
ErrorLog logs/error_log
```

The following line from httpd.conf sets the number of seconds before **httpd** send and receive requests time out. The numeric setting is set in seconds:

```
# Timeout: The number of seconds before receives and sends time out
```

```
Timeout 300
```

The following options are used when running the Apache server as standalone:

```
# Server-pool size regulation.  Rather than making you guess how
# many server processes you need, Apache dynamically adapts to the
# load it sees -- that is, it tries to maintain enough server
# processes to handle the current load, plus a few spare servers to
# handle  transient load spikes (e.g., multiple simultaneous
# requests from a  single Netscape browser).
```

```
# It does this by periodically checking how many servers are waiting
# for a request.  If there are fewer than MinSpareServers, it creates
# a new spare.  If there are more than MaxSpareServers, some of the
# spares die off.  These values are probably OK for most sites --
```

```
MinSpareServers 8
MaxSpareServers 20
```

The settings set how many spare **httpd** servers are running at any given moment. These spare servers are used to handle sudden rushes of requests, or other spikes of http traffic. The MinSpareServers setting sets the minimum number of spares to have at any given moment. The MaxSpareServers setting sets the maximum number of spares to have at any given moment. The following options also regulate the number of **httpd** servers running:

```
StartServers 10

# Limit on total number of servers running, i.e., limit on the
# number of clients who can simultaneously connect -- if this limit
# is ever reached, clients will be LOCKED OUT, so it should NOT BE
# SET TOO LOW. It is intended mainly as a brake to keep a runaway
# server from taking Unix with it as it spirals down...

MaxClients 150
```

The StartServers option sets how many servers to start Apache with. The MaxClients option is a little more important, as it sets the maximum number of running servers. This limits the number of clients who can simultaneously connect to your server. Therefore, you should not set this option too low, but keep the number reasonable enough to keep your Web server from crashing. Within the following eight lines, you can set up the virtual hosts on your Apache server:

```
NameVirtualHost 127.0.0.1
<VirtualHost www.test.com>
ServerAdmin webmaster@test.com
DocumentRoot /home/httpd/html/virtual/www.test.com
ServerName www.test.com
ErrorLog logs/www.test.com-error_log
TransferLog logs/www.test.com-access_log
</VirtualHost>
```

 This section is the most important section concerning setting up domains and Web sites on your Apache server!

We will discuss the use of virtual hosts more thoroughly in the next section of this chapter, titled "Virtual Hosts." The first line in the above code specifies the use of NameVirtualHost. This setting is usually either the main domain name of the machine, or the IP address that the Apache server is listening on. The NameVirtualHost is only required for entries on a machine that is using a single IP address for multiple domains.

The second line is the ServerAdmin entry. The ServerAdmin setting sets the email address for **httpd** to email if there are any **httpd** errors with the specific domain or IP. This is often set to root@localhost, and the mail is sent directly to the root account on the Web server. If you don't check root's email, however, you should set this to an appropriate email account you read.

The third line is <VirtualHost *xxx.xx.xxx* >. The VirtualHost setting specifies the new VirtualHost entry. The setting for this option (which replaces the *xxx.xx.xxx* in the preceding line) is typically either the full domain name for the site (**www.domain.com**) or the domain's IP address (192.168.0.1). The end of this VirtualHost entry is specified in the last line by </VirtualHost>.

The fifth line specifies the DocumentRoot entry. The Document Root is the location of the files on the Apache server for the particular entry's Web pages and data. Many times administrators use a single main directory for all Web pages, such as /home/html/, and then create a directory under the /home/ html/ directory for each domain. In this case, the DocumentRoot would be set to /home/html/*domain*. Other times administrators link the DocumentRoot into a user's home directory, and create a directory under the user's home directory to contain the documents. In this case, DocumetRoot would be set to / home/*user/domain* or something similar, where *user* is the username, and *domain* is the directory containing the domain HTML and Web data.

The fifth line specifies the ServerName entry. The ServerName is the full domain name of the particular Web site. This entry should always be set to the full domain name, such as **www.test.com, web.test.com, another.test.com**, or whatever the user enters in his browser to retrieve this site.

The sixth line specifics the location for the ErrorLog. The ErrorLog is the log where **httpd** stores any error messages received for that address. Many administrators place all their logs under a main "logs" directory. Therefore, an appropriate setting for ErrorLog would be **ErrorLog logs/www.test.com/ error_log**.

Entries and settings in any of the /etc/httpd/conf/ files use standard Linux rules for paths. For instance, logs/www.test.com/ error_log would assume the full path /home/httpd/conf/logs/ www.test.com/error_log, whereas an entry such as /logs/www .test.com/error_log would assume the simple path /logs/www.test .com/error_log. Notice the difference in the first character (/) pointing to an absolute path, and the absence of the character (/) pointing to a path relative to ServerRoot.

The seventh line specifies the location for the TransferLog. The TransferLog is the log where **httpd** stores all the access information for the particular Web site. If the administrator is keeping all the logs underneath a default "logs" directory as mentioned previously, a valid setting for this would be **TransferLog logs/www.test.com/access_log**.

srm.conf

The srm.conf file defines the name space the users see for the **httpd** services. The file also specifies other server defined file and mime types. The srm.conf file is quite lengthy. The following code lines are excerpts from the srm.conf file that are necessary for both setting up Apache properly and passing the RHCE 3000 exam. This entry in srm.conf specifies the DocumentRoot for the system:

```
DocumentRoot /home/httpd/html
```

This setting is the directory you will use to serve your Web documents. By default, all requests are taken from the /home/httpd/html/ directory, but symbolic links and aliases may be used to point to other locations. This entry from the srm.conf file specifies the User Directory:

```
UserDir public_html
```

The User Directory is used when the system receives a request for a *~user*, where *user* is a user on the Web server. The request is then routed to look in the public_html directory within the user's home directory (by default). This entry from the srm.conf file specifies the DirectoryIndex:

```
DirectoryIndex index.html index.shtml index.cgi
```

The DirectoryIndex is the default file that is automatically assumed to be loaded first within the Web directory. This means that if you go to **www.test.com**, **httpd** will look in the Document Root directory and automatically load the file named index.html, index.shtml, or index.cgi (whichever is present), as specified by the DirectoryIndex listing. The index.html, and so on, are the default options. If you wish to change this, or add files such as home.html, you would change this entry.

> *Note:* *After configuring Apache, or making changes, such as adding virtual hosts, you must restart **httpd** before your changes go into effect. To restart **httpd**, use the **restart** option by running /etc/rc.d/init.d/httpd restart.*

Virtual Hosts

As discussed in the previous section, virtual hosts are configured in the httpd.conf file. Virtual hosts are all the entries for enabling different hosts to be hosted on the same machine. Originally, Web servers could typically only host a single domain on a single machine. Though other Web servers were developing methods to host multiple hosts on a single server, Apache was the first to develop a simple interface to accomplish hosting multiple domains on a single machine. The concept of having more than one host on a single machine is called virtual hosting.

During early development of virtual hosting, Apache required individual IP addresses to be assigned to each host. Now Apache allows you to configure multiple hosts to share the exact same IP address. This means two domains could be assigned the exact same IP address, but have individual Web sites.

Configuring Virtual Hosts

Once you have Apache configured properly, there are eight simple steps to configure your virtual hosts by editing the httpd.conf file:

1. Set NameVirtualHost. The NameVirtualHost setting is only required when setting up virtual hosts with the same IP address. If you have individual IP addresses for each host, skip this step. The setting for NameVirtualHost can be either name-based (**www.example.com**), or IP-based (192.168.0.1). Use this setting to specify to **httpd** that there are multiple hosts under the specific name (**www.domain.com**), or IP (192.168.0.1). VirtualHost entries under the NameVirtualHost directive are then indexed by the ServerName setting. A request for an IP or domain listed under the NameVirtualHost directive will be matched by ServerName and the appropriate DocumentRoot settings. For example, **NameVirtualHost 192.168.0.1**.

2. Set VirtualHost. The setting for the VirtualHost can be either name-based (**www.example.com**), or IP-based (192.168.0.1). Administrators typically prefer to used name-based settings. This allows the administrator to change IP addresses for the host in DNS without having to change the httpd.conf file. Make sure you have registered the domain and set up DNS to ensure this option works properly. For example, **<VirtualHost www.example.com>**.

3. Set DocumentRoot. The setting for DocumentRoot points to the directory where the Web documents for the host can be found. This may point to a subdirectory for the host under a larger dedicated directory such as /home/httpd/*domain*, or to a dedicated subdirectory located

under a user's home directory such as /home/*user*/*domain*, or anywhere else you prefer. Within this dedicated directory, you should put any HTML or other Web files required for the Web site. Make sure the DocumentRoot directory, subdirectories, and files are world readable and executable (with permissions set to at least 755 for directories and 644 for files). For example, **DocumentRoot/home/exampleadmin/ example/**.

4. Set ServerName. The setting for ServerName is the name-based reference used by Web browsers to request your host's Web site. For instance, if a user would put **http://www.example.com/** to access your Web site, your ServerName would be **www.test.com** . This option is especially important when sharing IP addresses among hosts. For example, **ServerName www.example.com**.

5. Set ErrorLog. The setting for ErrorLog is to set the directory and file for **httpd** to store any errors for the specific host. By default, this setting is set for logs/*www.domain.com*/error_log. For example, **ErrorLog logs/ www.example.com/error_log**.

6. Set TransferLog. The setting for TransferLog is set to the directory and file for **httpd** to log all access information for the host. The default setting for the TransferLog is **logs/***www.example.com***/access_log**. For example, **TransferLog logs/www.example.com/error_log**.

7. Close VirtualHost Entry. To specify the end of the particular virtual host entry, you must close it by supplying the </VirtualHost> option as the last line of the virtual host entry. For example, **</VirtualHost>**.

8. Save and restart. Save the changes to the httpd.conf file, and restart httpd (*not* your system). To restart **httpd**, type **/etc/rc.d/init.d/httpd restart**.

There are several other options available to customize your individual virtual host entries. Three specific ones include the settings for Alias, Redirect, and ServerAlias:

➤ **Alias** */sublocation* /*alternate_document_root*   Using the Alias setting allows you to set an alternative DocumentRoot file for a path below your host. For instance, if you would like to have one DocumentRoot for **www.example.com,** but have an entirely different DocumentRoot for **www.example.com/example/,** you could supply the Alias option within the **www.example.com** virtual host entry to point /example to another directory for its Web files. For example, **Alias /example /home/test/ example**.

> ➤ Redirect */sublocation http://other.new.location*   Using the Redirect
> setting allows you to specify an alternative location for a subdirectory
> under the specific virtual host entry. For instance, if you want **www.**
> **example.com**/somewhere to redirect to www.somewhere.org, you could
> add the Redirect option to the virtual host entry for **www.example.com**.
> For example, **Redirect /somewhere http://www.somewhere.com**.

> ➤ ServerAlias *example.com *.example.com*   Using the ServerAlias setting
> allows you to specify additional ServerNames that could be used to
> access the same Web data. For example you could set the ServerAlias
> setting in the www.example.com virtual host entry to allow users to
> access not only **http://www.example.com**, but **http://example.com**, and
> **http://web.example.com/**. For example, **ServerAlias example.com**
> ***example.com**.

Sample Virtual Host Scenario

To better understand the layout of the virtual host entries in the httpd.conf
file, please consider the following scenario, and view the following snippet of
the example scenario httpd.conf file.

Scenario

Your Web server has been assigned three IP addresses. They include 123.12.12.1,
123.12.12.2, and 123.12.12.3. You want to host five domains. They include www
.choc.com, www.bar.net, www.baz.org, www.test.com, and www.iluvlinus.com.
You decide to assign www.choc.com its own IP address of 123.12.12.1. You
decide to share 123.12.12.2 with both www.bar.net and www.baz.org. You also
decide to share 123.12.12.3 with both www.test.com and www.iluvlinus.com.
You want each host to have its files in a home directory dedicated to a user
with the same host name (meaning choc, bar, baz, test, and iluvlinus) in a
directory named web. You decide to leave the logs in the standard location
beneath the logs directory under /etc/httpd/conf/. Notice you only need to use
the NameVirtualHost once above the entries that are sharing the specified IP.
(This IP setting can be replaced with a domain name whose address resolves to
the shared IP address.) Listing 10.2 lists the sample Virtual Hosts entries mentioned in the above scenario.

Listing 10.2   Virtual hosts entries in httpd.conf.

```
<VirtualHost www.choc.com>
DocumentRoot /home/choc/web
ServerName www.choc.com
ErrorLog logs/www.choc.com/error_log
```

```
TransferLog logs/www.choc.com/access_log
</VirtualHost>

NameVirtualHost 123.12.12.2
<VirtualHost www.bar.net>
DocumentRoot /home/bar/web
ServerName www.bar.net
ErrorLog logs/www.bar.net/error_log
TransferLog logs/www.bar.net/access_log
</VirtualHost>

<VirtualHost www.baz.org>
DocumentRoot /home/baz/web
ServerName www.baz.org
ErrorLog logs/www.baz.org/error_log
TransferLog logs/www.baz.org/access_log
</VirtualHost>

NameVirtualHost 123.12.12.3
<VirtualHost www.test.com>
DocumentRoot /home/test/web
ServerName www.test.com
ErrorLog logs/www.test.com/error_log
TransferLog logs/www.test.com/access_log
</VirtualHost>

<VirtualHost www.iluvlinus.com>
DocumentRoot /home/iluvlinus/web
ServerName www.iluvlinus.com
ErrorLog logs/www.iluvlinus.com/error_log
TransferLog logs/www.iluvlinus.com/access_log
</VirtualHost>
```

Email Services

Email services comprise three main parts: the Mail Transport Agent (MTA), the Mail Delivery Agent (MDA), and Mail User Agent (MUA). The MTA is responsible for the physical sending and receiving of user and system email. The MDA receives the incoming email from the MTA and delivers it to the appropriate user. The MUA retrieves the mail delivered by the MDA and allows the user to read it. In addition to incoming mail relaying from MTA to MDA to MUA, outgoing mail is submitted by the MUA, picked up by the MDA, transferred to the MTA, and sent to the appropriate recipient server. In this section we will briefly discuss the default Red Hat Linux MTA (**sendmail**), MDA (**procmail**), and popular MUAs (**elm, pine,** and Netscape).

sendmail

The most popular (default Red Hat Linux) Mail Transport Agent (MTA) is sendmail. The sendmail program is typically installed by default during installation and, when installed via the Red Hat 6.0 CD-ROM, requires no configuration to work properly.

If sendmail is not installed during your Red Hat Linux installation, you can install the RPM found on your Red Hat Linux 6.0 CD. The sendmail RPM file on the Red Hat 6.0 CD is sendmail-8.9.3-10.i386.rpm and is found in the /RedHat/RPMS/ directory on your Red Hat 6.0 CD-ROM.

Configuring sendmail

The main configuration file for sendmail is /etc/sendmail.cf. The /etc/sendmail.cf file is machine-readable code used to run sendmail. Since /etc/sendmail.cf is machine-readable code, it is not very administrator-reader friendly. Because of the complexity and sensitivity of this file, it is not recommended to edit this file by hand. For this task, there is a macro pre-processor available, m4, which should be used to recreate the sendmail.cf file from edited source (/etc/sendmail.mc).

To use m4, you must install the sendmail-cf RPM file, sendmail-cf-8.9.3-10.i386.rpm found on your Red Hat 6.0 CD in the /RedHat/RPMS/ directory. To make changes to your /etc/sendmail.cf file, follow these instructions:

1. Make backups. Make backups of your /etc/sendmail.cf and /etc/sendmail. mc files. Copy these files from sendmail.cf to sendmail.cf.old and from sendmail.mc to sendmail.mc.old, or something suitable.

2. Edit /etc/sendmail.mc. Edit the /etc/sendmail.mc to make any changes you need. If an option is in single quotes, be sure the first quote around the option is a back tick (`) and the last quote around the item is a forward tick ('). To disable (or comment) a line, insert dnl at the front of the line.

3. Generate new /etc/sendmail.cf. Generate the new /etc/sendmail.cf list from the edited /etc/sendmail.mc by using the m4 macro processor. To do this, execute: m4 sendmail.mc > sendmail.cf. (Please double-check to see that you have a backup of your current running sendmail.cf before overwriting your current one!)

4. Restart sendmail. Restart sendmail by running /etc/rc.d/init.d/sendmail restart.

procmail

The mail delivery agent used by default with Red Hat Linux 6.0 and sendmail is procmail. The procmail MDA is used to handle the mail between the MTA (**sendmail**) and the MUA (mail reader). Typically, **procmail** is installed by default during Red Hat Linux 6.0 installation. If necessary, however, you can install **procmail** via **rpm**. The RPM file included with Red Hat Linux 6.0 for **procmail** is procmail-3.13.1-2.i386.rpm, located in the /RedHat/RPMS/ directory on your Red Hat Linux 6.0 CD-ROM.

Configuring procmail

For the MDA services of **procmail**, there is nothing you need to configure. This means after installation, **procmail** is ready to go "out of the box." You can, however, customize how **procmail** handles each user's mail by editing a .procmailrc file within each user's home directory. By editing a user's home .procmailrc, you can enable mail sorting, blocking, and more. For an in depth description of filtering options available through **procmail**, run **man procmailrc**.

Email Clients

Email clients are the mail user agents used by the user to read her mail. There are a variety of MUAs available. Any MUA can be used as long as the MUA supports the POP or IMAP (discussed in Chapter 4) protocols to receive mail remotely. Some popular email clients used on Linux include **elm**, **pine**, and the Netscape mail reader.

elm

The MUA **elm** is a popular text-based mail reader used on Unix systems. The interface is text-based and commands are given by simple key commands as prompted by the mail reader. The text of the email is derived by editing a text file with your default editor (**emacs**, **vi**, and so on) which is automatically spawned when running **elm**. To install **elm**, install elm-2.5.0-0.2pre8.i386.rpm from the /RedHat/RPMS/ directory of your Red Hat Linux 6.0 CD-ROM. Figure 10.1 shows the interface used with the **elm** MUA.

pine

Another popular text-based MUA is **pine**. The **pine** mail reader is a little more user friendly than **elm** key combination menu-based options; it uses and uses a simpler text editor. To install **pine** from the Red Hat Linux 6.0 CD, install the pine-4.10-2.i386.rpm file. Figure 10.2 shows the text-menu based interface for **pine**.

Netscape

In addition to the multiple text-based MUAs that are found on most Unix systems, other graphical MUAs exist as well. Remember, any MUA that supports POP and IMAP (as discussed in Chapter 4) should work on your Red

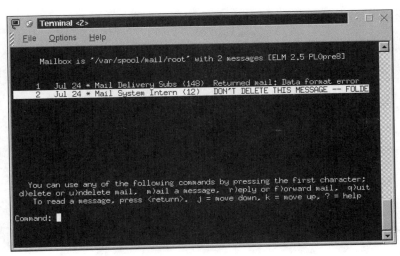

Figure 10.1   The **elm** interface.

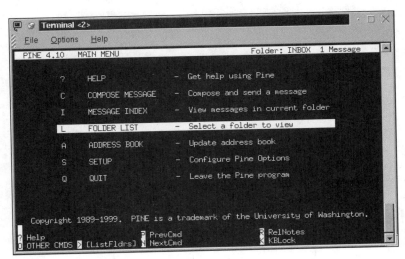

Figure 10.2   The **pine** interface.

Hat Linux system. One popular GUI-interfaced MUA is the Netscape mail reader that is included in Netscape Communicator. The Netscape MUA has a graphical window interface with directory style options for mailboxes on the left, and mail list indexes and mail content text on the right. Buttons at the top of the Netscape mail reader allow you to maneuver through the MUA program. To install the Netscape mail reader on your Red Hat Linux 6.0 CD, you must install Netscape Communicator 4.51 from the RPM file netscape-communicator-4.51-3.i386.rpm located in the /RedHat/RPMS/ directory on your CD. Figure 10.3 shows the GUI interface of the Netscape mail reader.

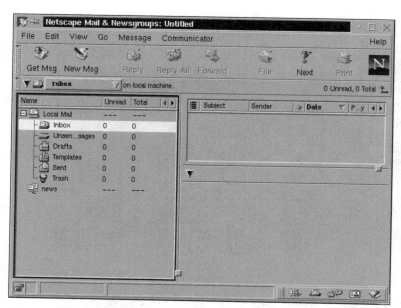

Figure 10.3   The Netscape mail reader.

Domain Name Service (DNS)

DNS is the service responsible for managing the host and domain name conversion to and from the mapped IP addresses. Therefore, DNS is responsible from converting an IP address to its domain name and converting a domain name to its assigned IP address. The server that is run on a Linux DNS server is **named**. The **named** server is a part of the BIND (Berkley Internet Name Domain) package used on more than 85 percent of all DNS servers in the world.

Configuring BIND 8.x

During the Red Hat Linux 6.0 installation, you are given the option of installing BIND automatically. However if BIND isn't installed during installation, you can install it from the Red Hat Linux 6.0 CD-ROM. There are three different RPMs you should install. The first, and most important, is the bind-8.2-6.i386.rpm file, which is the main BIND RPM. The second is recommended to be installed on every machine, even if the machine isn't planning on being a DNS server, as it is the bind utilities package. The bind utilities package is installed with bind-utils-8.3-6.i386.rpm. An optional (but highly recommended) package to be used with BIND is the caching name server package that configures your DNS server to cache DNS entries making name lookups and DNS access faster. The caching name server package to install is caching-nameserver-6.0-2.noarch.rpm.

The main configuration file for BIND 8.x is /etc/named.conf. In /etc/named.conf, you can specify options such as the default directory for **named** files and specify the zones for the **named** entries you are hosting. There are two types of **named** files that you host. The first is the database (db) entry specified for each domain you host. These db entries are typically named either db.*domain.com* or *domain.com*.db, depending on the naming scheme you use. The db entries are the forward DNS entries for your domain. The second type of **named** file you host is the reverse DNS file denoted typically by db.x.x.x.in-addr.arpa where x.x.x is the reverse subnet you are hosting. For example, if you host the 192.168.1.x subnet, you would have a db.1.168.192.in-addr.arpa reverse DNS file.

 Some DNS servers do not host the entire subnet. Therefore, the subnet provider (Internet Service Provider) hosts the reverse DNS information and the in-addr.arpa entries are not required on your machine.

named.conf

The /etc/named.conf file is the main configuration file for **named**. Within the named.conf file, you will specify options such as the default directory for **named** entries (Red Hat Linux 6.0 default is /var/named/) and zone entries for individual **named** files. The following is a sample /etc/named.conf file:

```
options {
        directory "/var/named";
};

zone "." {
        type hint;
        file "named.ca"'
};

zone "1.168.192.in-addr.arpa" {
        type master;
        file "db.1.168.192.in-addr.arpa";
};

zone "example.com" {
        type master;
        file "db.example.com";
};
```

```
zone "example.net" {
        type slave;
        file "db.example.net";
        masters {
                192.168.0.100;
        };
};
```

The above listed sample /etc/named.conf has five different types of entries. (For your convenience, each entry is highlighted separately.) The first two entries are mandatory configuration options for BIND. The first entry specifies BIND options. In the above example, the specified options sets where all **named** files will be placed. By default, this option is set to /var/named/. Many DNS administrators are accustomed to keeping named files under /etc/named/ and thus change this directory option to "/etc/named".

The second entry is a default zone entry to specify what file can be used as a "hint" for where to find root name servers. By default, BIND 8 uses /var/named/named.ca. This second entry is required, and it is not recommended to edit this entry or file unless necessary.

The third entry in the above example is a reverse DNS zone entry. The zone specified is the "1.168.192.in-addr.arpa". The reverse DNS is a primary DNS record, so the type entry is set to master. The file with the reverse DNS information is in /var/named/db.1.168.192.in-addr.arpa, so the file is set to "db.1.168.192.in-addr.arpa".

The fourth entry in the above example is a primary DNS zone entry. The zone specified is the "example.com". Since the entry is a primary DNS entry, the type is set to master. The file for the entry is found in /var/named/db.example.com, so the file is set to "db.example.com".

The fifth entry in the above example is a sample secondary DNS zone entry. The zone specified in the example is "example.net". Since the entry is a secondary DNS entry, the type is set to slave. The file for this secondary entry is found in /var/named/db.example.net, so the file option is set to "db.example.net". Since this entry is a secondary DNS entry, you must provide the primary DNS server information to retrieve the DNS information from. In this entry's case, the primary DNS server is 192.168.0.100 therefore; the masters option is set to 192.168.0.100.

Forward DNS Files

Forward DNS files are used to resolve domain names to the domain's assigned IP addresses. These files, by default, are found under the /var/named/ directory and are typically named db.*domain.com*, or *domain.com*.db. In these examples, we will use db.example.com. The following is a sample forward DNS file for a master (primary) record:

```
@           IN      SOA     ns.example.com.  root.example.com. (
                            1999080101      ; serial
                            10800   ; refresh (3 hours)
                            3600    ; retry (1 hour)
                            604800 ; expire (7 days)
                            86400 ) ; minimum (1 day)

            IN      NS              ns1.example.com.
            IN      NS              ns2.example.com.

            IN      MX              0       mail.example.com.
            IN      A               192.168.0.212
localhost   IN      A               127.0.0.1
www         IN      A               192.168.0.212
ns1         IN      A               192.168.0.10
ns2         IN      A               192.168.0.11
ftp         IN      CNAME           www
mail        IN      CNAME           www
irc         IN      CNAME           irc.example.net.
```

For better clarity, the sections of the /var/named/db.example.com file have been highlighted. The first section is the SOA (start of a zone authority) entry. The SOA entry contains the domain of the originating host, domain address of the maintainer, the file serial number, and various time parameters (refresh, retry, expire, and minimum TTL).

The second highlighted section of the above sample /var/named/ db.example.com specifies the domain's primary and secondary DNS server. These are denoted by the **NS** tokens. The first **NS** entry is the primary DNS server, and the second **NS** entry specifies the secondary DNS server. You can also add tertiary DNS servers and so forth with the same **NS** entries.

The third highlighted section includes other references, options, and settings for the domain entry. The **MX** (mail exchange) token points to the mail exchange server for the domain. The **A** tokens point to host addresses. For example the **A** token in this example sets the domain example.com to 192.168.0.212. Another **A** token sets the **www.example.com** to 192.168.0.212 as well. An additional token used in this example section is **CNAME** (canonical name). The **CNAME** token points an alias to the appropriate IP address or domain. In the above example, ftp.example.com is pointed to the same address as www, which was already defined as 192.168.0.212. Also, mail.example.com is directed to www. There is also a **CNAME** pointer for irc.example.com that redirects the request to a real IRC (Internet Relay Chat) server that is located in this example at irc.example.net.

Reverse DNS Files

Reverse DNS files are used to resolve IP addresses to their assigned host names. Reverse DNS is set up per subnet, meaning all 192.168.0.x addresses would have a single reverse DNS file defined, as would 192.168.1.x, 192.168.2.x, and so on (where x is equal to all nodes from .0 through .255).

Reverse DNS files are named by the subnet address (in reverse order) followed by the in-addr.arpafilename. For instance, the reverse DNS file for the 192.168.100.x subnet would be db.100.168.192.in-addr.arpa, and the reverse DNS file for the 205.23.12.x subnet could be db.12.23.205.in-addr.arpa.

Although the subnet and in-addr.arpa filenames are always used, many administrators replace the db. with rev., simply for clarification (for instance, rev.12.23.205.in-addr.arpa or 12.23.205.in-addr.arpa.rev). Regardless of which naming convention you use, simply keep the same naming convention throughout your system, and make sure all appropriate references (such as in /etc/named.conf) match appropriately.

The following is an example of the reverse DNS file (db.0.168.192.in-addr.arpa). You will notice that it looks similar to the forward DNS files, with the same SOA head entry, but has different tokens used in the body of the file.

```
@       IN      SOA     ns.example.com. root.example.com. (
                        199080101     ; serial
                        10800   ; refresh (3 hours)
                        3600    ; retry (1 hour)
                        604800 ; expire (7 days)
                        86400 ); minimum (1 day)
        IN      NS      ns.example.com.
1       IN      PTR     gateway.example.com.
2       IN      PTR     boss.example.com.
3       IN      PTR     node3.example.com.
;4      IN      PTR     node4.example.com.
212     IN      PTR     www.example.com.
254     IN      PTR     router.example.com.
```

In this example, the first six lines are identical to the forward DNS files. The first six lines of the file are the SOA entry information that includes the host information, file serial number, and various time settings. The remaining body of the example differs greatly from the forward DNS file, however. The remaining entries use the

PTR (pointer) token. The **PTR** token resolves the specific node on a subnet to a domain name. The first column in the above example of **PTR** entries specifies the node number on the subnet. For instance, 1 refers to 192.168.0.1, 2 refers to 192.168.0.2 and so forth. You'll notice that nodes that aren't assigned are either not listed, or the ones that are disabled are commented out (like the entry for 4 is commented out with the semicolon at the beginning of the line). Therefore the entry for 1 will resolve 192.168.0.1 to **gateway.example.com**, the entry for 212 will resolve 192.168.0.212 to **www.example.com**, and so forth.

Primary DNS

When you have a domain registered with your DNS server specified as the primary DNS server, you will need to set up your **named** files by following these steps:

1. Add zone to /etc/named.conf. As a primary entry, your zone entry in /etc/named.conf will look like this:

```
zone "example.com" {
        type master;
        file "db.example.com";
    };
```

2. Edit db.example.com. Create a file under /var/named named db.example.com. Add any necessary token entries and change the file serial number (highlighted in the next code section) to reflect the current date.

 The serial number (by standard convention) should be 10 characters–the first four (1999) reflect the year, the next two (08) reflect the current month; the next two (01) reflect the current day, and the last two (01) reflect the number of times you changed that file that day (for instance, if this is the first time you made a change, the digits would be 01, the second 02, the third 03, and so on).

3. Set your primary and secondary DNS servers. Add any hosts for this domain with appropriate tokens, and so forth. Your db.example.com should look something like this:

```
@           IN      SOA     ns.example.com. root.example.com. (
                            1999080101      ; serial
                            10800   ; refresh (3 hours)
                            3600    ; retry (1 hour)
```

```
                                    604800 ; expire (7 days)
                                    86400 ) ; minimum (1 day)
                IN      NS          ns1.example.com.
                IN      NS          ns2.example.net.
                IN      A           192.168.0.212
    www         IN      A           192.168.0.212
    ftp         IN      CNAME       www
    node2       IN      A           192.168.0.2
    router      IN      A           192.168.0.254
    ns1         IN      A           192.168.0.10
```

4. Set up reverse DNS. Create the db.0.168.192.in-addr.arpa file under /var/named/. Set up any and all reverse entries for each node, as specified in the forward DNS file. (Remember to change your file serial number accordingly!) Your reverse DNS file should look something like this:

```
    @           IN      SOA         ns.example.com. root.example.com. (
                                    1999080101      ; serial
                                    10800    ; refresh (3 hours)
                                    3600     ; retry (1 hour)
                                    604800   ; expire (7 days)
                                    86400 ) ; minimum (1 day)
                IN      NS          ns1.example.com.
    2           IN      PTR         node2.example.com.
    10          IN      PTR         ns1.example.com.
    254         IN      PTR         router.example.com.
```

5. Verify changes and restart **named**. Verify that your IPs, hosts, and serial number information are correct. Then restart **named** by running /etc/rc.d/init.d/named restart. To verify that you have your domain running properly, use **nslookup** (discussed in the "DNS Tools" section of this chapter) by running **nslookup www.example.com** and **nslookup 192.168.0.212**. You should receive the appropriate IP and domain information if DNS is set up properly.

Secondary And Tertiary DNS

When a domain is registered, it should be registered with not only a primary DNS server, but a secondary DNS server as well. Therefore, if the primary server is down, the secondary server will take over. For even more fail-over, a tertiary DNS server can be set up.

Setting up secondary DNS for a domain is even more simple than setting up primary DNS. Essentially you only have to do Step 1 and 4 from the above example of setting up primary DNS. There is a difference, however, from step 1 above. The following steps explain how to set up secondary DNS.

1. Add zone to /etc/named.conf. As a secondary entry, your type is slave. With a slave entry you have to specify the master (used to pull the DNS information for the domain from), which in this example is 192.168.2.50. As a secondary entry, your zone entry in /etc/named.conf will look like this:

```
zone "example.com" {
        type slave;
        file "db.example.com";
        masters {
                192.168.2.50;
        };
};
```

2. Verify changes and restart **named**. Verify that your IPs, and host information are correct. Then, restart **named** by running **/etc/rc.d/init.d/ named restart.**

DNS Tools

There are a variety of DNS tools available to help you utilize and test the DNS service. DNS tools should be installed on every Linux workstation, not just DNS servers. Tools such as **nslookup** are a great assistance for even users who want to look up an IP address or domain using a name server.

DNS tools can be installed on your system with the bind-utils-8.2-6.i386.rpm file found on your Red Hat Linux 6.0 CD in the /RedHat/RPMS directory. Some of the popular DNS tools included in this package are **dig, dnsquery, host,** and **nslookup.** Table 10.1 briefly explains these tools and gives an example of their usage.

Table 10.1   DNS tools.

Tool	Usage	Description
dig	dig @*nameserver domain*	Queries name server for domain name packet information
dnsquery	dnsquery –n *nameserver host*	Queries domain name server for host using resolver
host	host *domain*	Looks up host for domain name
nslookup	nslookup *domain* or nslookup *ipaddress*	Queries Internet name servers for IP and domain information

File Transfer Protocol (FTP)

FTP is the file transfer protocol used to connect two machines (a server and a client) to transfer files from one to the other. Typically, FTP works by a client connecting to a server (via an FTP client) and then either uploads files to the server or downloads files from the server to the client.

Two general types of FTP servers are user access and anonymous access. User access FTP servers require that the client accessing the FTP server have a valid user account (username and password) on the system. Anonymous access FTP servers simply allow any client to connect without needing a specific username and password to access the system. In this section, we will discuss how to set up the default Red Hat Linux FTP server (**wu-ftpd**) and how to set up the anonymous FTP.

Setting Up wu-ftpd

The default Red Hat Linux 6.0 FTP server is **wu-ftpd**. By default you can install the **wu-ftpd** package during the Red Hat Linux 6.0 installation. If you did not install **wu-ftpd** during your Red Hat Linux installation, you can install from the Red Hat 6.0 CD with the RPM wu-ftpd-2.4.2vr17-3.i386.rpm.

After the installation of **wu-ftpd** is finished, there is nothing to configure. With the default **wu-ftpd** installation, any user can then **ftp** to your server, and with his username and password authentication, gain FTP access to his own home directory (unless otherwise specified). There are three configuration files that are set up by **wu-ftpd**. The three files are /etc/ftpaccess, /etc/ftphosts, and /etc/ftpusers.

The /etc/ftpaccess File

The /etc/ftpaccess is the main **ftpd** configuration file. There are a number of options you can configure and customize in the /etc/ftpaccess file. You can specify the number of attempts to successfully log in to the FTP server with the **loginfails** option. (The default is **loginfails 5**, allows five attempts before the FTP server refuses connection.) You can also specify to allow or deny specific tool access (such as **compress**, **tar**, and **chmod**) to specific types of connections (such as **all**, **guest**, and **anonymous**). For more information about /etc/ftpaccess options, read the ftpaccess man page (**man 5 ftpaccess**).

The /etc/ftphosts File

The /etc/ftphosts file is used to allow or deny access to specific accounts from specified hosts. There are two types of entries in the /etc/ftphosts file. The first is **allow**, and the second is **deny**. The syntax used is **allow** *username host* or **deny** *username host.* For example, **allow kara 192.168.0.*** would only allow the user "kara" to log in from 192.168.0.* hosts. The entry **deny anonymous 192.168.1.*** would deny all anonymous user connections from any 192.168.1.* host. For more information about setting up the /etc/ftphosts file, read the ftphosts man page (**man 5 ftphosts**).

The /etc/ftpusers File

The /etc/ftpusers file is used to specify exactly what system user accounts can not log in to the server via **ftp**. By default, system users such as root, bin, deamon, adm, lp, sync, shutdown, halt, mail, news, uucp, operator, games, and nobody are automatically added to this list. If you create any users to whom you wish to deny FTP access, add them to the /etc/ftpusers file as well.

Setting Up Anonymous FTP

An anonymous FTP server does not require a specific user ID or password to access the server. This means the FTP server can be reached with anonymous FTP clients (such as Netscape) and by simply passing the generic usernames (such as "anonymous" and "ftp") along with the email address as the password.

To configure your FTP server as an anonymous FTP server, you can install the anonftp RPM, and the **wu-ftpd** server will be configured automatically. This RPM, can be found on your Red Hat Linux 6.0 CD as /RedHat/RPMS/anonftp-2.8.1.i386.rpm.

Network File System (NFS)

NFS is the Network File System, the standard method for sharing files between Unix (and Unix-like) systems. Linux can be an NFS server to other Linux (or Unix) systems, as well as an NFS client to other Linux (or Unix) systems.

The NFS Server

The NFS server can be installed by default during the Red Hat Linux 6.0 installation. If NFS was not installed during your Red Hat installation, you can use the RPM on the Red Hat installation CD. The NFS RPM can be found at /RedHat/RPMS/knfsd-1.2.2-4.i386.rpm.

Red Hat 6.0 uses the new kernel **nfsd** feature of the 2.2 Linux kernels. Therefore, in order to use the NFS server, the kernel must be configured with the appropriate kernel support. With the stock Red Hat 6.0 kernel, the kernel **nfsd** requires the nfsd.o module (which then requires the lockd.o and sunrpc.o modules). In addition, the NFS server requires the following specific user-space daemons and utilities.

➤ **Portmap** The NFS server system must be running the **portmap** daemon. It is included in the **portmap** package portmap-4.0-15.i386.rpm.

➤ **RPC** RPC daemons from the **knfsd** package must be running. They include **rpc.statd**, **rpc.rquotad**, **rpc.mountd**, and **rpc.nfsd**. (These may be started by running **/etc/rc.d/init.d/nfs start**).

Note: If for some reason the nfsd.o module is not available, rpc.nfsd will continue to run with the same behavior as the old user-space unfsd. Normally, it will pass control to the kernel nfsd and exit.

Configuring NFS Server Exports

The **knfsd** server uses /etc/exports to configure exported NFS filesystems. The format of the file entries is typically

```
/path/to/export  host(options)
```

The first field (/path/to/export) is the path that you want to make available via NFS. An example would be /mnt/cdrom. The second field (host) is the hostname (IP address or address/netmask) to which you want the filesystem to be made available. If nothing is supplied for host, the filesystem is exported to the world. The last field (options) is a comma-separated list of export options. Some standard examples are **ro** for read-only, **r** for read and, **w** for write. An example of the options field could be (ro) specifying that the exported filesystem is read-only or (rw) to specify that the exported filesystem is readable and writeable. The following is an example of an /etc/exports file:

```
/mnt/cdrom              (ro)
/tmp                    (rw)
/home                   192.168.0.0/255.255.255.0(rw)
```

The first line in the above example exports /mnt/cdrom read-only to the world. The second line in the above example exports /tmp read-write to the world. The third line in the above example exports /home read-write to only the 192.168.0.0 network. For more information about the format and options of /etc/exports, view the **exports** man page (**man 5 exports**).

After you have added your filesystem entries to /etc/exports, you must take the following steps:

1. Run **exportsfs –av**. To initially add all your entries in /etc/exports to the list of exported filesystems (assuming **mountd** is already running), run **exportfs -av**. The "a" option specifies **exportfs** to add the entries and the "v" option specifies to print the output verbosely.

2. Run **exportfs –rv**. After making changes to /etc/exports, you must update the NFS server using **exportfs -rv**. This command re-exports all directories in /etc/exports, syncing the server's list of exports (maintained by **mountd** in /var/lib/nfs/xtab) with the /etc/exports file.

To remove a filesystem from **mountd**'s list of exportable filesystems, use **exportfs -u**. More information about **exportfs** may be found in the exportfs(8) man page (**man 8 exportfs**).

The NFS Client

The NFS client is included in the NFS RPM knfsd-1.2.2-4.i386.rpm. In addition, an RPM package called knfsd-clients-1.2.2-4.i386.rpm is available. It contains useful NFS client tools such as **showmount**. The default NFS client on Linux consists of several parts. Some of the most important parts include the specific kernel modules **portmap** and **mount**.

Kernel Modules

The NFS client requires a specific set of kernel modules. These modules include nfs.o, lockd.o, and sunrpc.o. These kernel modules are installed in the default Red Hat 6.0 kernel installation and will automatically load when you mount a remote filesystem by the kernel module loader.

portmap

The NFS client (as well as the server) requires the system to be running the **portmap** daemon. The **portmap** daemon must be running for the NFS **lockd** (file locking over NFS) daemon to work properly. The **portmap** daemon is installed as /sbin/portmap on Red Hat 6.0 (included in the portmap RPM portmap-4.0-15.i386.rpm). To start **portmap**, run **/etc/rc.d/init.d/portmap start**.

mount

The utility required to use NFS is the **mount** utility. The **mount** utility is used to mount a remote NFS filesystem. Common use of the **mount** utility is **mount remotehost:/path /local/path**. There are several commonly used mount options for NFS. Table 10.2 lists the most common mount options used on NFS.

Using the above mount options, you could mount the filesystem /export on the NFS server linux.example.com with a 8k blocksize on /mnt/nfs, by issuing the following:

```
mount linux.example.com:/export /mnt/nfs -o rsize=8192,wsize=8192
```

Table 10.2   NFS mount options.

Mount Option	Description
rsize=num	Read *num* bytes at a time (instead of the default 1024 bytes).
wsize=num	Write *num* bytes at a time (instead of the default 1024 bytes).
soft	If a timeout occurs, return an I/O error to the calling program.
hard	If a timeout occurs, send a "Server not responding" to the console and continue to retry. (This is the default behavior.)
intr	For a hard mount that has timed out, allow I/O to be interrupted with a signal to the calling program. (The default is to not allow I/O on a hard mount to be interrupted.)

NFS Tools

In addition to the **mount** command used to **mount** the NFS filesystems, there are a few other useful NFS tools to help use and administer NFS filesystems. Table 10.3 lists a few extra tools to make your life with NFS easier.

SAMBA (SMB)

SAMBA is the Open Source server that implements SMB (Server Message Block). SMB allows you to set up your Red Hat Linux 6.0 machine to act as a server for Windows 95/98/NT for services such as file and print sharing.

Setting Up SMB

With Red Hat Linux 6.0, you have the option to install SAMBA during the installation ("Set up windows file and print sharing" option). If SAMBA wasn't

Table 10.3   NFS tools.

NFS tool	Usage	Description
df	*df*	Lists the filesystems mounted on your machine
showmount	*showmount –e host*	Shows export mount information for host
rpcinfo	*/usr/sbin/rpcinfo –p host*	Lists all RPC services running on host

installed during your Red Hat installation, you can install the SAMBA RPM from the Red Hat Linux 6.0 CD. The CD contains the RPM in /RedHat/ RPMS/samba-2.0.3-8.i386.rpm.

Installing the SAMBA RPM sets up the main configuration file for SMB as /etc/smb.conf. In addition to the main configuration file, a number of additional configuration files and tools are installed. Table 10.4 lists all the configuration files and tools installed by the SAMBA RPM file.

Setting Up A SAMBA Share

When setting up a SAMBA share, there are roughly five steps to follow (after the basic installation). To set up a SAMBA share for a specific directory (for this example /home), go through the following steps.

Table 10.4   SMB files.

File	Path	Description
smb.conf	/etc/smb.conf	Configuration file for SAMBA
smbpasswd	/etc/smbpasswd	Configuration file for Windows password file for server
smbuser	/etc/smbuser	Unix-to-NT user mapping
nmdb	/usr/sbin/nmbd	Windows NetBIOS names for sending and receiving names of machines on the network
smbd	/usr/sbin/smbd	SMB daemon for server shares
swat	/usr/sbin/swat	Web based configuration tool for SMB
smbadduser	/usr/bin/smbadduser	Tool for adding user to your system
smbclient	/usr/bin/smbclient	Client-side program to connect to SMB server from Linux
smbmount	/usr/bin/smbmount	Utility to mount SMB shares
smbpasswd	/usr/bin/smbpasswd	Utility used to add user to /etc/ smbpasswd allowing for Windows encrypted passwords
smbprint	/usr/bin/smbprint	Script used for printing
smbrun	/usr/bin/smbrun	Script used to start SMB server
smbstatus	/usr/bin/smbstatus	Tool used to print status information for the running SMB server
smbtar	/usr/bin/smbtar	Script used for backing up Windows machines to your SMB server
smbumount	/usr/bin/smbumount	Tool used to unmount SMB service

1. Check the workgroup setting in /etc/smb.conf. The default setting is "WORKGROUP." To set the workgroup (or domain) to MYGROUP, add a line in the [globals] section like

```
workgroup = MYGROUP
```

2. Add the share to the /etc/smb.conf. You first need to add the share entry beneath the **Share Definitions** section of /etc/smb.conf. The entry will have six lines. The first line will name your share, for example [USER_HOME]. The second line sets the comment that is the part seen by the Windows client. A sample comment could be Home Directories. The third line specifies the path to the shared directory. For this example, the setting would be/home. The fourth line specifies public access (also known as guest ok). The fifth line specifies if the share is printable (only used for printer shares). The sixth line in this entry specifies whether the share is writeable. A sample entry for a Share Definition may look like this:

```
[USER_HOME]
        comment = User Home Directories
        path = /home
        public = yes
        printable = no
        writable = yes
```

3. Check your /etc/smb.conf syntax. After you have saved your changes to /etc/smb.conf, you should check your smb.conf syntax. A tool that will allow you to do that is **testparm**.

4. Restart SAMBA. After your /etc/smb.conf has been set up appropriately, you need to restart the SMB server. To do this, run **/etc/rc.d/init.d/smb restart**

5. Test your SMB shares. First check to make sure SMB is running (**/etc/rc.d/init.d/smb status**). If SMB seems to be running properly, attempt to mount your own SMB share via **smbclient**. To do this, use **smbclient –L localhost**. (When you are prompted with a password, simply hit enter.) If your system is working properly, you should see everything your machine is offering as a SMB share.

Dynamic Host Configuration Protocol (DHCP)

DHCP is a superset of **bootp**, which is used to assign IP addresses to clients on a network. DHCP is used for dynamic hosts that can move, connect, and disconnect from networks. DHCP can dynamically assign IP addresses from pre-assigned IP address in /etc/dhcpd.leases and set up static IP addresses based on the NIC MAC (Media Access Controller) address. DHCP can even restrict access by accepting requests only from specified MAC addresses.

Setting Up DHCP Server

To set up a DHCP server, make sure that you have installed the DHCP RPM. The DHCP RPM packaged with Red Hat Linux 6.0 is dhcp-2.0b1pl6-6.i386.rpm. To finish setting your DHCP server, follow these steps:

1. Check to see that you have MULTICAST support in your kernel. To do this, run **ifconfig –a**. If you already have MULTICAST support, you will have a line that says "UP BROADCAST RUNNING MULTICAST MTU:1500 Metric:1" in the **eth0** section of the **ifconfig** output. If MULTICAST is not in your configuration, you must either reconfigure your kernel to support MULTICAST, replace your NIC (if not supported), or change your interface settings.

2. Add a route for 255.255.255.255 (required by Microsoft Clients). To do this, type **route add –host 255.255.255.255 dev eth0** (where eth0 is the device of your ethernet card).

   Note: If you get an "unknown host" error when adding this route, add the following entry to your /etc/hosts file: 255.255.255.255 all-ones.

3. Start the DHCP server. To start the server, type **/etc/rc.d/init.d/dhcpd start**.

4. Verify that DHCP is working properly. Type **/usr/sbin/dhcpd –d –f**.

5. Configure your /etc/dhcpd.conf file (an example for setting random IPs for clients follows).

Configuring dhcpd For Random IP Assignment

To set up DHCP to assign random IP addresses to DHCP clients on the network, you will need to configure the /etc/dhcpd.conf file, which is the main configuration file for DHCP. The following list contains sample settings for the /etc/dhcpd.conf that will allow DHCP to randomly assign IP addresses on your network that are between 192.168.1.10 and 192.168.1.100, as well as in the range 192.168.1.150 through 192.168.1.200. Listing 10.3 is a sample /etc/dhcpd.conf configuration.

Listing 10.3 Sample /etc/dhcpd.conf file.

```
default-lease-time 500;
max-lease-time 6000;
option subnet-mask 255.255.255.0
option broadcast-address 192.168.1.255
option routers 192.168.1.254
option domain-name-servers 192.168.1.1, 192.168.1.2;
option domain-name "example.com";
subnet 192.168.1.0 netmask 255.255.255.0 {
          range 192.168.1.10 192.168.1.100;
          range 192.168.1.150 192.168.1.200;
}
```

Using DHCP Client

The DHCP client used on Red Hat Linux is called **pump**. If you did not install **pump** during the Red Hat Linux installation, you can install the **pump** RPM from the Red Hat Linux 6.0 CD-ROM. The file is pump-0.6.4-1.i386.rpm and may be found in the /RedHat/RPMS/ directory on the Red Hat 6.0 CD-ROM. To configure your Linux DHCP client, take the following steps:

1. Execute **netcfg** by typing **netcfg** at the root prompt.

2. Choose the Interfaces button (See Figure 10.4 for Steps 2, 3, 8, and 9).

3. Select the ethernet interface of your network connection (typically eth0).

4. Choose the Edit button to pull up the configuration window for the ethernet interface. (See Figure 10.5 for Steps 4, 5, 6, and 7).

5. Using the down arrow next to "Interface configuration protocol," choose "dhcp" as shown in Figure 10.5.

6. Enable the option to "Activate interface at boot time."

7. Choose "Done."

8. Select the eth0 (or appropriate ethernet) interface and choose the "Activate" Button. (See Figure 10.4.)

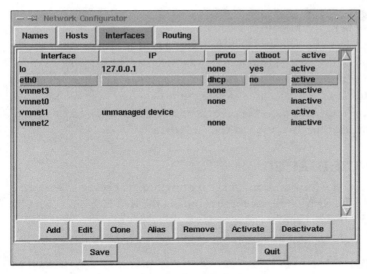

Figure 10.4   The **netcfg** interfaces window.

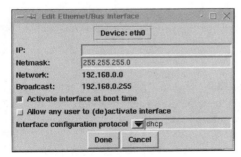

Figure 10.5   The **netcfg** eth0 configuration window.

9. Press the "Save" button to ensure your configuration is saved, and then press the "Quit" button.

10. To make sure that you are connected to the DHCP server, run **ifconfig**. The eth0 section of the output should have an **inet addr:** entry with your DHCP-assigned network address.

Time Services

There are a number of services available on Red Hat Linux that allow you to configure and synchronize time services on your machine. These tools are made available because few machines have atomic clocks attached to them, therefore computers often lose accurate time. There are three main time related tools included in Red Hat Linux 6.0—they are the time configuration tool **timetool** and the time synchronization tools **xntpd** and **rdate**.

Time Configuration

A GUI interface tool for time configuration, **timetool**, is packaged with Red Hat Linux 6.0. The RPM available for **timetool** on the Red Hat Linux 6.0 CD is timetool-2.5-5.noarch.rpm.

To change system time with **timetool**, execute it as root by typing **timetool** at the root prompt. At the GUI window, select the time setting you want to change (hour, minute or second), and then use the up and down arrows to change accordingly. When time is set appropriately, choose the "Set System Clock" button to save the time setting to the system. Then, choose the "Exit Time Machine" to exit. See Figure 10.6 for the interface of **timetool**.

Time Synchronization

Some administrators choose to use time synchronization tools to set the system time based on a specified host machine. One (older) tool used for this is **rdate**. A more popular package used to set up a continuously running synchronization daemon is **xntp3**.

Figure 10.6 The **timetool** interface.

rdate

The Red Hat Linux tool **rdate** is a tool to synchronize the system time with a specified machine. The **rdate** tool only synchronizes once when the tool is being used. The RPM used to install **rdate** on the Red Hat Linux 6.0 CD is rdate-0.960923-8.i386.rpm.

To use **rdate**, run **rdate –p –s** *host* where *host* is the machine with which you want to synchronize your time. The "-p" option prints the time set on the remote host you specify. The "-s" option synchronizes the time on your machine with the host you specify.

 rdate uses port 37 to send and receive **rdate** requests. Many administrators disable this port and service; therefore, finding a good **rdate** host may be troublesome, unless it is on your own network.

xntp3

The most popular package used for time synchronization is the **xntp3** package. The **xntp3** package contains several time-related tools such as **ntpdate** and the popular **xntpd** time daemon that runs continuously to synchronize your system time. The RPM used to install **xntp3** on the Red Hat Linux 6.0 CD is xntp3-5.93-12.i386.rpm, and it is found in the /RedHat/RPMS/ directory.

➤ ntpdate   Similar to **rdate**. The **ntpdate** tool is used to retrieve the date and time from the network by polling the Network Time Protocol Servers as specified in the command. The **ntpdate** command is often placed in /etc/rc.local's startup script or can also be run from the system **cron**.

➤ xntpd   Time synchronization daemon used to continuously adjust system time. Configuration for xntpd is done through /etc/ntp.conf.

Squid Proxy Server

Squid is a caching proxy server. Proxy servers are used to cache data streams such as FTP, gopher, and HTTP. Network clients can then be directed to the proxy server to aid in pulling up cached HTTP documents.

Setting Up Squid

To install **squid** via **rpm** from the Red Hat Linux 6.0 CD, use squid-2.2.STABLE1-1.i386.rpm from the /RedHat/RPMS/ directory. The main

configuration file that is automatically set up from the RPM is /etc/squid/
squid.conf. The squid.conf file consists of every configuration setting needed
to run Squid and contains excellent comment explanations for each setting
available.

After installing the Squid RPM, the default configuration file (squid.conf) is
already configured with default settings that allow you to run Squid "out of the
box." To start squid, type **/etc/rc.d/init.d/squid start**. When you start **squid** for
the first time, you automatically create the **squid** cache files as specified in the
/etc/squid/squid.conf settings. The **squid** daemon will automatically listen on
port 3128 for proxy requests.

Using Squid

The most popular use for Squid is as a Web proxy server. A Web proxy server
caches HTTP request information (such as images, HTML pages, and so on)
on a local machine to speed browsing download times and so forth to clients
on the network. This feature is especially useful when a specific Web site is
requested numerous times on a specific network.

When configuring a client to use a proxy server (such as Netscape), you simply
set the client to point its HTTP traffic to the proxy server's IP address and
port (3128). For instance, if your proxy server was on 192.168.0.1 and the
network client was running Netscape, you would take the following steps:

1. Load Netscape. After Netscape has loaded, use the menu options at the
   top of the window to choose "Edit," and then "Preferences." This
   presents you with a preferences menu where you can set up everything
   from identification information to advanced options such as using a
   proxy server. (See Figure 10.7.)

2. Select the Advanced option in the left frame of the Preferences window
   by selecting the arrow to the left of the Advanced option. Select the
   Proxies option (as displayed in the Figure 10.7) from beneath the
   Advanced directory. In the right frame of the window, select "Manual
   Proxy Configuration" and choose the "View" button. An "Edit Manual
   Proxy Configuration" window then appears, as shown in Figure 10.8.

3. In the HTTP: setting box, set the IP address to the Squid server on your
   network (in this example, the server is set to 192.168.0.1), and set the
   port to send to (by default, this is set to 3128).

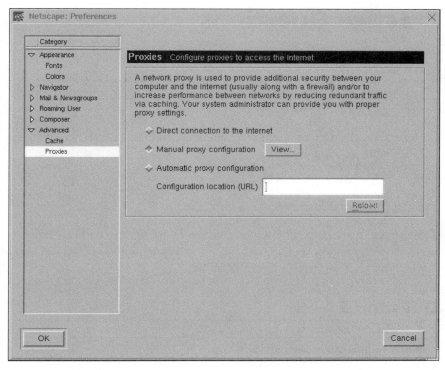

Figure 10.7   Netscape preferences.

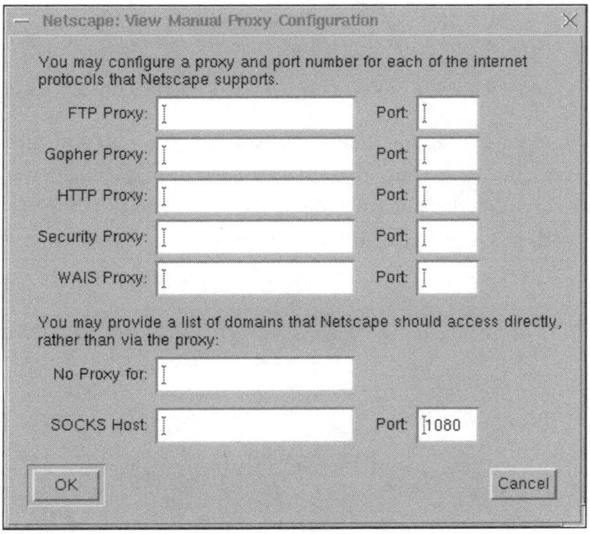

Figure 10.8   Edit manual proxy configuration in Netscape.

Practice Questions

Question 1

Which daemon is used for the Apache server?

○ a. apached

○ b. httpd

○ c. htmld

○ d. ftpd

The correct answer is b. The server used to set up an Apache Web server is httpd. Answers a and c are incorrect because they are not valid servers. Answer d is incorrect because ftpd is the FTP server.

Question 2

What is the main Apache configuration file?

○ a. httpd.conf

○ b. apache.conf

○ c. access.conf

○ d. conf.apache

The correct answer is a. The main Apache configuration file is /etc/httpd.conf. Answers b and d are incorrect because they are not valid options. Answer c is incorrect because while it is an Apache configuration file, it is used to configure the access levels for httpd, but not httpd itself.

Question 3

What is a DocumentRoot?

○ a. The file characteristics that indicate the root settings for the document

○ b. The header files of a document that indicate where the document should be kept

○ c. The default location where httpd files for a domain are to be kept

○ d. None of the above

The correct answer is c. The DocumentRoot setting is given in the httpd.conf file for setting up the default location for domain httpd files (such as HTML, CGI, and so forth) are to be found.

Question 4

What are the three required parts to a default Red Hat Linux Email system? [Check all correct answers]

❑ a. The MTA

❑ b. The MUA

❑ c. procmail

❑ d. pine

❑ e. The MBA

The correct answers are a, b, and c. The three main ingredients to a default Red Hat Linux system are the MTA (sendmail), the MDA (procmail), and the MUA (mail reader). Answer d is incorrect because while pine is an MUA, the particular program pine can be replaced by other MUAs on the system, such as elm or Netscape. Answer e is incorrect because it is not a valid option.

Question 5

> Which server is used with the BIND package?
>
> ○ a. httpd
> ○ b. bind
> ○ c. dnsd
> ○ d. named

The correct answer is d. The server used with BIND (DNS) is named. Answer a is incorrect because httpd is the Apache server. Answers b and d are incorrect because they are not valid entries.

Question 6

> What is an FTP server used for?
>
> _____

An FTP server is a File Transfer Protocol server. The FTP server is used to transfer files between a client and a server. The FTP server is capable of both uploading files from the client to the server, and downloading files from the server to the client.

Question 7

> NFS is used to share information between Unix servers and Windows clients.
>
> ○ a. True
> ○ b. False

The correct answer is b. NFS is used to share data and mounted directories between multiple Unix and Linux machines. To share data between a Linux and Windows client, you must use Samba.

Question 8

> What is xntpd?
>
> ○ a. An X Window Server
>
> ○ b. An X FTP server
>
> ○ c. A time Synchronization server
>
> ○ d. An X-based NT Administration tool

The correct answer is c. The xntpd is part of the xntpd3 package that includes tools for time synchronization between a client and host machine. Answers a, c, and d are all invalid answers.

Question 9

> What is Squid?
>
> ○ a. An HTTP proxy
>
> ○ b. An NIS proxy
>
> ○ c. A DNS caching proxy
>
> ○ d. The Linux mascot

The correct answer is a. Squid is a proxy server that is capable of caching HTTP, FTP, and gopher requests. Answer b is incorrect because there is no such thing as an NIS proxy. Answer c is incorrect because the DNS caching is handled by the name server. Answer d is incorrect; Tux (a penguin) is the Linux mascot.

Question 10

> What port does Squid listen to (by default)?
>
> ○ a. 3620
>
> ○ b. 3128
>
> ○ c. 6619
>
> ○ d. None of the above

The correct answer is b. The default port Squid listens on is 3128. Answers a, c, and d are incorrect because they are not valid answers.

Task 1

Install the DNS (BIND) server on your machine. Configure it to set up three primary domains and a secondary domain. Set up the reverse files for your subnet. Use nslookup to see that your three primary domains each have the appropriate IP addresses and domains assigned to them.

Task 2

Install the Apache Web Server. Configure Apache to host 3 different virtual hosts, each with their own IP on your subnetwork. Create unique DocumentRoot entries for each, so that when displayed on your system, each has a unique Web site. Now change the configuration files for the three to have the same IP address, but still have the three unique Web sites. Don't forget to set up any DNS and host files.

Task 3

Install the wu-ftpd FTP server. Set up a new user on your system to FTP from another machine on your network (if available). Upload a test file into the user's home directory. Now change to ftpaccess files to deny that user from the remote host. Try to connect again. What happens? Next configure the FTP server for anonymous user connections using the anon-ftp package. Now connect from the same remote system as an anonymous user. What happened? Why?

Task 4

Install the NFS server on your machine. Set up an NFS share for the /tmp directory on your system. Mount the NFS share from another machine on your network. Try to write a file to the /tmp directory. What happened? Change the NFS mount entry to (ro). Try to write another file to the /tmp directory from the remote host. What happens?

Task 5

Install the SMB server on your machine. Set up an SMB share to /usr/docs/. Make sure the docs are not writeable. Mount the SMB share from a Windows client on your network. Browse the /usr/docs/ entries and open a file. Try to write to it. What happens? Add another share to the /mnt/cdrom directory. Mount a Windows or Microsoft related CD-ROM in the SMB server CD-ROM. Access the /mnt/cdrom share from a Windows machine. Execute an .exe from the CD-ROM. Did it work?

Task 6

Set up two machines on your network. Set up the first machine to be a DHCP server. Set up the second machine to be a DHCP client. Bring the ethernet interface on the client up and down a few times, checking the assigned IP address to the machine each time. What happens? Why?

Need To Know More?

Albitz, Paul and Cricket Liu. *DNS and BIND*, O'Reilly & Associates, Sebastopol, CA, 1998. ISBN 1-56592-512-2. This book covers implementation and usage of DNS and BIND.

Baines, Dominic. *Samba Black Book*, The Coriolis Group, Scottsdale, AZ, 1999. ISBN 1-57610-455-9. This book covers the implementation and usage of Samba.

Costales, Bryan and Eric Allman. *Sendmail*, O'Reilly & Associates, Sebastopol, CA, 1997. ISBN 1-56592-222-0. This book covers all the technical aspects of compiling, configuring, and using Sendmail.

Kabir, Mohammed J. *Apache Server Bible*, IDG Books Worldwide, 1999. ISBN 0-76453-218-9. This book covers every aspect of Apache Web server administration, including configuration and administration. It also includes a CD-ROM with utilities covered in the book and third-party applications to assist with Apache installation and administration.

Kelly, Petter, P. Donham, David Collier-Brown. *Using Samba*, O'Reilly & Associates, Sebastopol, CA, 1999. ISBN 1-56592-449-5. This book covers implementation and usage of Samba.

Laurie, Ben and Peter Laurie. *Apache: The Definitive Guide*, 2nd Edition, O'Reilly & Associates, Sebastopol, CA, 1999. ISBN 1-56592-528-9. This book is a complete guide for how to obtain, configure, and secure Apache on both Unix and other operating systems.

Stern, Hal and Mike Loukides. *Managing NFS and NIS*, O'Reilly & Associates, Sebastopol, CA, 1991. ISBN 0-93717-575-7. This book provides required information for system administrators who need to set up and administer either NFS or NIS in a Unix environment.

http://squid.nlanr.net/

For more information about current development and documentation regarding Squid, visit the Squid Web site.

http://www.samba.org/

For more information about current development and documentation regarding Samba, visit Samba's Web site.

http://www.sendmail.org/

For more information about current development and documentation on Sendmail, visit Sendmail's Web site.

http://metalab.unc.edu/LDP

The Linux Documentation Project contains links, HOWTOs, and other documentation.

System Security
And Administration

11

Terms you'll need to understand:

√ Database

√ Query

√ Pluggable modules

√ tty devices

√ Daemons

√ Firewall

√ Route

Techniques you'll need to master:

√ Understanding NIS implementation

√ Implementing Name Server Switching options

√ Using Pluggable Authentication Modules (PAM)

√ Setting up secure tty sessions

√ Using INET services

√ Implementing tcp_wrappers

√ Setting up routing

√ Configuring a firewall

Security is an essential part of networking. Keeping your system secure from crackers and unavailable for unauthorized use is a must. Some very basic security problems can arise from standard daily activities. With such emphasis placed on network security today, it is important for an RHCE in the workplace to be comfortable with setting up network security. With this in mind, configuration and working knowledge of network security tools and concepts is essential. In this chapter, we will discuss security concepts, NIS (Network Information Service), PAM (Pluggable Authentication Modules), inetd, and tcp_wrappers. We will also discuss some advanced network options including routing, firewalling, and IP masquerading.

NIS

NIS is Sun's Network Information Service. It was formerly known as Yellow Pages, but after a trademark dispute with British Telecom, Sun changed the name to Network Information Service.

NIS is a small directory service whose main purpose is to allow remote authentication for users on local network systems. NIS allows configuration information such as passwd and group files, sendmail aliases, automount maps, and hosts files to be kept on a separate server. Each system map NIS domain runs the NIS client and ypbind to find a server and retrieve the appropriate maps on it.

Within a NIS domain, there must be at least one NIS server. In some cases, multiple NIS servers are set up with master and slave NIS servers. In the master-slave setup, the slave NIS servers make copies of the master NIS servers' database each time the master database changes.

You must run the RPC PortMapper (/usr/sbin/portmap) to run NIS. The RPC PortMapper servers convert the RPC program numbering to TCP/IP or UDP/IP protocol port numbers. Typically, the PortMapper servers are started by inetd. We will discuss network services on inetd later in this chapter.

NIS On Red Hat Linux

Red Hat Linux 6.0 ships with NIS v.2 compliant clients, servers, and tools. The three NIS packages in Red Hat Linux 6.0 include ypbind (the NIS client), ypserv (the NIS server), and yp-tools (the utilities for querying the NIS server). NIS is only used when specified by the /etc/nsswitch.conf file and ypbind. In this section, we will discuss the NIS client and NIS server commands.

NIS Client

The NIS client is responsible for querying the NIS server for information from the NIS system maps and other NIS information. There are five main tools that NIS clients use:

➤ **ypbind**   Finds and stores information about an NIS domain and server. Information is stored in /var/yp/binding.

➤ **ypwhich**   Returns the name of the NIS server used by the NIS client.

➤ **ypcat**   Prints the values of all keys in the specified NIS database.

➤ **yppoll**   Returns the version and master server of the specified NIS map.

➤ **ypmatch**   Prints the values of keys from an NIS map.

NIS Server

The NIS server is responsible for hosting the system maps and authentication files on its dedicated machine. The NIS server then responds to NIS client requests for authentication, system map, and other NIS information. In addition to the NIS client commands, the NIS server uses NIS commands such as:

➤ **ypserv**   The NIS server program.

➤ **yppasswd**   Server that handles the NIS password changes.

Other NIS Commands

There is a number of other NIS commands that are available for use on NIS networks. A couple of NIS commands that are commonly used are:

➤ **makedbm**   Translates ASCII databases, such as /etc/passwd to DBM databases.

➤ **yppush**   Notifies the slave servers when changes are made to master databases.

/etc/nsswitch.conf

NIS is only implemented when specified by the /etc/nsswitch.conf file or with ypbind. The GNU C library includes support for the Name Server Switch file (/etc/nsswitch.conf), which is patterned after the nsswitch.conf file on Solaris 2. The Name Server Switch file configures the order of lookups for various system services. The following snippet is the /etc/nsswitch.conf file that is shipped with Red Hat 6.0.

```
#
# /etc/nsswitch.conf
#
# An example Name Service Switch config file. This file should be
# sorted with the most-used services at the beginning.
#
# The entry '[NOTFOUND=return]' means that the search for an
# entry should stop if the search in the previous entry turned
# up nothing. Note that if the search failed due to some other
# reason (like no NIS server responding) then the search continues
# with the next entry.
#
# Legal entries are:
#
# nisplus or nis+     Use NIS+ (NIS version 3)
# nis or yp           Use NIS (NIS version 2), also called YP
# dns                 Use DNS (Domain Name Service)
# files               Use the local files
# db                  Use the local database (.db) files
# compat              Use NIS on compat mode
# [NOTFOUND=return]     Stop searching if not found so far
#
# To use db, put the "db" in front of "files" for entries you want
# to be looked up first in the databases
#
# Example:
#passwd:    db files nisplus nis
#shadow:    db files nisplus nis
#group:     db files nisplus nis

passwd:     files nisplus nis
shadow:     files nisplus nis
group:      files nisplus nis

#hosts:     db files nisplus nis dns
hosts:      files nisplus nis dns

services:   nisplus [NOTFOUND=return] files
networks:   nisplus [NOTFOUND=return] files
protocols:  nisplus [NOTFOUND=return] files
rpc:        nisplus [NOTFOUND=return] files
ethers:     nisplus [NOTFOUND=return] files
netmasks:   nisplus [NOTFOUND=return] files
bootparams: nisplus [NOTFOUND=return] files

netgroup:   nisplus
```

```
publickey:   nisplus

automount:   files nisplus
aliases:     files nisplus
```

The format of the preceding nsswitch.conf file uses the layout, database: location [result=action], where database is the name of the requested database, location is the location of the database, result is the requested result, and action is the action that occurs if the requested result is matched. Therefore, as in the above stock Red Hat 6.0 nsswitch.conf file, passwd lookups with the getpw*C library calls will first go to the local passwd file, and if not located, will second try NIS+, and if still not located will finally try NIS.

Tables 11.1 through 11.3 list the databases, locations, and results that the GNU C library can recognize.

Note: The action for any result will always either be RETURN or CONTINUE.

Table 11.1	NIS databases.
Database	**Database Explanation**
aliases	Mail aliases that are used by sendmail
ethers	Ethernet numbers
group	Groups of users used by getgrent functions
hosts	Host names and numbers used by gethostbyname and similar functions
netgroup	Network-wide list of hosts and users used for access rules
network	Network names and numbers, used by getnetent functions
passwd	User paswords used by getpwent functions
protocols	Network protocols used by getprotent functions
publickey	Public and secret keys for secure_rpc, used by NIS+ and NFS
rpc	Remote procedure call names and numbers used by getrpcbyname and similar functions
services	Network services uses by getservent functions
shadow	Shadow user passwords used by getspnam functions

Table 11.2 NIS locations.

Location	Location Description
nisplus (nis+)	lookup via NIS+
nis (yp)	lookup via NIS
compat	lookup via NIS in manner compatible with older versions of glibc
db	lookup via local database files
files	lookup via local text files
dns	lookup via DNS

Table 11.3 NIS results.

Result	Result Description	Default Action
SUCCESS	The error occurred and the wanted entry is returned.	Return
NOTFOUND	The lookup process works OK, but the needed value was not found.	Continue
UNAVAIL	The service is permanently unavailable. This can either mean the needed file is not available, or for DNS, the server is not available or does not allow queries.	Continue
TRYAGAIN	The service is temporarily unavailable. This could mean a file is locked or a server cannot accept any more connections.	Continue

Pluggable Authentication Modules (PAM)

PAM is the Pluggable Authentication Modules system that enables ruleset implementation without having to recode individual services. All security conscious programs (such as **login, su,** and **ftp)** are configured by PAM to do a variety of authentication and security checks.

When a service such as **login** is used, PAM will check its configuration files to determine how to authenticate the user. For instance, PAM may authenticate by checking /etc/passwd, kerberos, or NIS. After the method of authentication is determined, PAM will then return an answer to the service to indicate whether the user was authenticated.

PAM Configuration

All the PAM configuration files are located in /etc/pam.d/. Every application or service that can use PAM has a file entry in /etc/pam.d/ as well. Some of the most common entries that can be found under /etc/pam.d/ include **chfn, chsh, halt, linuxconf, login, passwd, ppp, reboot, rexec, rlogin, rsh, shutdown, su, xdm,** and **xscreensaver.** If installed, you may even find **kde, samba,** and **ssh** here as well. Looking at these files, you will see four columns of information. They include module-type, control-flag, module-path, and arguments. Take a look at the following example of the login entry under /etc/pam.d/:

```
#%PAM-1.0
auth       required     /lib/security/pam_securetty.so
auth       required     /lib/secuirty/pam_pwdb.so        shadow nullok
auth       required     /lib/security/pam_nologin.so
account    required     /lib/security/pam_pwdb.so
password   required     /lib/security/pam_cracklib.so
password   required     /lib/security/pam_pwdb.so nullok use_authtok
session    required     /lib/security/pam_pwdb.so
session    optional     /lib/security/pam_console.so
```

module-type

There are currently four types of modules that you will find under the module-type column in your PAM configuration files. These include **auth, account, session,** and **password.**

➤ **auth**   This module type provides two ways of authenticating the user. First, it establishes that the user is indeed who the user claims to be. It does this by instructing the application to prompt the user for a password. The module can then grant group membership (independent of /etc/ groups) or other privileges through its credential granting properties.

➤ **account**   This modules performs non-authentication-based account management. It is typically used to restrict or permit access to a service based on the time of day, maximum number of users, or even the location of the user (for instance, allowing user "root" to only log in from the console).

➤ **session**   This module is associated with performing duties that need to be done for the user before they can be given service. Services that are affected by this include the logging of information of a user opening and closing data, mounting directories, and so on.

➤ **password**   This module is required for updating the authentication token associated with each user. There is typically one module for each challenge- or response-based authentication (auth) module-type.

control-flag

The control-flag is used to indicate how the PAM library will react to the success or failure of the module with which it is associated. The four flags that are used to specify the module actions are **required, requisite, sufficient,** and **optional,** described here:

➤ **required**   This indicates that the success of the module is required for the module-type facility to succeed. If this module fails, the failure will not be apparent to the user until all the modules of the same module-type have been executed.

➤ **requisite**   This is similar to **required,** but if this module fails, control is immediately returned to the application. This flag is useful to protect against the possibility of a user being allowed to enter a password over an unsafe medium.

➤ **sufficient**   This indicates that the Linux-PAM library is satisfied that this module-type has succeeded in its purpose. If no previous module has failed, no more stacked modules of this type are invoked. If this module fails, the result is not deemed fatal to the application.

➤ **optional**   This control-flag marks the module as not being critical to the success or failure of the user's application for service. In fact, Linux-PAM will ignore such a module when determining if the module stack succeeds or fails.

module-path And Arguments

The **module-path** is the path name to the dynamically loadable module. The default path to the module is set to /usr/lib/security/, unless another path is mentioned. Typically the full path /usr/lib/security/ is listed regardless.

The argument column of each entry lists arguments that are passed to the module when the module is invoked. Typically, these arguments are optional and are listed specifically to each given module. If an argument is invalid, the module ignores it. If such an error is made, the module is required to write the error to **syslog,** the system logfile. The five generic arguments that are often used and understood by most modules are **debug, no_warn, use_first_pass, try_first_pass,** and **use_mapped_pass,** described here:

➤ **debug**   Use the **syslog** cal to log debugging information to the system log files.

➤ **no_warn**   Instruct module to not give warning messages to the application.

➤ **use_first_pass**   The module should not prompt the user for a password. Instead, it should obtain the previously typed password from the preceding auth module. If that does not work, the user will not be authenticated.

➤ **try_first_pass**   The module should attempt authentication with the previously typed password from the preceding auth module. If that does not work, the user is prompted for a password.

➤ **use_mapped_pass**   Instructs the module to take the clear text authentication token entered by a previous module and use it to generate an encrypted (or decrypted) key to safely store or retrieve the authentication token required for the module.

The **use_mapped_pass** argument is not currently supported by any of the modules in the Linux-PAM distribution because of possible consequences associated with U.S. encryption restrictions. Developers within the United States (or their own country) may implement it freely within their country.

A special argument listed in the example for auth was **shadow**. This refers to support for shadow passwords, which is supported by pam_pwdb.so. Shadow passwords utilize several methods to increase system security. Shadow passwords make system password files more difficult to extract system password information by replacing the password field of /etc/passwd (with an "x") and creating the file /etc/shadow to contain the password hash.

Red Hat 6.0 can be set to use shadow passwords during installation. If shadow passwords were not enabled during installation, the system can be converted to use shadow passwords by running the **pwconv** program. If needed, it can later be converted back to regular password by using **pwunconv**. The change should be transparent to all programs that use PAM.

/etc/securetty

As one of the most popular uses of PAM, the /etc/securetty file is used to specify settings for the secure tty access on the system. The /etc/securetty file is used by **login** to enable which tty devices that root is able to log in on. Typically, only the local consoles are listed. By limiting access to only local consoles, you disable direct login superuser privileges from anywhere except the console. This is not fail-safe however, as disabling virtual terminal console login does not restrict the user from using **su** to log in as root from the user account. The output of the /etc/securetty file is very simple, as it only lists the tty devices that allow root logins. Figure 11.1 shows a sample output of a default Red Hat 6.0 /etc/securetty file.

inetd

The daemon **inetd** is the Internet daemon that controls most of the network services that listen for incoming connections on your machine. The inetd daemon runs in the background, binding all relevant ports and calling the appropriate servers when necessary.

The /etc/inetd.conf configuration file controls the inetd daemon. This inetd.conf file specifies which services the machine is supposed to manage, and it contains a list of entries comprised of seven fields. The seven fields include the service name, socket type, protocol, wait/nowait, user, server program, and arguments, described here:

➤ **Service Name**   The service name is translated to a port number by looking the service name up in the /etc/services file.

➤ **Socket Type**   This specifies either the stream for TCP or dgram for UDP.

➤ **Protocol**   This specifies the name of the transport protocol used by the service.

➤ **wait/nowait**   This specifies the wait or nowait option for dgram sockets (it will not affect stream sockets).

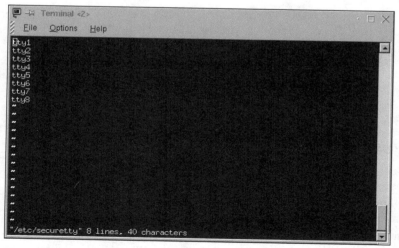

Figure 11.1   Sample output of /etc/securetty.

➤ **User**   Login ID of the user that the process will execute under.

➤ **Server Program**   Full path name to the server program to be executed.

➤ **Arguments**   Command and arguments to be passed to the server.

When a connection is requested from another machine over a network, the request is initially handled by inetd. First, inetd checks for proper tcpd granted access permissions. Second, inetd looks up the service by its port number in /etc/services/. It then starts the appropriate server listed in the /etc/inetd.conf file to connect with the incoming request.

To disable a network service handled by inetd is very simple: simply comment the specific line in /etc/inetd.conf that corresponds to the service with a hash (#) mark. The following is a snippet from a sample inetd.conf file. Notice that there are multiple entries for services such as ftp that can be used with both tcp and upd. In addition, notice that this /etc/inetd.conf file has several services disabled, such as finger and talk:

```
#
ftp     stream  tcp   nowait   root   /usr/sbin/tcpd    in.ftpd -l -a
telnet  stream  tcp   nowait   root   /usr/sbin/tcpd    in.telnetd
#
# Shell, login, exec, comsat and talk are BSD protocols.
#
shell   stream  tcp   nowait   root   /usr/sbin/tcpd    in.rshd
login   stream  tcp   nowait   root   /usr/sbin/tcpd    in.rlogind
#exec   stream  tcp   nowait   root   /usr/sbin/tcpd    in.rexecd
#talk   dgram   udp   wait     root   /usr/sbin/tcpd    in.talkd
ntalk   dgram   udp   wait     root   /usr/sbin/tcpd    in.ntalkd
#
# Pop and imap mail services et al
#
#pop-2  stream  tcp   nowait   root   /usr/sbin/tcpd    ipop2d
#pop-3  stream  tcp   nowait   root   /usr/sbin/tcpd    ipop3d
#imap   stream  tcp   nowait   root   /usr/sbin/tcpd    imapd
#
# Finger, systat and netstat give out user information which may be
# valuable to potential "system crackers." Many sites choose to
# disable some or all of these services to improve security.
#
finger stream  tcp   nowait    root   /usr/sbin/tcpd       in.fingerd
#cfinger stream tcp  nowait    root   /usr/sbin/tcpd       in.cfingerd
#systat stream tcp   nowait    guest  /usr/sbin/tcpd/bin/ps  -auwwx
#netstat stream tcp  nowait    guest  /usr/sbin/tcpd /bin/netstat -f
inet
```

```
#
# Authentication
#
auth  stream  tcp  nowait  nobody /usr/sbin/in.identd in.identd -l
#
# End of inetd.conf
```

Shadow Passwords

Shadow passwords have several purposes. First, the password field of /etc/passwd is removed (replaced by an "x"). The file /etc/shadow then contains the password hash. The permissions on the shadow file make it unreadable by anyone but root (and, on some distributions, the "shadow" group). This makes it more difficult to extract password hashes to run through crack or any other similar password guessing programs. The shadow file also contains password aging information.

A system can be converted to shadow passwords by running the pwconv program. If needed, it can later be converted back by using pwunconv. The change should be transparent to all programs that use PAM (discussed in Chapter 1). Password aging can be controlled with the **chage** program.

tcp_wrappers

The use of tcp_wrappers on your system allows you to perform specific actions when another machine attempts to connect, or actually connects, to your own. With the use of the /etc/hosts.allow and /etc/hosts.deny configuration files, you can determine who can and who cannot connect to your machine or who can and who cannot use specific services. The use of tcp_wrappers can only affect services that are controlled by **inetd** (as previously discussed in the section on **inetd**).

When a connection request is sent from another machine to your machine, **inetd** first checks to see that the service is enabled and all permissions are set properly. If so, **inetd** then passes off the request to tcp_wrappers. Next, tcp_wrappers checks the /etc/hosts.allow file to see if permission is granted specifically for that service to the requested user. If tcp_wrappers finds that the specific user is granted access to the service, the connection is granted. If no setting in /etc/hosts.allow is specified, then tcp_wrappers checks the /etc/hosts.deny file. If tcp_wrappers finds that the specific service has been denied to that user, the connection is refused. However, if no setting in /etc/hosts.deny specifies that that service to the requested user is denied, the connection is granted.

/etc/hosts.allow

The /etc/hosts.allow file is the first file that tcp_wrappers checks for allowed connections to specific services by specific users. If a service or user is specifically granted access in /etc/hosts.allow, the /etc/hosts.deny file is ignored.

In the /etc/hosts.allow file, permission is granted to either a specific service or to all services. The service setting is then granted to individual IP blocks, IP ranges, domains, local, or to all. The entries in the /etc/hosts.allow file are set up by *service:granted_to* where *service* specifies the name of the services and *granted_to* specifies whom (or what location) has permission to use the service.

Specifying Services

When specifying a service to provide access to, you have the option of specifying the particular service, such as ftpd, or to specify all services. To specify a particular service, you will use the syntax **in.***service*, where *service* is the service to be specified. To specify all services, you will use the syntax **ALL**.

To grant a specific services, such as ftpd, to everyone on your local 192.168.x.x network, you would have an entry in your /etc/hosts.allow file that looked like this: **in.ftpd: 192.168.0.0/192.168.255.255**. With this entry, tcp_wrappers will allow access to the ftp daemon that is connecting from any IP between 192.168.0.0 through 192.168.255.255.

To grant all services to everyone on your local 192.168.x.x network, you would have an entry in your /etc/hosts.allow file that looked like this: **ALL: 192.168.0.0/192.168.255.255**. With this entry, tcp_wrappers will allow access to all services granted by **inetd** that are connecting from any IP between 192.168.0.0 through 192.168.255.255.

Specifying User Access

When granting access to a service to a user, you have the option of specifying a specific domain, an IP, a range of IPs, or all. In addition, you can use an **EXCEPT** argument that allows you to specify specific domains and IPs to not grant access to.

To specify all services access to a specific domain such as redhat.com, you would use the following entry: **ALL: .redhat.com**. With this entry, any user from redhat.com can access all available services on your machine. To specify an additional domain, such as coriolis.com, you would use the following: **ALL: .redhat.com, .coriolis.com**.

To specify permission to all services to a specific IP such as 192.168.0.1, you would use the following: **ALL: 192.168.0.1**. With this entry, only users from

192.168.0.1 can access all services on the machine. To specify an additional IP, such as 192.168.0.100, you would use the following: **ALL: 192.168.0.1, 192.168.0.100**. To specify a range of IPs, such as 192.168.0.1 through 192.168.0.100, you would use **ALL: 192.168.0.1/192.160.0.100**.

To specify permission to all services to all users, you would use **ALL: ALL**. You can specify **EXCEPT** cases with any of the previously mentioned arrangements. For instance, **ALL: ALL EXCEPT LOCAL** would grant everyone access, except users on your local connection. In addition, **ALL: ALL EXCEPT .redhat.com** would grant all access, except anyone connecting from redhat.com. An additional use of **EXCEPT** can be used in the services specification **ALL EXCEPT in.ftpd: ALL**. Any combination of services and hosts can be used in the /etc/hosts.allow file. A sample /etc/hosts.allow file follows:

```
#
# hosts.allow  This file describes the names of the hosts which are
#              allowed to use the local INET services, as decided
#              by the '/usr/sbin/tcpd' server.
#
in.ftpd:ALL EXCEPT 204.28.2.23, 204.28.0.1
in.telnetd: .redhat.com
```

/etc/hosts.deny

If a service or user is not specified to have direct access in the /etc/hosts.allow file, tcp_wrappers will then check to see if the service or user is denied in the /etc/hosts.deny file. The format for the entries in /etc/hosts.deny is identical to the entries found in /etc/hosts.allow. To reference online syntax for /etc/hosts.deny, refer to the previous section "/etc/hosts.allow."

Any entry in /etc/hosts.deny can be overridden in the /etc/hosts.allow file. Therefore, if access is granted to **ALL:ALL** in /etc/hosts.allow, then an entry of **in.ftpd: .redhat.com** in /etc/hosts.deny will be ignored. However, if an entry exists in /etc/hosts.allow, such as **in.ftpd: 192.168.0.0/192.168.255.255**, and an entry exists in /etc/hosts.deny, such as **ALL:ALL**, the only service that can be accessed on your system is ftpd. The service can only be accessed by users on IPs ranging from 192.168.0.0 through 192.168.255.255. All other service requests or requests from any other IP will be rejected by the /etc/hosts.deny entry.

Linux Routing

Routing with Linux fully implements TCP/IP protocol routing. There are several routing services available in addition to simple "router" services. With routing on Linux, you can also set up Linux firewalls and IP masquerading (discussed in the "Linux Firewalling" and "IP Masquerading" sections later in this chapter).

Routing

To set up routing on Linux, you must have installed the net-tools packages. The net-tools package (net-tools-1.51-3.i386.rpm) can be found on your Red Hat Linux 6.0 CD under the /RedHat/RPMS/ directory. The two main tools found in the net-tools package are **route** and **netstat**.

The **route** command is used to add routes to your routing system. For example, let's say you have a system on the network with an IP address (192.168.1.1) on the ethernet interface (eth0). The router on your network has the IP address 192.168.2.1. If you wanted to send all traffic (that isn't destined to 192.168.1.0) to the 192.168.2.1 "gateway" host, you could issue

```
route add default gw 192.168.2.1 dev eth1
```

The **netstat** tool is used to list network connections and the routing tables used on your system. By viewing the routing table, all the routes that are set up on your system will print. To view the routing table, use the command **netstat -rn**. The Kernal IP routing table, shown in Listing 11.1, is one example.

Listing 11.1   Kernel IP routing table.

Destination	Gateway	Genmask	Flags	Metric	Ref	Use	Iface
192.168.1.1	0.0.0.0	255.255.255.255	UH	0	0	0	eth0
192.168.1.0	0.0.0.0	255.255.255.0	U	0	0	0	eth0
192.168.2.100	0.0.0.0	255.255.255.255	UH	0	0	0	eth1
192.168.2.0	0.0.0.0	255.255.255.0	U	0	0	0	eth1
127.0.0.0	0.0.0.0	255.0.0.0	U	0	0	0	lo
0.0.0.0	192.168.2.1	0.0.0.0	UG	0	0	0	eth1

Listing 11.1 has six routing entries. The first two entries specify that traffic destined for the 192.168.1.0 network should be sent through the eth0 interface. The second two entries specify that network traffic destined for the 192.168.2.0 network should be sent though the eth1 interface. The fifth entry is to specify to keep local traffic on the system, rather than sending it over the network. The sixth entry specifies that all other traffic should be routed to 192.168.2.1, and the host on that IP will have to decide where to route the information.

IP Forwarding

A router uses IP forwarding to route packets originating from a separate host to another host on the network. For instance, a system (without IP forwarding set up) using the above routing table would get a "host unreachable" error if a host on the 192.168.1.0 network would send a packet to any other host than 192.168.1.1. To enable this sample system to forward the packet as if it were originating from the system itself, you must enable network pack forwarding (IPv4). There are two methods you can use to enable packet forwarding:

➤ Issue a command to the ip_forward script to enable the system. You can manually do this by typing

```
echo>/proc/sys/net/ipv4/ip_forward
```

➤ Use netcfg. Execute netcfg to bring up the network configurator window. Under the "routing" option, enable the option that says "Network Packet Forwarding (IPv4)," as shown in Figure 11.2.

Routes

There are two different types of routes that can be established with Linux TCP/IP routing—static and dynamic. Static routes are "hard-coded" routes that are assigned on a router. They will not change, regardless if there is a failure on a network or if an alternate route is available. This means that a static route is the only path from one host to another. The most popular static route on a Linux network is the route to the machine's default gateway.

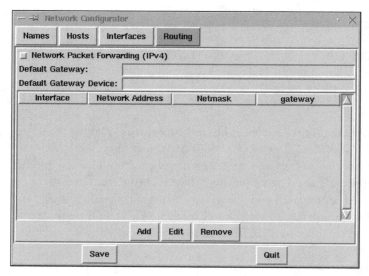

Figure 11.2   Enable packet forwarding in netcfg.

A dynamic route is a route that is assigned "on the fly," meaning no definitive route is set, and a route for a packet is assigned each time a packet is sent (not predetermined). A typical type of dynamic route is the route established with standard dial-up access to an ISP. When a request is made from the client for a particular Web site, for instance, the packet is sent from the client to the ISP router. The ISP router then looks for the next router that can accept the packet for the requested recipient. If that router does not respond, the ISP router then looks for an alternate router that can reach the host (or an additional router), until the host is reached. The ability to use an alternate route is the main difference between dynamic and static routes. A dynamic route may use a separate route each time a specific host is requested, whereas a static route will use the exact same route for the specified host.

Linux Firewalling

The Linux kernel can be set up to do firewalling, meaning that certain kinds of TCP/IP traffic are allowed, but other traffic is not. Firewall support is configured using **ipchains**. Support for **ipchains** is a new feature of 2.2.x (and very late 2.0.x kernels). Earlier kernels used the **ipfwadm** utility (which is now obsolete).

In order to perform firewalling on a Red Hat Linux system, you must have compiled the Linux kernel with firewalling support. To check if your kernel is already compiled for firewalling, do the following:

```
ls -l /proc/net/ip_fwchains
```

If the file exists, then your kernel already has compiled support for firewalling. If not, then you need to compile a kernel with firewalling support. If you need (or choose) to compile a new kernel for firewalling support, enable (or modularize) the following support:

➤ Networking support (CONFIG_NET)

➤ Network firewalls (CONFIG_FIREWALL)

➤ TCP/IP networking (CONFIG_INET)

➤ IP: firewalling (CONFIG_IP_FIREWALL)

➤ IP: always defragment (required for masquerading) (CONFIG_IP_ALWAYS_DEFRAG)

ipchains

The **ipchains** tool specifies firewall policies to the Linux kernel. With **ipchains**, you can filter depending on IP address, port, network, destination, source, subnet, connection state, domain names, sub-domain names, and so on. You can in-stall **ipchains** from the ipchains package on the Red Hat Linux 6.0 CD-ROM. The RPM for **ipchains** is ipchains-1.3.8-3.i386.rpm.

There are three different categories of rules in **ipchains**: the IP input chain, the IP output chain, and the IP forwarding chain. For each category, an individual table of rules is maintained:

➤ **IP input chain (Input firewall)**   The IP input rules regulate the accep-tance of incoming IP packets. All packets coming in via one of the local network interfaces are checked against the input firewall rules. A rule that matches a packet will cause the rule's packet and byte counters to be incremented appropriately.

➤ **IP output chain (Output firewall)**   The IP output rules define the permissions for sending IP packets. All packets that are to be sent via one of the local network interfaces are checked against the output firewall rules. A rule that matches will cause the rule's packet and byte counters to be incremented appropriately.

➤ **IP forwarding chain (Forwarding firewall)**   The IP forwarding rules define the permissions for forwarding IP packets. All packets sent by a remote host having another remote destination are checked against the forwarding firewall rules. A rule that matches will cause the rules packet and byte counters to be incremented appropriately.

Using ipchains

There are multiple options, rules, and so on that can be used for issuing **ipchains** commands. The standard syntax for using **ipchains** is:

```
ipchains -command chain [rule specification] [target]
```

There are several different commands that can be issued to **ipchains**. Table 11.4 lists the six most common commands, usage, and description of what the com-mand does. (For a complete list, view the **ipchains(5)** man page – **man 5 ipchains**.)

Rule specifications are required when you add (-A) or delete (-D) a rule. There are several parameters that may be used for rule specifications (for a complete list, view **man 5 ipchains**). Three popular rule specifications are –**p** (protocol), –**s** (specify), and –**j** (jump), described here:

➤ -p   Specifies protocol. Protocol could be tcp, udp, icmp, or all. For example, usage= ipchains –A input –p icmp –s *source* –j *target*.

➤ -s   Specifies the source. Source can be name of host or network, or an IP address. For example, usage= ipchains –A input –s 192.168.100.0 –j *target*.

Table 11.4	Commands for ipchains.	
Command	**Usage**	**Description**
-A	ipchains –A *chain rule*	Append rule specification to end of specified chain.
-D	ipchains –D *chain rule*	Delete rule from specified chain.
-L	ipchains –L *chain*	List all rules in selected chain. (If no chain is specified, all rules are listed.)
-F	ipchains –F *chain*	Flush all rules from selected chain.
-P	ipchains –P *chain target*	Set policy of specified chain to given target (see Table 11.5).
-h	ipchains –h	Help.

➤ **-j** Specifies a target to a rule, meaning what to do if packet matches. For example, usage=ipchains –A input –s 192.168.100.0 –j DENY.

When specifying your rule, there are several types of "targets" that you can specify. The target is what happens when your rule specifications are matched. Five of the most common target values are ACCEPT, DENY, REJECT, MASQ, and REDIRECT. Table 11.5 lists and explains each of the five targets.

Table 11.5	ipchains targets.
Target	**Description**
ACCEPT	Allows packet through.
DENY	Drops packet.
REJECT	Similar to DENY, but sends an ICMP message back to sender stating that the packet was dropped.
MASQ	Only used in forward chains (or user defined chains). Requires CONFIG_IP_MASQUERADE to be compiled in the Linux kernel. Packets are masqueraded as if they were originated from local host. (Reverse packets are also demasqueraded automatically, bypassing the forwarding chain.) See the section in this chapter titled "IP Masquerading" for more information.
REDIRECT	Only used in forward chains (or user defined chains). Requires CONFIG_IP_TRANSPARENT_PROXY to be compiled in Linux kernel. Packets are redirected to a local socket.

Sample ipchains

The following are some sample **ipchains** rules and their explanations. The sample scenario is being set up on a router (192.168.0.254) controlling a 192.168.0.x network:

➤ **ipchains –P input –j REJECT**   This line will reject all incoming packets unless otherwise specified with an ALLOW in the input chain.

➤ **ipchains –A input –p icmp –j DENY**   This line will add a rule to the input chain that denies all ICMP packets coming into the network.

➤ **ipchains –A output –p tcp –j ALLOW**   This line will add a rule to the output chain that ALLOWS all TCP packets to go out of the network.

➤ **ipchains –A input –s 192.168.50.2 –j REJECT**   This line will add a rule to the input chain that REJECTS all packets from 192.168.50.2 to come into the network.

IP Masquerading

IP masquerading is a specialized version of NAT (Network Address Translation), where all packets on a network are forwarded through a firewall and modified to appear as if the packet originated from the firewall itself. IP masquerading relies on the firewalling and **ipchains** packages to be installed (explained in section in this chapter titled "Sample ipchains").

Setting Up IP Masquerading

In addition to the support for firewalling and the **ipchains** package installation, you must have specific options compiled (or modularized) into the Linux kernel. The four options required are as follows:

➤ IP: transparent proxy support
(CONFIG_IP_TRANSPARENT_PROXY)

➤ IP: masquerading
(CONFIG_IP_MASQUERADE)

➤ IP: masquerading special modules support
(CONFIG_IP_MASQUERADE_MOD)

➤ IP: ipportfw masq support
(EXPERIMENTAL)(CONFIG_IP_MASQUERADE_IPPORTFW)

Using ipchains For IP Masquerading

Setting up an **ipchains** rule to masquerade is simple. Let's say you have an internal network assigned with 192.168.0.x addresses. You want to give each

machine in your internal network access to the Internet through a single gateway server (a Linux router dialed in via modem to the Internet). You can forward
all traffic from the internal ethernet interface (eth0) to the external network
interface (ppp0), masquerading all the packets to look as if it was generated by
the router with the following **ipchains** command (all on one line):

```
ipchains -A forward -p all -s 192.168.0.0/24 -d 0.0.0.0/0 -i ppp0
        -j MASQ
```

Practice Questions

Question 1

What line in /etc/hosts.allow would specifially grant access to ftpd for users from redhat.com?

○ a. ALL EXCEPT in.ftpd: .redhat.com

○ b. in.ftpd: ALL EXCEPT .redhat.com

○ c. ALL: in.ftpd

○ d. None of the above

The correct answer is d. Answer a is incorrect because it specifies permission for all services except ftpd to redhat.com. Answer b is incorrect because it specifies access to ftpd from all except redhat.com. Answer c is incorrect because it is an invalid format.

Question 2

What command do you use to add routes to a Linux router?

○ a. addroute

○ b. route

○ c. netstat

○ d. net

The correct answer is b. The route command is used for adding routes to a Linux router. Answers a and d are incorrect because they are invalid options. Answer c is incorrect because netstat is used to print network information, such as routing tables and so forth, but does not add routes to the system.

Question 3

> In what file could you deny all INET services from all network connections? [Check all correct answers]
>
> ❑ a. /etc/hosts.allow
>
> ❑ b. /etc/hosts.deny
>
> ❑ c. /etc/inetd.conf
>
> ❑ d. /etc/pam.d

The correct answers are b and c. In answer b, you could deny all services to all users with an ALL:ALL entry. However, with answer c, you could simply disable all network services that would deny access to all INET services to all users as well. Answer a is incorrect because /etc/hosts.allow only specifies permission, not deny. Answer d is incorrect because pam.d sets up authentication for services, not permissions for them.

Question 4

> How do you disable a service in /etc/inetd.conf?

To disable a service in /etc/inetd.conf, simply apply a hash (#) mark in front of the line that specifies the service.

Question 5

> It is invalid to have duplicate services listed under /etc/inetd.conf.
>
> ○ a. True
>
> ○ b. False

The correct answer is b. A service may be listed twice under /etc/inetd.conf, once for the tcp protocol and once for the udp protocol, if applicable.

Question 6

PAM authentication is used by:

O a. passwd

O b. ppp

O c. su

O d. All of the above

The correct answer is d. All the above answers, passwd, ppp, and su, use PAM for authentication.

Question 7

What is IP forwarding?

IP forwarding is the process of forwarding a packet from one source and redirecting it to the appropriate destination host.

Question 8

What is used to convert RPC programming numbering to TCP or UDP protocol port numbers?

O a. /etc/inetd.conf

O b   /etc/pam.d

O c. /usr/sbin/proto

O d. None of the above

The correct answer is d. The program used to convert the RPC programming numbering to TCP or UPD protocol port numbers is /usr/sbin/portmap.

Question 9

What can be used to set up a firewall on a Linux system?

○ a. tcp_wrappers

○ b. route

○ c. ipchains

○ d. NIS

The correct answer is c. When setting up a firewall on a Red Hat Linux system with a 2.2 (or newer) kernel, you use ipchains. Answer a is incorrect as tcp_wrappers are used to allow or deny services on a single system to specific hosts, but it does not firewall traffic from (or to) a network. Answer b is not correct as it is used to establish routes, not manage them. Answer d is incorrect because it is used in authentication, not firewalling.

Question 10

How is a network connection request handled when using tcp_wrappers?

When a network connection request is made to a server, the request is accepted by **inetd**. If access is passed by **inetd**, then the request is handed to tcp_wrappers. Then tcp_wrappers checks the service and the user access grant permissions in /etc/hosts.allow. If no specifications are made in /etc/hosts.allow, the tcp_wrappers checks for any deny entries for the service or user in /etc/hosts.deny. If no deny entry is found in /etc/hosts.deny, the connection is granted.

Task 1

Set up some basic security options on your machine. Disable any tools that you don't want anyone to use in **inetd**. Disable telnet in **inetd** and attempt to connect via telnet from another system. What happens?

Task 2

Set up tcp_wrappers to deny connections from all except your local network. Attempt to connect to your machine from another network. What happens?

Need To Know More?

Stern, Hal. *Managing NFS and NIS*, O'Reilly & Associates, Sebastopol, CA, 1991. ISBN 0-93717-575-7. This book details how to configure and administer NIS systems for Unix system administrators.

http://metalab.unc.edu/LDP

The Linux Documentation Project. Excellent resource for finding guides, HOWTOs, and more Linux-related information.

http://metalab.unc.edu/LDP/HOWTO/IPCHAINS-HOWTO.html

The ipchains (firewalling) HOWTO. Excellent guide for using ipchains.

Installation And Configuration Exam

As we discussed in the first chapter, the majority of the RHCE 300 Exam is performance based. This means that sections of the exam are hands on and graded by how well you do (or don't) perform the tasks.

There is a great deal of things to manage when taking performanced based examinations such as the RHCE 300. Not only do you need to be fluent with the skills at hand, but you need to manage your time well, know where to go when the going gets tough, and know what to do to when things are not going well.

One of the hands-on portions of the RHCE 300 centers on the installation and configuration of Red Hat Linux. In this chapter we will discuss methods, planning, and skills relating to the installation and configuration of Red Hat Linux.

Installation And Configuration

The root of one of the two hands-on portions of the RHCE 300 exam is the installation and configuration of a networked Red Hat Linux system. Topics at hand will cover everything from the base Red Hat Linux installation to software configuration (as we will cover in the next section). Until you get started, you won't be sure what is available for you to use, how you'll have to install the system, and what (if any) documentation will be available. In addition, the installation and configuration portion of the performanced-based exam is time limited. By default, you are given only two hours to perform the system installation and configure whatever options (hardware, software, and so on) are specified.

What You Can Expect

When you go in for the exam portion on installation and configuration, simply feel prepared. Feel confident that you can successfully achieve all the primary goals of each section in this book. Don't walk in expecting any surprises. You shouldn't find any surprises or extenuating circumstances in this exam.

On the exam, you will be presented with all (if any) tools you may use for your installation. What types of tools could you be presented with? You may have items available, including scratch paper, writing utensils, floppy disks, CD-ROMs, network information, server information, and more.

You will then be given your list of objectives. Nope, you can't start yet! Once everyone in the class has received their objectives, you will be asked to turn over the objective packet to fill out the front information. The first sheet of the packet is for you to fill out your name and other basic personal information and such, and you will fill out the time you start (provided by the instructor). In addition, you will be asked to sign a non-disclosure agreement stating you will not share the contents of your exam.

When you are finished with the exam, you are asked to place your objectives sheet upside down on your desk and check in with your instructor before leaving the exam room. The instructor will then check whether and how you completed your objectives, by sitting at your machine and testing each one.

How To Handle It

Your installation and configuration exam objectives will be very straightforward. Remember, don't expect anything tricky for this part of the exam. When your instructor signals for you to begin, follow these steps:

1. Read through each objective.

2 Note which objectives you can perform the easiest, and which ones you'll find difficult.

3. Make any quick notes for any objectives you may find useful as "reminders" once you have gotten deep into the exam. (Especially ones that you may not have media, documentation, or **man** pages for.)

4. Make note of any objectives that you can do simultaneously. Remember, this is a timed exam. If any objective requires you to wait for a result, do something else at the same time. Also, if any objectives can be related, finish both in one step (rather than returning to the subject and finishing later).

5. Don't spend more than 5 minutes doing this. Pick your first obvious objective and begin. With this exam, you'll have a few more minutes to plan out the rest of your test during the software installation.

Software Configuration Objectives

The biggest (and most difficult) parts of this exam are the software configuration objectives. The greatest percentage of your software configuration topics is covered in Chapter 10 with networking services. In addition, you can expect objectives ranging anywhere from installation and configuration options in Chapter 6, to advanced configuration options from Chapter 8, and X options in Chapter 9, as well as security features from Chapter 11. You should expect to see objectives (and probably more than one) from each of these chapters. Spend your time wisely.

Managing Your Time

You are given two hours for the installation and configuration portion of the exam. Use some of the following guidelines, and budget your time to allow you to finish all objectives in the exam.

➤ **Plan**   While previewing your objectives, make a mental (or paper) note of how long that task should take you. Objectives which take longer, or that make you wait, can probably be done at the same time as another objective, saving overall time. Make sure to plan to leave the last 15 minutes of the exam available to double-check your work.

➤ **Begin**   Begin your exam within five minutes of receiving your objectives. Do not preview too long or you will risk running out of time to complete the exam. Installation and configuration all take time.

➤ **When you get stuck**   If you are stuck on an objective, or it just isn't working right, spend no longer than five minutes trying to work on it. If you are unable to solve the objective, concentrate on getting through the rest of the objectives, and then go back to the ones you had problems with.

Sample Lab Objectives

Please review and complete the following objectives. (In addition, you will want review the tasks from each chapter and feel comfortable completing them.) The following objectives, like the objectives of the exam, are performance-based. This means there are no right or wrong, yes or no answers. The credit is given for making it work, and making it work right, not necessarily the steps you took to get there or what tools you used. Therefore, you will not find an answer key for this section in the back of the book (as you will for the multiple-choice element of the exam in Chapter 14).

Objective 1

Install Red Hat Linux with the CD-ROM media provided. Set up the machine with separate partitions dedicated for /boot, /home, /(root), /var, and swap. Configure the Red Hat machine to support networking via DHCP, X Window system, and printing.

Objective 2

Your mom wants an account on your machine. Set her up with a non-privileged account where she can browse the Internet and receive email. Well, Linux is catching on at your house—Dad and little sister Pam want accounts too! Set dad up with an account. He wants his email forwarded to his dad@example.com account. Little sister Pam wants an email-only account on your machine. That way she can download her email to her computer at school.

Objective 3

Compile a custom modularized kernel. Customize options such as machine type and so on, while disabling options that may not be available on your machine, such as ISDN and Infrared. The main objective is to have a kernel configured specifically for your machine. Set up the machine to have a choice to boot from either your new or old kernel.

Objective 4

Your mom is really tired of using WindowMaker. She wants to try KDE instead. Your little sister Pam decides she wants to browse the Internet when she's at home too, but she prefers fvwm95. Dad just doesn't like change, so he wants to keep WindowMaker. Set each of these users up to automatically start up their favorite window managers when they log in.

Objective 5

It's time to start setting up a network server. You want to set up a family Web site to help keep you, your mom and dad, and your sister in contact while little sister Pam is off to school and you move away from home. Set up an FTP server that allows each family member to **ftp** their Web files into their own home directories. Set up Apache for the Web site http://family.example.org/ . Set up /mom, /dad, and /pam under the domain to point to their Web entries in their own home directories that you set up for FTP. Set up your FTP server to allow anonymous connections to download photos of you and your family.

Objective 6

Guess what? Your boss saw what you set up for home, and wants you to set it up for him too. Set up another domain, http://boss.example.org/, to access Web files that your boss can upload to his own Web directory. Don't forget to set up your DNS.

Objective 7

Your boss decides he wants you to share your Linux box as a file server with the Windows clients on the network. Set up Samba on your system to share your /home directory with all Windows clients on your network.

Objective 8

Your sister has been using your server to connect to chat-rooms. Some kids in the chat-rooms saw her connection information and decided to start trying to access your Linux server. The kids are trying to connect from cracker.example.com, as well as from an unknown network IP of 192.168.250.250. Set up some low-level security on your system that denies all access from people on either cracker.example.com or 192.168.250.250. Take that a step further and deny access to everyone except your boss (from boss.example.org) and family (from family.example.org). Also allow your sister to connect from school from her static IP address of 192.168.2.23. Only allow your family FTP access.

13

The Debugging Exam

As we discussed in Chapter 12, the majority of the RHCE 300 Exam is performance based. Whereas the installation and configuration exam is graded by completing objectives and specific goals as specified in your objectives sheet, the debugging exam is different—you are not presented with an exact list of what to do. Instead, you are presented with an end goal (of what needs to work) and have to work your way through a number of (unspecified) problems to get to your end goal.

There are a great deal of things to manage when taking a performance based examination such as the debugging element. Not only do you need to be fluent with the skills at hand, but you need to manage your time well, know where to go when the going gets tough, and know what to do to when things are not going well.

This hands-on portion of the RHCE 300 focuses on the troubleshooting of Red Hat Linux. In this chapter, we will discuss methods, planning, and skills relating to the debugging of Red Hat Linux.

The second performance-based exam involves debugging Red Hat Linux. Preparing for this section of the exam is difficult as you cannot be sure what element of Red Hat Linux will be broken, you won't be sure exactly what tools you will have to fix the problems, and under no circumstances can you simply re-install the broken component (or system). The debugging portion of the RHCE 300 exam allows you three hours (total) to fix two separate debugging issues.

What To Expect

When you go to take your debugging element of the exam, remain calm. Your debugging skills work best when you have a clear mind. The biggest mistake people make during the debugging element is to worry about what will be broken on the system and being stressed about the exam before taking it. Don't make any presumptions about what you can or cannot do for the exam.

When you enter the examination room, you will be seated at your machine and asked to stow away any tools, books, or other materials you brought with you. You will then be presented with any tools you are allowed to use during the exam. As with the installation and configuration exam, you will be issued an objectives sheet, and when instructed to do so, will turn it over and sign the non-disclosure agreement on the front page. When permitted, you can open the objectives hand-out and start the exam.

When you are finished with the first objective, you will be asked to document what the problem was and how you fixed it. The instructor will then come to your machine, sign off on your objectives sheet, verify that you did or did not fix the problem, and send you off for a quick break while he (or she) prepares your system for the next debugging objective.

How To Handle It

After opening your objectives sheet, you will be given an end result objective. A sample of an end result objective could be something similar to "establish a networking connection from the workstation to the server using DHCP." This may sound simple, but the machine has been "pre-broken" to not simply configure this task. The machine may first not boot properly, and second have something configured improperly in networking that doesn't allow a simple configuration for DHCP (or it might not).

Regardless of what your objectives will be or what part of your system will be broken, there are several steps that could help you determine your problem and recover your system. Following these steps in order should help you successfully find the problem and give you the opportunity to fix it as necessary. Not all of the following steps will be required each time you troubleshoot a machine (in real life or on the exam):

1. Boot your machine. See what happens, what errors you get, and where the system seems broken. Do you know where the error is? Can you fix the machine as is? If not, perhaps you need to boot the system into single user mode and fix the problem. You may need to use system rescue disks.

2. Obtain (2 floppy) rescue disk set.

   This set is created from your system and a rescue image from the Red Hat 6.0 CD-ROM. (You will either create these disks from your installation and configuration exam or have them made available to you by the instructor.)

   Use **mkbootdisk** for the first disk, which creates a boot disk for your system (used for emergencies, to boot without LILO, and such). To create your boot-disk, type **mkbootdisk** *image* where *image* is the image of your bootable kernel located in /boot.

   Use the rescue.img image from the Red Hat 6.0 CD-ROM for the second rescue disk. Type:

   ```
   dd if=/mnt/cdrom/images/rescue.img of=/dev/fd0
   ```

3. Boot your machine. If you can fix your problem by booting from single user mode, type **linux single** at the LILO prompt, and proceed to the next step. Otherwise, check the system BIOS to see that it is set to boot from floppy disk as its first option. Then, boot with the first of the two-disk rescue set (the **mkbootdisk** disk). When prompted, provide the rescue disk (created from rescue.img).

 When booting via the system rescue disks, you do not have **vi** or **emacs** available. You must use **pico (pico –w)** to edit any necessary files.

4. Do you need to check your filesystem? First, use **fdisk –l** to print your partition table. Verify what you believe to be the filesystem partitions. Once you have decided which is your root filesystem (will most likely be the largest one), you can use **fsck** to check the filesystem. If /(**root**) is /dev/hda4, then use **fsck /dev/hda4**.

5. Do you need to check a second extended filesystem? If so, use **fdisk –l** to verify what your second extended filesystem may be. Once you have decided which filesystem you want to check, you can use **e2fsck** to check the second extended filesystem. If perhaps /dev/hda4 is your second extended filesystem, use **e2fsck –y /dev/hda4**.

   Note: The "–y" option used in the above e2fsck option is used to specify the answering of "yes" to any prompts. The e2fsck program prompts you several times for various options such as "check this filesystem," "fix this error," and so forth, which should all be answered "yes."

6. Do you need to mount your filesystems? (If you booted via the rescue disks, then yes, you do.) You can mount your filesystems using **mount**. First verify your partition table using **fdisk –l**. You must mount your devices in a specific order.

First, mount your root partition. Then, mount any other filesystems under your root (/) partition. First create a mount directory to mount your filesystems. For instance, if you wanted to mount root (/) and /boot, create a directory called /mnt/ harddrive (for root), and /mnt/harddrive/ boot (for /boot). Next mount your filesystems. If /dev/hda4 is your root (/) partition and /dev/hda2 is your /boot partition on the system, then first mount root (**mount /dev/hda4 /mnt/ harddrive**), and then mount /boot (**mount /dev/hda2 /mnt/harddrive/boot**).

7. Regardless of boot method (single or with rescue disks), you will then need to make any appropriate changes to your system to fix whatever your problem is (if the problem was something other than a corrupt filesystem, which is most likely the case for the RHCE 300 exam).

8. Did you have to change LILO? If you did, you have to rerun **lilo** to save the changes to the system. Simply run **/sbin/lilo** if you are in single user mode. If you are in rescue boot mode, you will have to use **lilo –r** to specify where the root filesystem is (since you mounted it to /mnt/ harddrive). To use **lilo** on the separate mounted filesystem use **/mnt/ harddrive/sbin/lilo –r /mnt/harddrive**.

9. Have you made changes to the disk? If so, then you need to sync your disk to ensure that the system buffers (changes you made) are written to the hard disk. To do this, use **sync**. From the prompt run **sync**. You may wish to run this another time or two to be absolutely positive all of your system buffers were flushed and written to the disk.

10. Are you ready to reboot? Well, if you are in single user mode, go for it. If you are in rescue mode, you have to unmount your mounted filesystem. You have to do this in a specific order as well. Whereas when you mounted them, you mounted root (/) first, when you unmount them, you have to unmount root (/) last. To unmount the /boot partition (from these examples), use **umount /mnt/harddrive/boot**. Next unmount the root (/) partition using **umount /mnt/harddrive**.

11. Now remove all disks (if necessary) and exit from the system. Power the system off, and try out the repaired system.

Does your system boot properly now? Good. You may not be through, however. Your objective sheet may list something in particular (such as networking, video, sound, etc) that isn't working right on the system. Since your system is now booting properly, fix whatever is specified using your knowledge of setting up and configuring the item (covered in our previous chapters, such as items listed in Chapters 6, 8, 9, and 10).

Managing Your Time

You are given three hours to complete two separate sets of objectives in the debugging portion of the exam. Try to use some of the following guidelines, and budget your time to allow you to finish all objectives in the exam.

➤ **Plan** While previewing your objectives, make a mental (or paper) note of how long that task should take you. Try to budget only half (1.5 hours) for each objective sheet. (Remember, you won't know what the second set of objectives is until you have completed the first.)

➤ **Begin** Begin your exam within 5 minutes of receiving your objectives. Do not preview too long or you will risk running out of time to complete the exam. Installation, configuration, and such all take time.

➤ **When you get stuck** Each set of objectives will have two types of debugging elements involved. With this in mind, try to budget 25 percent of your time for each mini-objective. If you have spent more than half of your total time (50 percent of three hours) on the first mini-objective, then you may want to consult the instructor for help. Consulting for help on a mini-objective, however, means you don't get credit for that mini-objective. (If there are two mini-objectives in an objective, and you get help on one of them, you lose 50 percent for the single objective). While completing each mini-objective is critical to your score, running out of time and not completing the remaining objectives is detrimental.

Sample
Written Test

In this chapter, we provide pointers to help you develop a successful test-taking strategy, including how to choose proper answers, how to decode ambiguity, how to work within the Red Hat testing framework, how to decide what you need to memorize, and how to prepare for the test. At the end of the chapter, we include 50 questions on subject matter pertinent to the RHCE 300 exam. Good luck!

Questions, Questions, Questions

There should be no doubt in your mind that you are facing a test full of specific and pointed questions. The written element of the RHCE 300 exam will consist of 50 questions and take somewhere between 30 and 60 minutes.

When taking the exam, you may be presented with various types of questions, such as:

➤ Multiple choice with a single answer.

➤ Multiple choice with multiple answers.

➤ Statement with a choice of "true" or "false."

Always take the time to read a question at least twice before selecting an answer. Remember, not every question has only one answer; many questions require "the best" answer. Therefore, you should read each question carefully, determine how many answers are valid, and look for hints in the question when selecting answers.

Choosing Proper Answers

The only way to pass any exam is to select enough of the right answers to obtain a passing score. However, Red Hat's exams are not standardized like the SAT and GRE exams; they are far more diabolical and convoluted. In some cases, questions are strangely worded, and deciphering them can be a real challenge. In those cases, you may need to rely on answer-elimination skills. Almost always, at least one answer out of the possible choices for a question can be eliminated immediately because it matches one of these conditions:

➤ The answer does not apply to the situation.

➤ The answer describes a nonexistent issue, an invalid option, or an imaginary state.

➤ The answer may be eliminated because of information in the question itself.

After you eliminate all answers that are obviously wrong, you can apply your retained knowledge to eliminate further answers. Look for items that sound correct but refer to actions, commands, or features that are not present or not available in the situation that the question describes.

If you're still faced with a blind guess among two or more potentially correct answers, reread the question. Try to picture how each of the remaining answers would alter the situation. Be especially sensitive to terminology; sometimes the choice of words, such as "remove" instead of "disable," can make the difference between a right answer and a wrong one.

Only when you've exhausted your ability to eliminate answers but remain unclear about which of the remaining possibilities is correct should you guess at an answer. An unanswered question offers you no points, but guessing gives you at least some chance of getting a question right; just don't be too hasty when making a blind guess.

 If you're taking a multiple-choice test, you can wait until the last round of reviewing questions (just as you're about to run out of time or out of unanswered questions) before you start making guesses. Guessing should be a last resort.

Working Within The Framework

The test questions appear in random order, and many elements or issues that receive mention in one question may also crop up in other questions. It's not uncommon to find that an incorrect answer to one question is the correct answer to another question, or vice versa. Take the time to read every answer to each question, even if you recognize the correct answer to a question immediately. That extra reading may spark a memory or remind you about a Linux feature or function that will help you on another question in the exam.

For the multiple-choice exam, you can revisit any question as many times as you like. If you're uncertain of the answer to a question, circle it and come back to it later.

 For written tests, we strongly recommend that you first read through the entire test quickly, before getting caught up in answering individual questions. This will help to jog your memory as you review the potential answers and can help identify questions that you want to mark for easy access to their contents. It will also let you identify and mark the tricky questions for easy return as well. The key is to make a quick pass over the territory to begin with—so that you know what you're up against—and then to survey that territory more thoroughly on a second pass, when you can begin to answer all questions systematically and consistently.

Preparing For The Test

The best way to prepare for the test—after you've studied—is to take at least one practice exam. We've included one in this chapter for that reason. The test questions are located in the pages that follow. (Unlike the preceding chapters in this book, the answers don't follow the questions immediately; you'll have to flip to Chapter 15 to separately review the answers).

Give yourself an hour to take the exam, and keep yourself on the honor system—don't look at earlier chapters in the book or jump ahead to the answer key. When your time is up or you've finished all the questions, you can check your work in Chapter 15. Pay special attention to the explanations for the incorrect answers; these can also help to reinforce your knowledge of the material. Knowing how to recognize correct answers is good, but understanding why incorrect answers are wrong can be equally valuable.

Taking The Test

Relax. Once you're sitting in front of the test, there's nothing more you can do to increase your knowledge or preparation. Take a deep breath, stretch, and start reading that first question.

You don't need to rush, either. You have plenty of time to complete each question and to return to those questions that you skip or mark for return. If you read a question twice and remain clueless, you can circle it and come back to it later. Both easy and difficult questions are intermixed throughout the test, in random order. When taking a multiple-choice test, don't cheat yourself by spending too much time on a hard question early in the test, thereby depriving yourself of the time you need to answer the questions at the end of the test.

On the multiple-choice test, you can read through the entire test, and, before returning to circled questions for a second visit, you can figure out how much time you've got per question. As you answer each question, move on to the next. Continue to review the remaining marked questions until you run out of time or complete the test.

That's it for pointers. Here are some questions for you to practice on.

Sample Written Test

Question 1

In order to increase the amount of memory available for a system, what is the maximum size of a swap partition (with kernel version 2.2.x)?

- ○ a. 32M
- ○ b. 64M
- ○ c. 128M
- ○ d. 512M
- ○ e. 2GB

Question 2

To create a 'swap' partition using fdisk, what must the partition's system id type be?

- ○ a. 4
- ○ b. 5
- ○ c. 82
- ○ d. 83
- ○ e. c

Question 3

How many primary partitions can exist on one drive?

- ○ a. 1
- ○ b. 2
- ○ c. 4
- ○ d. 16
- ○ e. None of the above

Question 4

How many extended partitions can exist on one drive?

○ a. 1

○ b. 2

○ c. 4

○ d. 16

○ e. None of the above

Question 5

How many logical partitions can exist on one drive?

○ a. 1

○ b. 12

○ c. 4

○ d. 16

○ e. None of the above

Question 6

Under Linux, hard drives and their partitions have a specific naming convention. What would the device name for the first IDE hard-drive's first primary partition?

○ a. hda

○ b. hda1

○ c. sda

○ d. sda1

○ e. hda5

Question 7

What is the device name for the first logical partition on the first IDE hard-drive?

- ○ a. hda1
- ○ b. hda2
- ○ c. sda
- ○ d. sda1
- ○ e. hda5

Question 8

To create a boot disk for Linux using DOS or Windows, what command could you use?

- ○ a. transdisk
- ○ b. fdisk
- ○ c. copy
- ○ d. diskcopy
- ○ e. rawrite

Question 9

To create a installation boot floppy disk from Linux (or another Unix) machine, what command could you use?

- ○ a. rawrite
- ○ b. dd
- ○ c. fsck
- ○ d. fdisk
- ○ e. copy

Question 10

Which of these type of installs requires a special installation boot image other than boot.img?

○ a. NFS

○ b. FTP

○ c. harddisk

○ d. Both answers a and b

○ e. All of the above

Question 11

You install the Linux bootloader to the first sector of the boot partition when:

○ a. multiple operating systems are on the system.

○ b. this is a trial run for installing Linux.

○ c. there is a fear of losing data or the superblock.

○ d. another boot loader is already on the system.

○ e. booting by floppy is used.

Question 12

To build a modularized kernel, the kernel-headers and kernel-source packages must first be installed. Where will you find the kernel-headers and kernel-source?

○ a. /usr/bin

○ b. /usr/src/redhat

○ c. /usr/src/linux

○ d. /usr/local

○ e. /usr/local/src

Question 13

What command do you use to build a kernel configuration file? [Choose the best answer.]

○ a. make config

○ b. make menuconfig

○ c. make xconfig

○ d. Both answers a and c

○ e. All of the above

Question 14

After you have compiled your kernel, what do you have to edit to boot your new kernel image?

○ a. /etc/lilo.conf

○ b. /etc/named.boot

○ c. /etc/conf.modules

○ d. /boot/lilo.conf

○ e. /boot/conf.modules

Question 15

What file specifies the order to use specified name services?

○ a. /etc/hosts

○ b. /etc/nsswitch.conf

○ c. /etc/nsorder

○ d. /etc/services

○ e. /etc/inetd.conf

Question 16

What file contains the list of port numbers (and associated names) monitored by inetd?

○ a. /etc/hosts

○ b. /etc/nsswitch.conf/

○ c. /etc/nsorder

○ d. /etc/services

○ e. /etc/inetd.conf

Question 17

What service is not monitored by inetd?

○ a. finger

○ b. ntalk

○ c. time

○ d. ssh

○ e. telnet

Question 18

In which tcp_wrappers file can you specify to allow all connections from all hosts?

○ a. /etc/tcp.conf

○ b. /etc/hosts

○ c. /etc/hosts.deny

○ d. /etc/hosts.allow

○ e. None of the above

Question 19

What are the three types of chain rulesets defined by default in ipchains?

- ○ a. accept, deny, reject
- ○ b. accept, deny, forward
- ○ c. deny, forward, masq
- ○ d. input, output, forward
- ○ e. None of the above

Question 20

Which command allows you to print your routing table?

- ○ a. route-add
- ○ b. netstat-rn
- ○ c. print route
- ○ d. Both answers a and b
- ○ e. None of the above

Question 21

You just added a new user, kara, to the system. What group is kara added to by default?

- ○ a. user
- ○ b. group
- ○ c. kara
- ○ d. root
- ○ e. None of the above

Question 22

How do you change the group set bit on a directory?

○ a. chmod +x

○ b. chmod +s

○ c. chmod +b

○ d. setbit +1

○ e. None of the above

Question 23

Which command can you use to view a system log continuously (in real time)?

○ a. cat

○ b. head

○ c. view

○ d. tail

○ e. tail −f

Question 24

How would you create a boot disk for a specific kernel image on your system?

○ a. dd

○ b. mkbootdisk

○ c. mkkickstart

○ d. cp

○ e. cat

Question 25

Which command can you use to view your system's partition table?

○ a. fdisk

○ b. df

○ c. du

○ d. dd

○ e. fdisk –l

Question 26

Which command can force all buffers to disk?

○ a. flush

○ b. edbuff

○ c. sync

○ d. save

○ e. None of the above

Question 27

Which methods can you use to install Red Hat Linux?

○ a. CD-ROM

○ b. FTP

○ c. Samba

○ d. Both answers a and b

○ e. All of the above

Question 28

Which boot image is required for a network install?

- ○ a. boot.img
- ○ b. netboot.img
- ○ c. bootnet.img
- ○ d. network.img
- ○ e. None of the above

Question 29

Which file is used to configure mounted filesystems?

- ○ a. /etc/fstab
- ○ b. /etc/sysconfig
- ○ c. /etc/filesys
- ○ d. /etc/mount.sys
- ○ e. None of the above

Question 30

With which file can you edit your systems' virtual console specifications?

- ○ a. /etc/consoles
- ○ b. /etc/inittab
- ○ c. /etc/inetd.conf
- ○ d. Both answers a and b
- ○ e. None of the above

Question 31

Which tool can be used to add a user to the system?

○ a. adduser

○ b. linuxconf

○ c. useradd

○ d. Both answers b and c

○ e. All of the above

Question 32

In which directory can you store system user default files used for creating user directories?

○ a. /etc/users

○ b. /etc/skel

○ c. /etc/default

○ d. /usr/tmp

○ e. None of the above

Question 33

How could you install the file ipchains-1.3.8-3.i386.rpm?

○ a. rpm –e ipchains-1.3.8-2.i386.rpm

○ b. rpm –i ipchains*.i386.rpm

○ c. rpm –Uvh ipchains

○ d. rpm –qip ipchains

○ e. None of the above

Question 34

What could you use to list all the files in an RPM package?

○ a. rpm –qa

○ b. rpm –qi

○ c. rpm –ql

○ d. rpm –L

○ e. None of the above

Question 35

Which boot image would you need to use a PCMCIA network card during installation?

○ a. bootnet.img

○ b. pcmcia.img

○ c. boot.img

○ d. Both answers a and b

○ e. None of the above

Question 36

Which runlevel reboots the system?

○ a. 1

○ b. 2

○ c. 3

○ d. 4

○ e. None of the above

Question 37

Which option can you pass at the LILO: prompt to boot into single user mode?

- ○ a. linux 1
- ○ b. init 1
- ○ c. linux single
- ○ d. Both answers a and c
- ○ e. All of the above

Question 38

Which is the system initialization script that is run at boot time?

- ○ a. /etc/rc.d/rc0.d
- ○ b. /etc/rc.d/init.d
- ○ c. /etc/rc.d/start
- ○ d. /etc/rc.d/rc.sysinit
- ○ e. None of the above

Question 39

Which type of kernel has all support compiled into the kernel image?

- ○ a. monolithic
- ○ b. modular
- ○ c. bzImage
- ○ d. zImage
- ○ e. boot

Question 40

Which program is used to automatically install Red Hat Linux on identical hardware?

○ a. mkkickstart

○ b. ghost

○ c. tar

○ d. bzImage.img

○ e. None of the above

Question 41

Which is used to schedule particular jobs or programs at particular times on the system?

○ a. cron

○ b. scheduler

○ c. outlook

○ d. vi

○ e. None of the above

Question 42

Which is the main sendmail configuration file?

○ a. /etc/pine.conf

○ b. ~/.sendmail.rc

○ c. /etc/sendmail.cf

○ d. Both answers a and c

○ e. None of the above

Question 43

In what file can you specify which users are not allowed to access a system via FTP?

○ a. /etc/ftpaccess

○ b. /etc/hosts.deny

○ c. /etc/ftpusers

○ d. All of the above

○ e. None of the above

Question 44

Which command is used to see which services an NFS server is running?

○ a. nfserv

○ b. getnfs

○ c. rpcinfo

○ d. nfsmount

○ e. None of the above

Question 45

Which command is used to mount NFS filesystems?

○ a. nfsmount

○ b. knfsd

○ c. mount

○ d. Both answers a and b

○ e. None of the above

Question 46

Which is used to access a SMB share on a Linux system?

- ○ a. NFS
- ○ b. SMBD
- ○ c. smbclient
- ○ d. smbserver
- ○ e. None of the above

Question 47

Which cannot be assigned by a DHCP server?

- ○ a. IP address
- ○ b. gateway
- ○ c. netmask
- ○ d. DNS
- ○ e. None of the above

Question 48

Which command lists your configured network interfaces, such as IP address, broadcast address, and netmask?

- ○ a. netstat –rn
- ○ b. route
- ○ c. ichains
- ○ d. ifconfig
- ○ e. None of the above

Question 49

What symbolic links points to the pathed filename of the system preferred display manager?

○ a. Xdefaults

○ b. /etc/X11/prefdm

○ c. Xclients

○ d. Xdisplay

○ e. None of the above

Question 50

What is the main Apache configuration file?

○ a. /etc/srm.conf

○ b. /etc/httpd/conf/httpd.conf

○ c. /etc/httpd/conf/apache.conf

○ d. Both answers a and b

○ e. None of the above

15

Answer Key To Written Test

This chapter is an answer key to Chapter 14's multiple-choice exam. Please note that no answer keys are available for exam situations in Chapters 12 and 13. The performance-based exams do not have answer keys, as they are graded by the outcome result of the required objective (as specified in the exam), and not by a specific answer or method.

1. e	14. a	27. d	40. b
2. c	15. b	28. c	41. a
3. c	16. d	29. a	42. c
4. a	17. d	30. b	43. c
5. b	18. d	31. e	44. c
6. b	19. d	32. b	45. c
7. e	20. b	33. b	46. c
8. e	21. c	34. c	47. e
9. b	22. b	35. b	48. d
10. d	23. e	36. e	49. b
11. d	24. b	37. d	50. b
12. c	25. e	38. d	
13. e	26. c	39. a	

Question 1

The correct answer is e. Kernel versions 2.2 and higher can support up to 2GB on Intel machines; therefore answers a, b, c and d are incorrect.

Question 2

Answer c is correct. ID type 82 is Linux swap. Partition ID type 4 is FAT16, therefore answer a is incorrect. ID type 5 is Extended, therefore b is incorrect. ID type 83 is Linux native, therefore answer d is incorrect. ID type c is Win95 FAT32, therefore answer e is incorrect.

Question 3

Answer c is correct. A Linux system uses the DOS style partition table, which limits the system to a maximum total of four primary partition support, therefore answers a and b are incorrect. The total amount of partitions that can be used (including extended and logical) is 16, so answer d is incorrect.

Question 4

Answer a is correct. A Linux partition table can support up to four primary partitions, one of which can be extended.

Question 5

Answer b is correct. A Linux partition table can support a total of 16 partitions. This includes 3 primary, 1 extended (which counts as the fourth supported primary partition), and 12 logical.

Question 6

Answer b is correct. The first primary partition on the first IDE hard-drive would be hda1. Answer a, hda, refers to the first hard-drive, but not the first primary partition on the first IDE hard-drive, therefore a is incorrect. Answers c and d are sda and sda1, which refer to the first SCSI hard-drive and first SCSI hard-drive partition, therefore both c and d are incorrect. Answer e, hda5, refers to the first logical partition and therefore is incorrect.

Question 7

Answer e is correct. The device name for the first logical partition on the first IDE hard-drive is hda5. The answers hda1 and hda2 refer to the first and second (primary or extended) partitions, therefore answers a and b are incorrect. The answers sda and sda1 refer to the first and second (primary or extended) partitions, making answers c and d incorrect.

Question 8

Answer e is correct. To create a boot disk for Linux using DOS or Windows, you use rawrite. The tool transdisk is not valid, therefore answer a is incorrect. The fdisk tool is used for disk partitioning, therefore answer b is incorrect. Answer c, copy, is used for copying files, not creating images, and therefore is incorrect. The option diskcopy is not a valid tool, therefore answer d is incorrect.

Question 9

Answer b is correct. To create a boot disk from Unix, you would use dd. The rawrite tool is used to write images on a DOS or Windows machine, therefore answer a is incorrect. Answer c, fsck, is used to check Unix filesystems, and therefore is incorrect. Answer d, fdisk, is used for manipulating partitions, and therefore is also incorrect. The copy tool is used for copying files, therefore answer e is incorrect.

Question 10

Answer d is correct. Special installation diskettes are required when an install is to be performed either over the network or via a PCMCIA device (such as CD-ROM or NIC). NFS is a network service. FTP is also a network service, therefore answer b is also correct. Answer c does not require a boot disk other than boot.img, therefore answer c is incorrect. Answer d selects both answers a and b; therefore answer d is correct. Answer e selects all of the above, and (since c is incorrect) is incorrect.

Question 11

Answer d is correct. You should only need to install the Linux bootloader within the first sector of the boot partition when you are planning to use an alternative bootloader (such as NT) to manage the multi-boot system. The Linux bootloader is capable of booting multiple operating systems, therefore answer a is incorrect. The bootloader has nothing to do with the trial run of Linux,

therefore answer b is incorrect. Installing the Linux bootloader to the superblock (MBR) does not lose data, therefore answer c is incorrect. If using another
bootloader instead of Linux, install Linux to the boot partition, therefore, answer d is correct. Using a boot floppy bypasses the installed Linux bootloader,
thus installing in the MBR or the boot partition is irrelevant, making answer e
incorrect.

Question 12

Answer c is correct. To build a modularized kernel, the installed kernel-headers
and kernel-source packages will be found in /usr/src/linux. Answer a, /usr/bin,
contains system binaries, therefore it is incorrect. Answer b, /usr/src/redhat,
stores information for source RPMs, and therefore is incorrect. Answer d,
/usr/local/, contains various user tools and information and therefore is incorrect. Answer e, /usr/local/src/, does not contain data, by default, and is incorrect.

Question 13

Answer e is correct. To build a kernel configuration command, you use make
and the configuration option. Answer a, make config, presents you with a text-
based configuration and therefore is correct. Answer b, make menuconfig,
presents you with a menu-based configuration and therefore is correct. Answer c, make xconfig, presents you with an X-based configuration tool and is
also correct. Answer e, All of the above, encompasses all the answers, and therefore is the best answer.

Question 14

Answer a is correct. To boot your new kernel image, you must edit /etc/lilo.conf.
Answer b, /etc/named.boot, is the BIND 4 configuration file, and is therefore
incorrect. Answer c, /etc/conf.modules, lists kernel modules and is incorrect.
Answers d and e are invalid options and are incorrect.

Question 15

Answer b is correct. To specify the order which to use specified name servers,
you must add them appropriately to /etc/nsswitch.conf, therefore answer a is
incorrect. Answer b, /etc/nsswitch.conf, is therefore correct. Answer c is invalid, and therefore is incorrect. Answer d, /etc/services, configures network
services, and therefore is incorrect. Answer e, /etc/inetd.conf, manages network services, and is therefore is incorrect.

Question 16

Answer d is correct. The file /etc/inetd.conf contains the list of port numbers monitored by inetd. The /etc/hosts file specifies hosts used by the system, and is therefore incorrect. The /etc/nsorder option is invalid, therefore answer c is incorrect. Answer e, /etc/inetd.conf, specifies what services are enabled, but not their port numbers, and therefore is incorrect.

Question 17

Answer d is correct. inetd monitors a great number of services. The programs finger, ntalk, time, and telnet (answers a, b, c, and e, respectively) are incorrect. SSH is not monitored via inetd, therefore answer d is correct.

Question 18

Answer d is correct. The file where you can specifically allow all connections from all hosts using tcp_wrappers is /etc/hosts.allow. Answer a, /etc/tcp.conf, is an invalid option, and is therefore incorrect. Answer b, /etc/hosts, specifies system hosts and therefore is incorrect. Answer c, /etc/hosts.deny, specifies who to deny, and therefore is incorrect.

Question 19

Answer d is correct. The three main chains defined by default in ipchains are input, output, and forward. The options accept, deny, and masq are invalid as they are used as targets, not chains. This makes answers a, b, c, and e incorrect.

Question 20

Answer b is correct. To print your routing table, use netstat-rn. Answer a, route-add, is used to add a route to the routing table and therefore is incorrect. Answer c, print route, is invalid. Answer d includes answer a, and therefore is incorrect.

Question 21

Answer c is correct. When you create a user, the user is automatically added to a group by the same name. Therefore, adding user "kara" will be added to group "kara" by default. Unless otherwise specified, "kara" will not be added to groups named user, group, or root, therefore answers a,b, and d are incorrect.

Question 22

Answer b is correct. To change the group setbit on a directory, use the +s option with chmod. Answer a, chmod +x, makes the file (directory) executable, therefore answer a is incorrect. Answer c, chmod +b, is invalid, and is therefore incorrect. Answer d, setbit +1, is invalid, and is therefore incorrect.

Question 23

Answer e is correct. To view a system log continuously (in real time), use the –f command option with tail. Answer a, cat, is used to concatenate a file, and therefore is incorrect. Answer b, head, prints the first 10 lines of a file, and therefore is incorrect. Answer c, view, is invalid. Answer d, tail, is incorrect as it only prints the last 10 lines of a file, but with the –f option (answer e), continuously prints the file (in real time) and therefore is correct.

Question 24

Answer b is correct. To create a boot disk for your running system, use mkbootdisk. While dd is used to create boot disks for installation and so forth, you cannot create a system disk with it, and therefore is incorrect. Answer c, mkkickstart, creates kickstart installation disks, and therefore is incorrect. Answer d, cp, is used to copy files and is incorrect. Answer e, cat, is used to concatenate files and is incorrect.

Question 25

Answer e is correct. To view your system's partition table, use the command fdisk –l, making answer e the best answer. Answer a, fdisk, by itself, only opens fdisk where you have the option to view your partition table, but must enter the command to do so, and therefore is incorrect. Answer b, df, is used to print the disk space available on the machine, and therefore is incorrect. Answer c, du, is used to print disk space used on the system and is incorrect. Answer d, dd, is used for converting and copying a file and is incorrect.

Question 26

Answer c is correct. When you need to flush the system buffers to disk, use the sync command, making answer c incorrect. Answer a, flush, is a Tcl command, and therefore incorrect. Answer b, edbuff is invalid, and therefore incorrect. Answer d, save, is invalid and incorrect.

Question 27

Answer d is correct. There are various ways you can install Red Hat Linux. You can install via CD-ROM, therefore answer a is correct. You can also install via FTP, therefore answer b is also correct. Answer c, SAMBA, is not supported, and therefore is incorrect. Answer d selects both answers a and b, and therefore is the best answer.

Question 28

Answer c is correct. When performing a network based install, a boot disk using the bootnet.img image is required. Answer a, boot.img, is used for a standard installation disk. Answer b is invalid. Answer d is invalid.

Question 29

Answer a is correct. To configure mounted filesystems, edit the /etc/fstab file. Answer b, /etc/sysconfig/, is a directory and incorrect. Answers c and d are invalid.

Question 30

Answer b is correct. To edit your virtual consoles setting, edit the /etc/inittab file. Answer a is invalid. Answer c, /etc/inetd.conf, configures inetd settings and is incorrect.

Question 31

Answer e is correct. When adding a user, you can use adduser, linuxconf, and useradd (equivalent to adduser), which makes answers a, b, and c correct. Answer e includes all the answers and is the single best answer.

Question 32

Answer b is correct. Default user files (used when creating user directories) are kept in /etc/skel, making answer b correct. Answer a is invalid. Answer c, /etc/default, only contains the command useradd (by default), and answer d, /usr/tmp, is used for temporary user files, therefore both are incorrect.

Question 33

Answer b is correct. To install an RPM, use **rpm –i** or **rpm –U**. Answer a, rpm -e ipchains-1.3.8-3.i386.rpm, deletes the file, and therefore is incorrect. Answer b, rpm –i ipchains*.i386.rpm, installs the package (which fits the * wildcard) and is correct. Answer c, rpm –Uvh ipchains, doesn't specify a valid package and is incorrect. Answer d, rpm –qip ipchains, queries a package for information and is incorrect.

Question 34

Answer c is correct. To list all files in an RPM package, use rpm –ql, therefore answer c is correct. Answer a, rpm –qa, lists all files installed on a system and is incorrect. Answer b, rpm –qi, queries for information and is incorrect. Answer d, rpm –L, is invalid.

Question 35

Answer b is correct. To use a PCMCIA device during installation, you must use a pcmcia.img boot image. Answer a, bootnet.img, is used for network installations and is incorrect. Answer c, boot.img, is used for regular installation and is incorrect.

Question 36

Answer e is correct. The runlevel to reboot the system is runlevel 6, and therefore answer e, None of the above, is correct. Runlevel 1 boots the system in single-user mode, 2 into multi-user mode (no networking), 3 multi-user full networking mode (and 4 is invalid), making answers a, b, c, and d incorrect.

Question 37

Answer d is correct. To boot into single user mode from the LILO: prompt, use either answer a, linux 1, or answer c, linux single. This makes answer d the best answer. Answer b, init 1, is used to boot the system into single user mode from runlevels 2 through 5, but is invalid for the LILO: prompt.

Question 38

Answer d is correct. The rc.sysinit is the system initialization script run during boot time. Answer a, /etc/rc.d/rc0.d/, is a runlevel directory and incorrect. Answer b, /etc/rc.d/init.d/, is a daemon directory, incorrect. Answer c is invalid.

Question 39

Answer a is correct. A monolithic kernel has all support compiled into the kernel image. Answer b, modular, is a kernel that makes use of modules for support. Answer c and d are types of kernel images, but not a type of kernel, and are therefore incorrect. Answer e is invalid.

Question 40

Answer b is correct. When installing Red Hat Linux on multiple (identical) machines, you can use kickstart to automate the install. Answer a, mkkickstart, is used to create the boot floppy for kickstart, but isn't the program that runs, and therefore is invalid. Answer b, ghost, is a commercial software package not used by Linux to create hard-drive images and is not correct. Answer c, tar, is a compression tool, but is not used to install Red Hat Linux, and is incorrect. Answer d is invalid. Therefore, the answer is None of the above.

Question 41

Answer a is correct. To schedule jobs or for programs to run at specific times, use cron. Answer b and c are invalid. Answer d, vi, is a Linux editor and is incorrect.

Question 42

Answer c is correct. The main sendmail configuration file is /etc/sendmail.cf. Answers a and b are invalid (which also makes d invalid).

Question 43

Answer c is correct. To specify what users are not allowed to access a system via FTP, edit the /etc/ftpusers file. Answer a, /etc/ftpaccess, is used to configure FTP access options and is not correct. Answer b, /etc/hosts.deny, specifies what domains, networks, and such that cannot access FTP, but not individual users, and therefore is incorrect.

Question 44

Answer c is correct. To see what services an NFS server is using, use rpcinfo. Answers a, b, and d are invalid.

Question 45

Answer c is correct. To mount an NFS filesystem, use the command mount in answer c. Answer a is invalid. Answer b, knfsd, is an NFS daemon, and therefore is incorrect.

Question 46

Answer c is correct. To view an SMB share from a Linux (or other Unix) system, use smbclient. Answer a is a separate network service and is incorrect. SMBD is the SMB server and is incorrect. Answer d is invalid.

Question 47

Answer e is correct. Many settings can be assigned with a DHCP server. Some of these items include the IP address (answer a), the gateway (answer b), the netmask (answer c), and DNS (answer d). The best answer is answer e, None of the above.

Question 48

Answer d is correct. To view your configured network interfaces, use ifconfig. Answer a, netstat –rn, prints the routing table and is incorrect. Answer b, route, prints the routing table and is used for route configuration, and therefore is incorrect. Answer c is invalid.

Question 49

Answer b is correct. The symbolic link used to link to the path for the system preferred display manager is /etc/X11/prefdm. Answers a and c, .Xdefaults and .Xclients, are used to configure a user's X Window system. Answer d is invalid.

Question 50

Answer b is correct. The main Apache configuration file is /etc/httpd/conf/httpd.conf. Answers a and c are invalid.

Appendix
GNU General
Public License

The GPL is the license that most open source projects use for their software. Developed in the late 1980s, it has not been revised since its publication in 1991. The GPL is quite extensive, and many of its users interpret the document in different ways. Read on for a better understanding of the foundation of the Open Source community.

Version 2, June 1991
Copyright (C) 1989, 1991 Free Software Foundation, Inc.
59 Temple Place - Suite 330, Boston, MA 02111-1307, USA

Everyone is permitted to copy and distribute verbatim copies of this license document, but changing it is not allowed.

Preamble

The licenses for most software are designed to take away your freedom to share and change it. By contrast, the GNU General Public License is intended to guarantee your freedom to share and change free software—to make sure the software is free for all its users. This General Public License applies to most of the Free Software Foundation's software and to any other program whose authors commit to using it. (Some other Free Software Foundation software is covered by the GNU Library General Public License instead.) You can apply it to your programs, too.

When we speak of free software, we are referring to freedom, not price. Our General Public Licenses are designed to make sure that you have the freedom to distribute copies of free software (and charge for this service if you wish), that you receive source code or can get it if you want it, that you can change the software or use pieces of it in new free programs; and that you know you can do these things.

To protect your rights, we need to make restrictions that forbid anyone to deny you these rights or to ask you to surrender the rights. These restrictions translate to certain responsibilities for you if you distribute copies of the software, or if you modify it.

For example, if you distribute copies of such a program, whether gratis or for a fee, you must give the recipients all the rights that you have. You must make sure that they, too, receive or can get the source code. And you must show them these terms so they know their rights.

We protect your rights with two steps: (1) copyright the software, and (2) offer you this license which gives you legal permission to copy, distribute and/or modify the software.

Also, for each author's protection and ours, we want to make certain that everyone understands that there is no warranty for this free software. If the software is modified by someone else and passed on, we want its recipients to know that what they have is not the original, so that any problems introduced by others will not reflect on the original authors' reputations.

Finally, any free program is threatened constantly by software patents. We wish to avoid the danger that redistributors of a free program will individually obtain patent licenses, in effect making the program proprietary. To prevent this, we have made it clear that any patent must be licensed for everyone's free use or not licensed at all.

The precise terms and conditions for copying, distribution and modification follow.

Terms And Conditions For Copying, Distribution, And Modification

This License applies to any program or other work which contains a notice placed by the copyright holder saying it may be distributed under the terms of this General Public License. The "Program", below, refers to any such program or work, and a "work based on the Program" means either the Program or any derivative work under copyright law: that is to say, a work containing the Program or a portion of it, either verbatim or with modifications and/or translated into another language. (Hereinafter, translation is included without limitation in the term "modification".) Each licensee is addressed as "you".

Activities other than copying, distribution and modification are not covered by this License; they are outside its scope. The act of running the Program is not restricted, and the output from the Program is covered only if its contents constitute a work based on the Program (independent of having been made by running the Program). Whether that is true depends on what the Program does.

1. You may copy and distribute verbatim copies of the Program's source code as you receive it, in any medium, provided that you conspicuously and appropriately publish on each copy an appropriate copyright notice and disclaimer of warranty; keep intact all the notices that refer to this License and to the absence of any warranty; and give any other recipients of the Program a copy of this License along with the Program.

   You may charge a fee for the physical act of transferring a copy, and you may at your option offer warranty protection in exchange for a fee.

2. You may modify your copy or copies of the Program or any portion of it, thus forming a work based on the Program, and copy and distribute such modifications or work under the terms of Section 1 above, provided that you also meet all of these conditions:

   a) You must cause the modified files to carry prominent notices stating that you changed the files and the date of any change.

   b) You must cause any work that you distribute or publish, that in whole or in part contains or is derived from the Program or any part thereof, to be licensed as a whole at no charge to all third parties under the terms of this License.

   c) If the modified program normally reads commands interactively when run, you must cause it, when started running for such interactive use in the most ordinary way, to print or display an announcement including an appropriate copyright notice and a notice that there is no warranty (or else, saying that you provide a warranty) and that users may redistribute the program under these conditions, and telling the user how to view a copy of this License. (Exception: if the Program itself is interactive but does not normally print such an announcement, your work based on the Program is not required to print an announcement.)

   These requirements apply to the modified work as a whole. If identifiable sections of that work are not derived from the Program, and can be reasonably considered independent and separate works in themselves, then this License, and its terms, do not apply to those sections when you distribute them as separate works. But when you distribute the same sections as part of a whole which is a work based on the Program, the distribution of the whole must be on the terms of this License, whose permissions for other licensees extend to the entire whole, and thus to each and every part regardless of who wrote it.

Thus, it is not the intent of this section to claim rights or contest your rights to work written entirely by you; rather, the intent is to exercise the right to control the distribution of derivative or collective works based on the Program.

In addition, mere aggregation of another work not based on the Program with the Program (or with a work based on the Program) on a volume of a storage or distribution medium does not bring the other work under the scope of this License.

3. You may copy and distribute the Program (or a work based on it, under Section 2) in object code or executable form under the terms of Sections 1 and 2 above provided that you also do one of the following:

a) Accompany it with the complete corresponding machine-readable source code, which must be distributed under the terms of Sections 1 and 2 above on a medium customarily used for software interchange; or,

b) Accompany it with a written offer, valid for at least three years, to give any third party, for a charge no more than your cost of physically performing source distribution, a complete machine-readable copy of the corresponding source code, to be distributed under the terms of Sections 1 and 2 above on a medium customarily used for software interchange; or,

c) Accompany it with the information you received as to the offer to distribute corresponding source code. (This alternative is allowed only for noncommercial distribution and only if you received the program in object code or executable form with such an offer, in accord with Subsection b above.)

The source code for a work means the preferred form of the work for making modifications to it. For an executable work, complete source code means all the source code for all modules it contains, plus any associated interface definition files, plus the scripts used to control compilation and installation of the executable. However, as a special exception, the source code distributed need not include anything that is normally distributed (in either source or binary form) with the major components (compiler, kernel, and so on) of the operating system on which the executable runs, unless that component itself accompanies the executable.

If distribution of executable or object code is made by offering access to copy from a designated place, then offering equivalent access to copy the source code from the same place counts as distribution of the source code, even though third parties are not compelled to copy the source along with the object code.

4. You may not copy, modify, sublicense, or distribute the Program except as expressly provided under this License. Any attempt otherwise to copy, modify, sublicense or distribute the Program is void, and will automatically terminate your rights under this License. However, parties who have received copies, or rights, from you under this License will not have their licenses terminated so long as such parties remain in full compliance.

5. You are not required to accept this License, since you have not signed it. However, nothing else grants you permission to modify or distribute the Program or its derivative works. These actions are prohibited by law if you do not accept this License. Therefore, by modifying or distributing the Program (or any work based on the Program), you indicate your acceptance of this License to do so, and all its terms and conditions for copying, distributing or modifying the Program or works based on it.

6. Each time you redistribute the Program (or any work based on the Program), the recipient automatically receives a license from the original licensor to copy, distribute or modify the Program subject to these terms and conditions. You may not impose any further restrictions on the recipients' exercise of the rights granted herein. You are not responsible for enforcing compliance by third parties to this License.

7. If, as a consequence of a court judgment or allegation of patent infringement or for any other reason (not limited to patent issues), conditions are imposed on you (whether by court order, agreement or otherwise) that contradict the conditions of this License, they do not excuse you from the conditions of this License. If you cannot distribute so as to satisfy simultaneously your obligations under this License and any other pertinent obligations, then as a consequence you may not distribute the Program at all. For example, if a patent license would not permit royalty-free redistribution of the Program by all those who receive copies directly or indirectly through you, then the only way you could satisfy both it and this License would be to refrain entirely from distribution of the Program.

If any portion of this section is held invalid or unenforceable under any particular circumstance, the balance of the section is intended to apply and the section as a whole is intended to apply in other circumstances.

It is not the purpose of this section to induce you to infringe any patents or other property right claims or to contest validity of any such claims; this section has the sole purpose of protecting the integrity of the free software distribution system, which is implemented by public license practices. Many people have made generous contributions to the wide range of software distributed through that system in reliance on consistent application of that system; it is up to the author/donor to decide if he or she is willing to distribute software through any other system and a licensee cannot impose that choice.

This section is intended to make thoroughly clear what is believed to be a consequence of the rest of this License.

8. If the distribution and/or use of the Program is restricted in certain countries either by patents or by copyrighted interfaces, the original copyright holder who places the Program under this License may add an explicit geographical distribution limitation excluding those countries, so that distribution is permitted only in or among countries not thus excluded. In such case, this License incorporates the limitation as if written in the body of this License.

9. The Free Software Foundation may publish revised and/or new versions of the General Public License from time to time. Such new versions will be similar in spirit to the present version, but may differ in detail to address new problems or concerns.

Each version is given a distinguishing version number. If the Program specifies a version number of this License which applies to it and "any later version", you have the option of following the terms and conditions either of that version or of any later version published by the Free Software Foundation. If the Program does not specify a version number of this License, you may choose any version ever published by the Free Software Foundation.

10. If you wish to incorporate parts of the Program into other free programs whose distribution conditions are different, write to the author to ask for permission. For software which is copyrighted by the Free Software Foundation, write to the Free Software Foundation; we sometimes make exceptions for this. Our decision will be guided by the two goals of preserving the free status of all derivatives of our free software and of promoting the sharing and reuse of software generally.

No Warranty

11. BECAUSE THE PROGRAM IS LICENSED FREE OF CHARGE, THERE IS NO WARRANTY FOR THE PROGRAM, TO THE EXTENT PERMITTED BY APPLICABLE LAW. EXCEPT WHEN OTHERWISE STATED IN WRITING THE COPY-RIGHT HOLDERS AND/OR OTHER PARTIES PROVIDE THE PROGRAM "AS IS" WITHOUT WARRANTY OF ANY KIND, EITHER EXPRESSED OR IMPLIED, INCLUDING, BUT NOT LIMITED TO, THE IMPLIED WARRANTIES OF MERCHANTABILITY AND FITNESS FOR A PARTICULAR PURPOSE. THE ENTIRE RISK AS TO THE QUALITY AND PERFORMANCE OF THE PROGRAM IS WITH YOU. SHOULD THE PROGRAM PROVE DEFECTIVE, YOU ASSUME THE COST OF ALL NECESSARY SERVICING, REPAIR OR CORRECTION.

12. IN NO EVENT UNLESS REQUIRED BY APPLICABLE LAW OR AGREED TO IN WRITING WILL ANY COPYRIGHT HOLDER, OR ANY OTHER PARTY WHO MAY MODIFY AND/OR REDISTRIBUTE THE PROGRAM AS PERMITTED ABOVE, BE LIABLE TO YOU FOR DAMAGES, INCLUDING ANY GENERAL, SPECIAL, INCIDENTAL OR CONSEQUEN-TIAL DAMAGES ARISING OUT OF THE USE OR INABILITY TO USE THE PROGRAM (INCLUDING BUT NOT LIMITED TO LOSS OF DATA OR DATA BEING RENDERED INACCU-RATE OR LOSSES SUSTAINED BY YOU OR THIRD PARTIES OR A FAILURE OF THE PROGRAM TO OPERATE WITH ANY OTHER PROGRAMS), EVEN IF SUCH HOLDER OR OTHER PARTY HAS BEEN ADVISED OF THE POSSIBILITY OF SUCH DAMAGES.

How To Apply These Terms To Your New Programs

If you develop a new program, and you want it to be of the greatest possible use to the public, the best way to achieve this is to make it free software which everyone can redistribute and change under these terms.

To do so, attach the following notices to the program. It is safest to attach them to the start of each source file to most effectively convey the exclusion of warranty; and each file should have at least the "copyright" line and a pointer to where the full notice is found.

one line to give the program's name and an idea of what it does.
Copyright (C) *yyyy   name of author*

This program is free software; you can redistribute it and/or
modify it under the terms of the GNU General Public License as
published by the Free Software Foundation; either version 2 of
the License, or (at your option) any later version.

This program is distributed in the hope that it will be useful,
but WITHOUT ANY WARRANTY; without even the implied warranty of
MERCHANTABILITY or FITNESS FOR A PARTICULAR PURPOSE.
See the GNU General Public License for more details.

You should have received a copy of the GNU General Public License
along with this program; if not, write to the Free Software
Foundation, Inc., 59 Temple Place - Suite 330, Boston, MA
02111-1307, USA.

Also add information on how to contact you by electronic and paper mail.

If the program is interactive, make it output a short notice like this when it starts in an interactive mode:

Gnomovision version 69, Copyright (C) *yyyy name of author*
Gnomovision comes with ABSOLUTELY NO WARRANTY;
for details type 'show w'.
This is free software, and you are welcome to redistribute it
under certain conditions; type 'show c' for details.

The hypothetical commands 'show w' and 'show c' should show the appropriate parts of the General Public License. Of course, the commands you use may be called something other than 'show w' and 'show c'; they could even be mouse-clicks or menu items—whatever suits your program.

You should also get your employer (if you work as a programmer) or your school, if any, to sign a "copyright disclaimer" for the program, if necessary. Here is a sample; alter the names:

Yoyodyne, Inc., hereby disclaims all copyright interest
in the program 'Gnomovision' (which makes passes at compilers)
written by James Hacker.

signature of Ty Coon, 1 April 1989
Ty Coon, President of Vice

This General Public License does not permit incorporating your program into proprietary programs. If your program is a subroutine library, you may consider it more useful to permit linking proprietary applications with the library. If this is what you want to do, use the GNU Library General Public License instead of this License.

Glossary

/bin/sh—The path to the standard shell on Linux (and Unix) systems.

/etc/conf.modules—File specifies commands, options, and paths for modules. This file sets up any module aliases and parameters that may be required.

/etc/crontab—File used to configure system cron (task schedule).

/etc/fstab—File for configuration of filesystems on a machine

/etc/group—File assigning users to specific (or shared) groups.

/etc/hosts—File that contains hosts found on your system.

/etc/httpd/conf/httpd.conf—Main httpd server configuration file.

/etc/inittab—File containing system configuration information, including virtual consoles.

/etc/lilo.conf—File responsible for the configuration of LILO.

/etc/named.conf—Configuration file used to configure DNS.

/etc/passwd—File containing user information such as user ID, user name, group ID, and password.

/etc/printcap—File used to configure printers.

/etc/rc.d/rc.local—Script used for local startup configuration.

/etc/rc.d/rc.sysinit—The main startup script.

/etc/securetty—File used to specify which tty root is allowed to login on.

/etc/sendmail.cf—Main configuration file for sendmail.

/etc/skel—Directory containing default user files used when creating new accounts.

/etc/smb.conf—Configuration file for SAMBA.

/etc/smbpasswd—File containing password information for Windows users connecting to the Samba server.

/etc/sysconfig—Directory containing script configuration files.

a.out—The old executable style of Linux and Unix systems. (The name comes from the default outpost file name of the C compiler.)

alias—A filename created as a "nickname" for another filename.

Apache—Popular hyper-text transport protocol (HTTP) server based originally on the popular web server NCSA's httpd 1.3.

APM (Advanced Power Management)—System used to manage CPU calls, shutdown options, suspend options, and other power-related functions.

ARP (Address Resolution Protocol)—The protocol used to resolve IP addresses to MAC addresses on ethernet.

autoprobe—Term referring to system capability to make calls to a specific device, receiving identification, and other information from the device automatically.

Bash (The Bourne Again Shell)—The GNU implementation of the Bourne/POSIX shell (/bin/sh).

BIND (Berkeley Internet Name Domain)—The standard, free reference DNS server implementation used by the vast majority of sites on the Internet.

BIOS (Basic Input/Output System)—The code in ROM or Flash RAM on a PC that initializes the hardware and starts the boot process.

BSD (Berkeley Software Distribution)—The Unix derivative created by the University of California at Berkeley. (The portions of BSD not derived from AT&T code are open-source software.)

build—Term used for compiling, or creating programs, RPM files, database files, and so on.

bzip—Compression utility for files.

character-cell mode—Console based menu system.

CIDR—Classless Inter-Domain Routing.

CISC (Complex Instruction Set Computing)—The CPU architecture used in the Intel 80x86 line of microprocessors which has variable-length instructions that may require several clock cycles to complete.

clear—Tool used to clear all text from an xterm or console.

clone—Machine configured with exact hardware and software configuration as another machine.

COFF (Common Object File Format)—The binary format used by some Unix systems, also used in a modified form by Windows NT, and introduced in Unix System V Release 3. Linux supports COFF executables of some other systems, but does not use the format natively.

compile—To convert the source code of a program to machine code.

conf.modules—The file in /etc with configuration information for loadable kernel modules.

control-panel—Red Hat menu used to configure Red Hat networking, users, and printing.

CPU—Central processing unit.

crackers—Term used to identify people who attempt to or succeed at breaking into computer systems unlawfully.

crontab—The file or files that specify commands to be run by cron at certain times. Also the command used to manipulate those files.

daemon—A program which runs in the background, whose parent process is **init**. Usually daemons provide some kind of system services.

device—A block or character special file that generally points to a piece of hardware.

DHCP (Dynamic Host Configuration Protocol)—A superset of bootp that is used to assign IP addresses to clients on a network. DHCP is used for dynamic hosts that can move, connect, and disconnect from networks.

dig—Tool used to query name server for domain name packet information.

disk druid—Graphical tool used to format and partition hard-drive during Red Hat installation.

distribution—A collection of software built into a complete system. Examples of Linux distributions include Red Hat Linux, Caldera OpenLinux, SuSE Linux, Debian GNU/Linux, Stampede, and Slackware.

DNS (Domain Name Service)—The protocol used to resolve domain names to IP addresses.

dnsquery—Tool used to query domain name server for host using resolver.

domain—Name assigned to an IP to identify a machine to an IP address.

dual boot—Method where a computer is set up to boot from a choice of operating systems.

dynamic route—Route that is assigned "on the fly," meaning no definitive route is set, and a route for a packet is assigned each time a packet is sent (not predetermined).

edquota—Tool used to edit disk quotas.

ELF (Executable and Linkable Format)—The binary format of Linux executables, as well as the standard binary format of many other Unix (and Unix-like) systems.

elm—Text-based mail reader used on Unix systems. The interface is text-based and commands are given by simple key commands as prompted by the mail reader.

eth0—Ethernet device name.

ethernet—The dominant LAN hardware protocol.

ext2—Mount type associated with Linux filesystems.

FDDI—A networking hardware layer that uses fiber optic cable as the physical media.

fdisk—The program that is used to manage partitions on a disk.

filesystem—Refers to the on-disk structures that store information such as file properties and the location of file data.

firewall—System used to monitor and control access to and from a network.

Free Software Foundation—*See* FSF.

fsck—The program that is used to check the consistency of filesystems.

FSF (Free Software Foundation)—Foundation established to promote the development and use of Free Software.

fstab—The file in /etc that contains mappings from device names to mount points.

FTP (File Transfer Protocol)—A protocol used to transfer files between two hosts.

GDM (GNOME Display Manager)—Tool used to replace default XDM (X Display Manager) that allows the user to log in to GNOME, KDE, or AnotherLevel.

GIMP—Linux tool used to manipulate graphics to that similar of Adobe Photoshop.

GMC (GNOME Midnight Commander)—GNOME file manager that allows capabilities such as drag and drop to the desktop features and file browsing similar to the Windows Explorer.

GNOME (GNU Network Object Model)—Window environment based on CORBA.

GnoRPM—GUI tool that replaces glint as the package management tool.

GPL (General Product License)—License established to preserve the rights of free software and free software authors.

group—Associates multiple users with one identification method allowing files and services to be accessed via group permissions rather than individual user permission.

groupdel—Tool used to delete all users in a group.

gzip—Compression utility for files.

Hardware address (MAC address)—A vendor-assigned 6-byte number in firmware on ethernet hardware that uniquely identifies the ethernet controller on a network.

home—Directory dedicated to a user.

host—Tool used to look up host for domain name.

hostname—Name assigned to identify your machine to a local network.

HTTP (HyperText Transport Protocol)—The protocol used to transfer files for the World Wide Web.

IANA (Internet Assigned Numbers Authority)—Body that sets standards used on the Internet.

IBM (International Business Machines)—The creators of the IBM PC, which most x86-based systems are based on (and compatible with).

ICMP (Internet Control Message Protocol)—The control (non-data) message protocol of TCP/IP.

IDE (Integrated Drive Electronics)—The standard PC bus for hard drives and other disk devices.

ifconfig—Tool used to view and configure active network interfaces.

ifdown—Tool used to disable a specified network interface (such as eth0).

ifup—Tool used to enable a specified interface (such as eth0).

IMAP (Internet Message Access Protocol)—A protocol used to read electronic mail on a remote server.

inetd—Internet daemon that controls most of the network services that listen for incoming connections on your machine.

init—Tool used to access various runlevels.

initrd—File used as the initial ram disk used to boot a system that uses SCSI during the boot process.

inode—A filesystem structure that uniquely identifies a file and its properties (permissions, size, and so on).

insmod—Tool that is used to load a specific module manually.

InterNIC—The organization responsible for managing the non-governmental US top-level domains (such as .com, .net, and .org).

I/O (Input/Output)—Often used to refer to a device's I/O address, which is the location in memory where the CPU can access the memory on the device.

IP forwarding—Routing system used to route packets originating from a separate host to another host on the network.

ipchains—Tool that specifies firewall policies to the Linux kernel.

IPv6—The next generation of TCP/IP, which is more secure than the current generation (IPv4) and which uses 128-bit addresses (instead of the current 32-bit addresses).

IPX—Network protocol used primarily on Netware.

IRQ—Hardware interrupt request.

ISA—Industry Standard Architecture PC bus interface.

ISDN (Integrated Services Digital Network)—Digital telephony service with 128k bandwidth.

iso9660—Mount type associated with CD-ROM devices.

ISP (Internet Service Provider)—Organization that charges fees for providing Internet access service and other Internet related services.

kbdconfig—Tool to configure system keyboard.

KDE—The K Desktop Environment.

kernel—The heart of an operating system. The kernel controls access to hardware, handles hardware events (such as interrupts), schedules timeslices for processes, and manages resources.

kernelcfg—GUI tool used to configure Linux kernel.

kerneld—Daemon used up to Red Hat Linux 5.2 to handle kernel modules.

kickstart—Tool used to automate Red Hat Linux installation.

kmod—kernel task that handles loading the kernel.

LDP (Linux Documentation Project)—On-line Linux resource for information. See **http://metalab.unc.edu/**.

LILO—(The LInux Loader)—Used to boot the kernel on x86 hardware.

lilo.conf—The file in /etc that describes kernels and other operating systems for **LILO** to boot.

linuxconf—Tool used to configure Linux networking, users, programs, and more.

lo—Local host device name.

login—Refers to username.

lpd—Print daemon.

lsmod—Tool used to tell you what modules are loaded.

make config—Command used for text based kernel configuration.

make menuconfig—Console-based tool used for kernel configuration.

make xconfig—GUI-based tool used for kernel configuration.

masquerading—Routing option set up to masquerade internal network traffic as a single system.

MBR (Master Boot Record)—Superblock of the hard-disk that contains system boot information.

MDA (Mail Delivery Agent)—Responsible for receiving (and sending) mail for the user to and from the MTA.

minix—Modular Unix-like system developed by Andrew Tanenbaum.

mkfs—The program used to create filesystems.

modprobe—Tool used to automatically load a model and all its dependancies.

modular—Type of kernel whose drivers compiled in that are required at boot time. Remaining drivers and support are installed as modules, and only loaded when needed.

modules—Loadable kernel object files that can be inserted and removed from a running kernel and that can contain device drivers, filesystem drivers, and other kernel code.

monolithic—Type of kernel whose system support is compiled directly in the kernel.

mount—Command used to mount filesystems and view lists of mounted filesystems.

mountpoint—Directory where a filesystem or device is mounted.

mouseconfig—Menu based tool used to configure system mouse.

msdos—The MS-DOS compatible filesystem.

MTA (Mail Transport Agent)—System responsible for the physical sending and receiving of user and system mail.

MUA (Mail User Agent)—Responsible for providing "front end" interface to user to create and read mail.

nameserver—Server dedicated to resolving DNS and hostnames via DNS.

netcfg—Tool used to configure networking.

netmask—A bitmask which is used to define an IP segment.

netstat—Tool used to report network information.

NetWare—Network based operating system developed by Novell.

NFS (Network File System)—The native Unix filesystem-sharing protocol.

NIC (Network Interface Card)—Adapter card used to connect a system to the network.

NIS (Network Information Service)—Formerly known as Yellow Pages, a protocol used to store shared configuration information (such as the passwd, group, and hosts files) on a server.

nmbd—Windows NetBIOS names for sending and receiving names of machines on the network.

nslookup—Tool used to queries Internet name servers for IP and domain information.

ntpdate—Tool similar to rdate. The ntpdate tool is used to retrieve the date and time from the network by polling the Network Time Protocol Servers as specified in the command.

Open Source Software—See OSS.

operating system (OS)—A software program that controls the operations on a computer system.

OSS (Open Source Software)—Established to promote the development and use of Open Source Software.

output—Term used to describe the text result from a console command.

PAM (Pluggable Authentication Modules)—System that enables ruleset implementation without having to recode individual services.

Partition—A piece of a disk. Under Linux, each partition on disk shows up as a separate device.

passwd—Tool used to change (or set) a user password.

PCI (Peripheral Component Interconnect)—The 32- or 64-bit, 33 MHz bus designed by Intel that is used in most current PCs and workstations.

PCMCIA—Slot style hardware used in laptops.

peripheral—Device attached externally to a computer.

Perl—Programming and scripting language developed by Larry Wall.

permissions—Access levels granted to a file, program, or directory, for a user or group. Can be changed with chmod.

pine—Text-based mail reader used on Unix systems. The pine mail reader is a little more user friendly than elm using key combination menu-based options, and uses a simpler text editor.

plug and play—Term used to describe hardware that is software (not jumper) configurable.

PMS (Package Management System)—Package management system project led by Rik Faith. It was predecessor to RPM.

Pointer—The arrow or other indicator that represents the location of your mouse, trackball, glide point, or other pointing device that corresponds to the location on the screen. Quite often the shape, color, or size of the pointer will change to indicate that the mouse has a particular function on that specific area of the screen.

POP (Post Office Protocol)—A protocol used to retrieve electronic mail from a remote server. (Currently there are two POP protocols supported on Linux, POP2 and POP3. POP2 is obsolete, although it is still supported.)

ppp0—ppp interface name.

printtool—Tool used to configure printing.

prototype—Machine configured as a test, or base model, used for cloning.

pwconv—Tool used to convert /etc/passwd to using shadow passwords.

pwunconv – Tool used to convert /etc/passwd from using shadow passwords.

query—Term used when a program sends a request to another program or package for information.

RAM (Random Access Memory)—Memory used on a system for storing temporary data for programs and files.

ramdisk—Required when support is needed, such as SCSI support during boot. The ramdisk is noted in your /etc/lilo.conf file as an initrd= comment.

RARP (Reverse ARP)—A protocol used to discover the IP address of a device given its **MAC address**. (This protocol is obsoleted by bootp and DHCP, although it is still somewhat commonly used.)

rdate—The Red Hat Linux tool used to synchronize the system time with a specified machine. The rdate tool only synchronizes once when used.

rebuild—Term used for recompiling.

RIP (Routing Information Protocol)—A protocol used to dynamically reconfigure routing information.

RISC (Reduced Instruction Set Computing)—The CPU architecture used in the Alpha, Sparc, and other CPUs, which has short, fixed-length instructions that perform simple tasks. More complex instructions must be built out of simpler instructions. This allows the CPU to be simpler and generally faster than a CISC CPU, at the cost of often needing to execute many more instructions than a CISC CPU.

rmmod—Tool used to remove a loadable kernel module.

root—The superuser, whose user ID is 0. File permissions are ignored for root.

root directory—The / directory.

root window—The background of your screen. The root window doesn't have any of the standard characteristics of any other window, but does have some unique applications. The root window is where you can customize your background images, among various other tasks.

route—The program that is used to manage the kernel's routing tables.

router—System responsible for managing and relaying network packets.

routing rules—Assignments specified to your server for how (and where) to handle network packets.

routing table—The kernel's mapping of IP addresses to network interfaces. The routing table tells the kernel how to send IP traffic to its destination.

RPM (Red Hat Package Manager)—Program used to manage Red Hat Linux packages for system programs and tools.

SAMBA—Open Source tool that implements SMB (Server Message Block).

screen—Term used to refer to your whole desktop. The terms screen and desktop are often interchanged. Technically, it is the primary video display that you use to view your X Window system.

SCSI (Small Computer Systems Interface)—The bus used to connect disk drives and other peripherals on some PCs and most workstations and other non-x86-based systems.

sendmail—Program responsible for mail transfer between servers.

services—Names associated with particular TCP/IP protocol and port number pairs. Also the name of the file in /etc with mappings from those names to particular protocols and port numbers.

shadow passwords—System used to move /etc/passwd information to a non-world-readable file, allowing options such as password aging.

shell—The command interpreter.

SMB (Server Message Block)—The standard filesystem and printer sharing protocol of LanManager and Windows.

smbadduser—Tool for adding Windows Samba users to your system.

smbclient—Client-side program to connect to SMB server from Linux.

smbmount—Utility to mount SMB shares.

smbpasswd—Utility used to add user to /etc/smbpasswd, allowing for Windows encrypted passwords.

smbprint—Script used for printing through SMB share.

smbrun—Script used to start SMB server.

smbstatus—Tool used to print status information for the running SMB server.

smbtar—Script used for backing up Windows machines to your SMB server.

smbumount—Tool used to unmount SMB service.

smbuser—Unix-to-NT user mapping.

SMP (Symmetric Multiprocessing)—Support for machines with more than one CPU.

sndconfig—Red Hat tool used to configure sound.

source code—Also known simply as Source, the text files that contain instructions that are converted to machine code by a compiler.

spec file—Refers to file containing specification for given package, file, or program for use by RPM.

SQL—Simple Query Language used for databases.

squid—Caching proxy server that caches data streams such as FTP, gopher, and HTTP.

static route—Preconfigured mandatory path for specified network requests and/or packets.

superuser—Also known as root. Special system user with privileged access to configure all parts of a Linux system.

supplementary group—Additional assigned group used in addition to the main user group

swap—The process of paging memory to disk as virtual memory. Also used to refer to the spaces on disk used for paging.

SWAT—Web-based configuration tool for SMB

switchdesk—Tool used to switch between installed desktops.

symbolic link—Also known as symlink, a directory entry that points to a path to another file.

SysLinux—Boots the Linux kernel from a DOS filesystem.

System Commander—Commercial bootloader that you can purchase from a local software vendor.

tar—Compression utility used for files.

TCP (Transmission Control Protocol)—The connection-oriented protocol of TCP/IP.

TCP/IP (Transmission Control Protocol/Internet Protocol)—The network protocol of the Internet, and the native networking protocol of Linux and Unix.

tcp_wrappers—Uses system files /etc/hosts.allow and /etc/hosts.deny to control who can and cannot access services managed by inetd.

terminal emulator—Window with just text that basically emulates a console. An example of a terminal emulator would be an xterm.

TeX—Special text formatting and typesetting program.

timeconfig—GUI tool used to configure system time.

tools—Software commands used to administer a program or computer services.

TOS—Type of service.

TTL (Time To Live)—A field in an IP packet that defines the number of routers the packet should pass through before being rejected. (The traceroute command works by repeatedly sending an ICMP echo packet, incrementing the TTL by one until the host is reached.)

UDP (User Datagram Protocol)—The stream-oriented, connectionless protocol of TCP/IP.

umask—File creation mask used to set up default file permissions based on the umask setting subtracted from full file permissions of 777.

Unix—The operating system developed in the late 60s and early 70s at Bell Labs that is the inspiration for Linux.

URL (Uniform Resource Locator)—A Web address such as **http://www.coriolis.com/**.

user—Individual with an account on a machine.

User ID—This is the number associated with individual user accounts. The system automatically sets this when the account is created.

useradd—Tool used to add user accounts to a system. (Equivalent to adduser.)

userdel—Tool used to delete a system user.

vfat—Mount type associated with Windows partitions and filesystems.

virtual consoles—Multiple text-based logins located on separate virtual screens on your system.

virtual hosts—Apache feature allowing a single machine to host multiple domains.

visual bell—Visual alarm, such as a screen flash, used to specify a system beep without using the speaker.

vmlinuz—A compressed vmlinux kernel file (compressed files often have the last character changed to z, or a .z or .Z appended to the filename), which is a play on vmunix, the standard kernel name on Unix systems.

window—A frame where any given application resides and is managed by the window manager. The active window is the window that you are currently using on your desktop. The active window is usually indicated by being on top, in focus, or highlighted compared to the inactive windows on the screen.

window manager—The main interface between the X Window system and the user. The window manager provides functionality such as window borders, menus, icons, desktops, and button and tool bars, and allows the user to customize them all.

X—The X Windowing system, originally developed at MIT as a client-server protocol for building graphical user interfaces.

xf86config—Text-based configuration tool that is used to configure the XF86Config file.

xhost—Tool used to grant X permission to host applications for other machines.

xntp3—Tool used to set up a continuously running synchronization daemon.

ypcat—Tool used to print the values of all keys in the specified NIS database.

ypmatch—Prints the values of keys from an NIS map.

yppoll—Tool used to return the version and master server of the specified NIS map.

yppush—Tool used to notify the slave servers when changes are made to master databases.

ypwhich—Tool used to return the name of the NIS server used by the NIS client.

Index

O

P